1974

SAMPLER OF
AMERICAN
SONGS

BOOKS BY MAYMIE R. KRYTHE

All About American Holidays

All About Christmas

All About the Months

What So Proudly We Hail:
All About Our American Flag,
Monuments and Symbols

SAMPLER OF

AMERICAN

SONGS

*

MAYMIE R. KRYTHE

1817

HARPER & ROW, PUBLISHERS

NEW YORK, EVANSTON, AND LONDON

To

FRANCES N. NIELSEN

"one of those rarely gifted persons . . ."

—GEORGE DU MAURIER

Give me the makings of the songs of a nation, and I care not who makes its laws.

—ANDREW FLETCHER OF SALTOUN

Our country is rich in patriotic and national music—songs which are a very part of our history and our development as a nation, for they have been born of the great events which have shaped our destiny and have flowed spontaneously from hearts and souls inspired by the events of the moment.

New periods of national enthusiasm and fervor will come—new songs will be sung—but there will always remain a deeper reverence for the older songs, for they are the very essence of that something which we call love of country. . . .

—*Patriotic Songs of America*

Contents

SAMPLER OF AMERICAN SONGS

*

1

*

"Yankee Doodle"

"Yankee Doodle" is the most famous and best-known song of all those associated with our American Revolution, and the only one that has retained its wide popularity down to the present time.

A catchy song, whose perennial popularity dates from the time of the American Revolution, was first sung by the red-coated British soldiers in derision of the Colonists in homespun.

—*American People's Encyclopedia*

The derivation of the word "Yankee" has long been a bone of contention; no one seems absolutely certain of its origin, although several have been suggested.

Some dictionaries say it stems from the Scottish word "yankie," meaning "a sharp or clever woman." Others maintain that the Massachusetts Indians corrupted the French word *Anglais* (for "English") into "Yankee."

Or it may have been of Dutch origin. The early Flemish sometimes called persons from Holland, *Jan Kees*—a shortened form of the two Dutch names, "Jan" and "Cornelius." Some authorities believe the Flemish used the expression in connection with the Dutch who emigrated to the New World. Or it may have derived from the Dutch *Jankee,* denoting "Little John."

3

The term "nankey," or "nankie," so some sources say, was contemptuously applied to the short-haired Roundheads, the Puritan followers of Oliver Cromwell. Among the varying forms of a reference to Cromwell, during the 1600's, when he rode from Canterbury to Oxford to head the Puritan forces, is the following:

> Nankey (or Yankee) Doodle came to town,
> Upon a Kentish pony;
> Stuck a feather in his cap
> And called it macaroni.

("Macaroni" in this instance is said to refer to the fact that Oliver Cromwell wore a single plume in his hat, fastened to a kind of knot called a "macaroni.")

"Yankee" is the best known of national nicknames, all around the globe. It was first given to the people of New England in the eighteenth century by British soldiers stationed there, as a nickname of contempt; later it was merely a descriptive expression. (It was widely used by the English during our Revolutionary War.)

One writer asserts that the American colonists did not apply the expression to themselves but to persons of other colonies; for "Yankee" was not considered complimentary. New Yorkers, for instance, thought themselves superior to the New Englanders; so they rather scornfully gave the latter this nickname. But especially after the Battle of Bunker Hill, the inhabitants of the Northeast adopted the name and took much pride in it. The British came to use the term in reference to all Americans, and this usage continued into the twentieth century. During and after the Civil War, the Southerners called all Northerners "Yankees."

A current dictionary gives this definition for the word: "A native of New England, by extension, of the Northern States; sometimes among foreigners, any inhabitant of the United States."

Many Europeans call all Americans "Yankees"; but in our country, the word is applied mainly to those living in the Northeastern states. According to one source, it really means anyone living north of the Mason-Dixon Line, or any Northerner.

The people in the northern part of the country had to develop much cleverness and shrewdness in their struggle to make homes and create industries in that "rocky wilderness." Yankee peddlers roamed through the thirteen American colonies selling their wares, which were made by fellow craftsmen in New England. These men were known as sharp bargainers and had the reputation of getting high prices for their goods. Because of this the expression "shrewd as a Yankee" came into use.

There is a story that a farmer of Cambridge, Massachusetts, Jonathan Hastings, was given the nickname "Yankee" when he attended Harvard in 1713. He spread the term widely and used it to express his idea of "excellence." Thus, "Yankee" cider or a "Yankee" horse denoted superior quality. The Harvard students who rented horses from "Yankee Jonathan" called them "Yankee" horses.

During World War I the use of "Yankee" increased. Both in Europe and at home our armed forces were given the name of "Yankees." When the American troops reached Paris in 1917, the French newspaper reporters hailed them as "Yankees" or "Yanks"; and Europeans have continued to use the word in this connection.

"Doodle," in one old English dictionary meant "a trifling, simple fellow." Samuel Johnson in his famous *Dictionary* defined a "doodle" as "a simpleton, silly, foolish fellow, generally of the rural type." Thus "Yankee Doodle," in accordance with this definition, meant a foolish, or simple, New Englander.

There are varied accounts as to the origin of the song "Yankee Doodle." In a file of old newspapers—the Albany *Statesman,* of July, 1824—it was reported that during the French and Indian Wars (before the Americans rebelled against the mother country), the British forces stationed in the colonies decided to reduce the French power in Canada by attacking Forts Niagara and Frontenac.

Their general, Lord Amherst, was in charge of the expedition and called in colonial forces to assist in the conflict. During the summer of 1755, the combined troops were encamped on the east bank of the Hudson River, south of Albany, at Camp Crailo, situated on land owned by the well-known Van Rensselaer family.

When the American militiamen, under Governor William Shirley, arrived at the camp to aid the British soldiers, the latter termed them "an ungainly lot . . . strangely clad in many colors. . . ." They declared that "such a motley assembly of men never before thronged together on such an occasion."

Some of the colonials, it was related, "had long coats, some short, while others had none at all . . . some with their hair cropped like the army of Cromwell, and others with wigs . . . their march, their accoutrements . . . furnished a matter of much amusement to the wits of the British army." Members of the latter made up some doggerel, declaring the old Continentals marched "in their ragged regimentals," or no regimentals at all!

The story is told that Dr. Richard S. Schuckburgh, a surgeon attached to the English forces, wrote the original words of "Yankee Doodle" (sung to a tune already known in the colonies) at Camp Crailo, in New York State, in order to ridicule the colonial soldiers, ill-clad in comparison with the Red Coats.

(As early as 1735, Dr. Schuckburgh, with a Captain Barrow, had done some prospecting on the Delaware River. From June 25, 1737, he had a commission as surgeon to some infantry companies. In 1761, he resigned this post and was placed in charge of Indian affairs. When he died, in 1773, at Schenectady, New York, he was praised as "a gentleman of a very genteel family . . . of infinite jest and humor . . . and a natural genius.")

In addition to his medical work, the doctor was something of a musician. He thought he would play a joke on the raw, untrained colonials, and composed four stanzas with a refrain. The song began:

> Yankee Doodle came to town,
> Riding on a pony,
> Stuck a feather in his cap
> And called it macaroni.

One source tells that Dr. Schuckburgh's poem consisted of "some rather silly verses which he set to the tune of 'Lucy Locket lost her pocket' "; and another writer declared they were "crude verses, mocking the shabby Colonists, who fought alongside the British."

In one issue of the Albany *Statesman,* a reporter wrote:

> . . . to please Brother Jonathan [nickname for an American colonial] he composed a tune, and, with much gravity, recommended it to the officers as one of the most celebrated airs of martial music. The joke took, to the no small amusement of the British Corps. Brother Jonathan exclaimed that it was "nation fine" and in a few days nothing was heard in the Provincial camp but "Yankee Doodle."

During the French and Indian Wars (1754–1763), the British forces played the song in derision; and such usage went on for years before the Revolution broke out. However, the American militiamen cleverly turned the joke against the English. They liked the piece and enthusiastically used it for their field music. They also wrote numerous additional stanzas that were more complimentary to themselves and their great cause of trying to gain their independence.

When the American Revolution started, "Yankee Doodle" was known throughout all the thirteen colonies. It is claimed that the first printed version appeared on October 12, 1768, in the New York *Journal.*

In 1885 and 1887, Dr. George Moore read a paper entitled "The Origin and History of 'Yankee Doodle' " before the New York and New England historical societies. Later Albert Mathews reproduced parts of this paper, and declared that Dr. Richard Schuckburgh had had an important role in making "Yankee Doodle" a national song; for in it he gave a picture of men and events of the times. Mathews also said that "the song was a satire, more or less clever, of the New Englander and his supposed ways."

Some sources have tried to discredit the stories of Dr. Schuckburgh's connection with "Yankee Doodle." But a granddaughter of Robert Van Rennselaer wrote Albert Mathews in Boston that there was no doubt in her mind about the surgeon's having written the piece. She said he had been a guest at their family home, and also that the room he had occupied had been pointed out to the children of the family because of his association with this patriotic composition. And she concluded: "All that we claim for Fort Crailo is that it was the birthplace of the original composition. . . ."

The beginning of the air of "Yankee Doodle" is still a moot question; and various origins have been assigned to it. "The rollicking tune is said to have been much older than the words" and may have started during the Middle Ages in southern Europe. About 1500, it was sung in Holland and began with the meaningless words, "Yankee dudel, doodle doun." German laborers who went to the neighboring country to work at harvest time are said to have sung it. It has also been credited to Persia.

Once, while Louis Kossuth, the famous Hungarian patriot and statesman, was in this country, he stated that our patriotic song, "Yankee Doodle," resembled an air of his native land.

On June 3, 1858, Buckingham Smith, the secretary of the American Legation at Madrid, Spain, wrote:

> The tune, "Yankee Doodle," from the first of my showing it here, has been acknowledged by persons acquainted with music to bear a strong resemblance to the popular airs of Biscay; and yesterday a professor from the north recognized it as being much like the ancient sword dance played on solemn occasions by the people of San Sebastian. He says the tune varies in the provinces. . . .
>
> Our national air certainly has its origin in the music of the free Pyrenees; the first strains are identically those of the heroic "Danza Esparta," as it was played to me, of brave old Biscay.

During Shakespeare's time the melody of "Yankee Doodle" was sung to children with the well-known nursery rhyme:

Lucy Lockett lost her pocket,
Kitty Fisher found it.
Nothing in it, nothing in it,
Save the binding round it.

As mentioned before, the tune was known at the time of Charles I in England. One tale goes that after Oliver Cromwell and his Roundheads rebelled, in the 1600's, the Cavaliers made fun of the Puritans in such a song; also the latter ridiculed the Cavaliers, using the same tune.

The melody was played as a march as early as 1750 by the Grenadier Guards. Its first known appearance in print under the title of "Yankee Doodle" is said to have been in Scotland in 1775 (or 1776) in James Aird's *Selection of Scotch, English, Irish, and Foreign Airs, for Fife, Violin, or German Flute.*

It was mentioned in a letter, written on April 16, 1776, and described as "a song composed in derision of New Englanders, scornfully called 'Yankees.' "

There were not many printed editions of the composition, which had the same air as the Irish number, "The Way to Galway." The tune occurred in at least two operas. In George Colema's work, entitled *Two to One,* printed in 1784, there was a song, "Adzooks, Old Crusty, Why So Rusty?" sung to the same tune as "Yankee Doodle."

Not much secular music was published in the American colonies before 1790. The first known printing of this national air in the new republic is said to have been a part of Benjamin Carr's "Federal Overture," a medley of patriotic songs. It was composed in 1794, and published in Baltimore in January, 1795, as an arrangement for the piano.

The New York *Journal* for October 13, 1768, reported that visitors to the English ships in Boston Harbor had been pleased by hearing "Yankee Doodle" played by the British musicians. So the tune soon became well known in Boston. However, as the ill feeling between the mother country and the Americans grew, the Red Coats often retaliated. They had been made to feel they had no business being there. So at times they took revenge on the citizens.

They knew many of the Bostonians were quite religious; and often on Sunday, the English bands would stand just outside the churches and loudly play "Yankee Doodle." They also used this tune to drum culprits out of town.

These British soldiers enjoyed concocting other verses and singing them to insult the colonists. One went as follows:

> Yankee Doodle came to town
> For to buy a firelock;
> We will tar and feather him
> And so we will John Hancock.

According to one source, "the sprightly, impudent tune" had become popular in the colonies by 1770; and another says "that verses composed and written in derision of New Englanders must have existed before April, 1775 in the form of a specific well-known song. . . ."

A fifteen- (or sixteen-) stanza poem, called "The Yankee's Return from Camp" contained the "original" words and began

> Father and I went down to camp,
> Along with Captain Gooding,
> There we see the men and boys
> As thick as hasty pudding.

> CHORUS

> Yankee Doodle, keep it up
> Yankee Doodle dandy,
> Mind the music and the step,
> And with the girls be handy.

This version may have originated at the provincial camp near Cambridge. There are differences as to dates; some say it was written in 1765; others, in 1775 or 1776. This long poem gives the reactions of recruits to military life. One writer calls it "hardly less than a jumble of almost idiotic words," but "the hilarious character of the song created a sensation on two continents."

The use of "Yankee Doodle" as a means of making fun of Americans continued in the early days of the Revolution. But, at the Battle of Lexington, "by a strange irony of fate, the colonists made the British dance to the tune of 'Yankee Doodle.' "

In April, 1775, Lord Percy's troops left Boston as reinforcements to relieve Major Pitcairn "in great stress" at Lexington. "The brigade marched out, playing by way of contempt 'Yankee Doodle.' " At Concord the British troops were routed by the colonial militiamen. As they beat a disorderly retreat to Boston, the Yankees followed them singing the patriotic air.

Copies of the song were printed as broadsides, sold in the streets, and played and sung in every American camp. The colonials whistled it in battle, made it their rallying cry, and ever since American Revolutionary days, "Yankee Doodle" has been a favorite patriotic air.

One story goes that the British had to hear the song so much during their retreat from Lexington and Concord that General Gage exclaimed, "I hope I never hear that song again!"

But it was heard again at Bunker Hill; and it is reported that, while the British had used the term "Yankee" as one of reproach, after the affair at Bunker Hill the Americans gloried in the song, and it became their favorite march. Its most famous stanza was

> Yankee Doodle came to town
> Riding on a pony.
> Stuck a feather in his cap
> And called it macaroni.

(One meaning of "macaroni" was "dandy" or "dude.")

Many stanzas were adapted to the tune; one such favorite began in this fashion:

> Yankee Doodle is the tune
> Americans delight in;
> 'Twill do to whistle, sing, or play.
> And is just the thing for fighting.

An amusing song was written by the gifted composer and statesman Francis Hopkinson (1737–1791), a signer of the Declaration

of Independence. It was a humorous political satire in verse, called
"The Battle of the Kegs" and sung to the tune of "Yankee
Doodle."

Some Philadelphians, in an attempt to destroy the British ships
on the Delaware River, hit on a plan of filling kegs with gun
powder, then floating them down the river, so that when they hit
the ships they would explode and destroy them. This poem, a witty
parody gaily mocking the Red Coats, had this opening stanza:

> Gallants attend and hear a friend
> Trill forth harmonious ditty;
> Strange things I'll tell which late befell
> In Philadelphia City.

On October 17, 1777, when General Burgoyne had to surrender
his forces to the Americans after the Battle of Saratoga, it was
mortifying—to say the least—for the English soldiers to have to
hear "Yankee Doodle" played during the ceremony. The story has
been told various times that this song was also heard at Yorktown
at the end of the war, when Lord Cornwallis surrendered to
General George Washington. However, this has not been con-
firmed by historians; an appropriate air played on that historic
occasion was "The World Turned Upside Down."

It happened, after the War of 1812, that Europeans heard
"Yankee Doodle" played as our national American song. In 1814,
Henry Clay and John Quincy Adams met with the British Ambas-
sador at Ghent, in Belgium; they were to sign the Treaty of Peace
between the United States and Great Britain on December 24,
1814.

The citizens of Ghent, who had sympathized with us in our
second war with England, were proud that the signing was to occur
in their city. On that important day, the burgers wanted to honor
the two embassies with serenades. Naturally, they were familiar
with the British national anthem, but they did not know what the
American song was.

Therefore, the bandmaster went to see Henry Clay, asked him about it, and was told that the song was "Yankee Doodle." Then the musician asked Clay to hum the tune so that he could write it down. That great statesman—so the story goes—tried to do so and failed. The secretary of the American Legation also was not able to "warble the melody" properly.

At once Henry Clay called in his Negro body servant and said, "Bob, whistle 'Yankee Doodle' for this gentleman!" The man whistled the tune; the bandmaster took it down, harmonized it, and made copies for his band members; and the serenade went off beautifully as planned at the American Embassy.

Today "Yankee Doodle" is no longer considered a national song, but it is still a favorite—second only to "Dixie" in national popularity. For countless decades it has appealed to Americans, and it shows no signs of passing into oblivion. Its great popularity at the period when we were making our supreme effort for national independence "clothes it with imperishable historical associations."

Even though it had so much derision heaped upon it, it became the chief marching song of our victorious American forefathers; and today it is "one of the most indestructible institutions of America."

Richard Grant White, an authority on American national songs, has criticized its words as "mere childish burlesque"; but he adds that "it has the claim of long association, and will probably always retain a certain degree of favor."

Here is a fine tribute to this old song:

> Throughout our Revolution, the song that tyranny had made to ridicule the champion of religious and political freedom was the march to greater victories of the same principles.
> —Helen K. Johnson

In her work, *The First Book of America,* Edith Heal has paid another fine tribute to this early patriotic song:

Rollicking "Yankee Doodle," our first national song, was written by a British army doctor, in the fiery years before the American Revolution. He chose a gay folk melody and wrote words for it, mocking the colonial Yankees. But the Yankees adopted the merry little tune, sang it, thought up more words for it, and made it the marching song of the American Revolution.

Yankee Doodle

Old English Tune

1. Fa - ther and I went down to camp, A - long with Cap - tain Good - win, And
2. And there was Cap - tain Wash - ing - ton Up - on a strap - ping stal - lion, And
3. And then the feath - ers on his hat, They looked so tar - nal fi - ney, I
4. And there I see a lit - tle keg, Its heads were made of leath - er, They
5. And there they had a swamp - ing gun, As big as a log of ma - ple, Up -
6. And ev - 'ry time they fired it off It took a horn of pow - der, It
7. It scared me so, I run the street, Nor stopped, as I re - mem - ber, Till

there we saw the men and boys As thick as hast - y pud - din'.
giv - ing or - ders to his men, I guess there was a mil - lion.
want - ed pesk - i - ly to get, To give to my Je - mi - my.
knocked up - on it with two sticks To call the men to - geth - er.
on a deu - ced lit - tle cart, A load for fa - ther's cat - tle.
made a noise like fa - ther's gun, On - ly a na - tion loud - er.
I got home and safe - ly locked, In gran - ny's lit - tle cham - ber.

Chorus

Yan - kee Doo - dle keep it up, Yan - kee Doo - dle dan - dy,

Mind the mu - sic and the step, And with the girls be han - dy.

2

*

"The Star-Spangled Banner"

In 1899, eighty-five years after our national anthem was written, Colonel Nicholas Smith declared that " 'The Star-Spangled Banner' probably has the firmest hold on the American people; for it is a product of one of the most romantic and thrilling events in our national history." And the poet who wrote this hymn was truly inspired in his creation of the song.

Francis Scott Key was born in Frederick County (now Carroll County) in western Maryland, on his father's estate, Terra Rubra. The Key family were among the earliest settlers in this section. Francis S. Key's great-grandfather, Philip Key, arrived in the colony of Maryland about the year 1720. His parents were John Ross Key (an officer in the Revolutionary War) and Ann Phoebe Charlton.

Until the boy was ten years old, he was educated at home; then he attended a preparatory school at Annapolis. While a student at St. John's College in the same town, from 1789 to 1796, he lived with his grandmother, Ann Ross Key, at her estate, Belvoir, on the Severn River. He also spent some time with her sister, Mrs. Upton Scott, in Annapolis.

After his graduation from St. John's, he studied law in the office of Judge Jeremiah Chase in order to prepare himself for the profession. One of his fellow law students was Roger Brooke Taney, who married Key's only sister. (Later he became the renowned Chief Justice Taney of the United States Supreme Court.)

On January 19, 1802, young Key married Mary Tayloe Lloyd. The wedding took place in stately Chase House, in Annapolis, then the property of Colonel Edward Lloyd. The Keys had six sons and five daughters. Key began his practice of law in Frederick, Maryland; but not long after the marriage, he moved from Frederick to Georgetown, D.C. The family resided on Bridge Street, and Francis Scott Key practiced law with his uncle, Philip Barton Key.

He had a flourishing law practice. At their home, he and Mrs. Key entertained notable visitors, including John Randolph of Roanoke, Virginia, and the Roger B. Taneys.

The young man was a brilliant attorney and had an extensive practice in the federal courts in Washington, D.C. He served as United States district attorney for the District of Columbia from 1833 to 1841. In October, 1833, President Andrew Jackson sent him to Alabama to negotiate a settlement between that state and the federal government in regard to Creek Indian lands.

Francis Scott Key was known as an excellent and effective speaker; several of his addresses are still in existence; they show that he had an unusually quick and logical mind. He was a devoutly religious man, a member of the Episcopal Church and a delegate to its General Conference from 1814 to 1826. For many years he acted as lay reader in St. John's Episcopal Church at Georgetown. Key, a man of real Christian character, was "fervent in public prayer." He once thought seriously of becoming a clergyman.

Key was kind in all his personal relations with different classes of people, and a sincere friend of Negroes. He served as an active member of the American Colonization Society, an organization whose purpose was to help Negroes settle in Liberia in the 1800's.

In fact—as someone once remarked—he was "just such a man as we would have chosen to write our national anthem."

One of his ancestors, John Key, had been an English poet laureate. From his youth, the lawyer wrote verses as a hobby; much of his poetry was of a religious nature. However, he never took his poetry writing seriously.

After Key's death, "the slender collection" was published as *Poems of the Late Francis Scott Key, Esq*. The volume contained an obituary, several religious poems, some "amatory and mildly facetious verse, respectable in meter, but of light consequence, save perhaps the hymn 'Lord, with Glowing Heart, I'd Praise Thee.' "

It is said that he was slender and carried himself erectly. He had dark blue eyes, and "thin, mobile features, expressive of his ardent and generous nature."

At sixty-three, Francis Scott Key was still active; but when visiting a daughter, Mrs. Charles Howard, at Mount Vernon Place in Baltimore, he caught cold and died of pleurisy on January 11, 1843. At first his body was interred in the Howard vault in Baltimore. Then in 1866, it was transferred to Mount Olivet Cemetery in Frederick, Maryland.

The bronze statue over his grave reveals Key with his hand outstretched, as at the moment he discovered that the flag "was still there." His other hand is waving his hat exultantly. When this memorial was unveiled, on August 9, 1898, the noted Colonel Henry T. Watterson of Kentucky made an outstanding address in his honor.

There are other monuments to the memory of the composer of "The Star-Spangled Banner"—at Fort McHenry, at Eutaw Place in Baltimore, and at Golden Gate Park in San Francisco. James Lick gave $150,000 for this last monument and its maintenance.

The period during which our national anthem was written was a most trying one for the young republic. We had won the Revolutionary War and gained our independence from England; but in

1812 we were forced into another conflict with the mother country.

For Great Britain claimed she had the right to interfere with American trade on the Atlantic Ocean and to search our vessels on the high seas for deserters from her navy. Also, the British incited Indians against us in the western part of our country.

To avenge such outrages, the United States declared war on England in 1812, a war which lasted two years, although many Americans opposed it. Encounters with the British took place both on land and sea, on Lakes Erie and Champlain, along the Atlantic Coast and at New Orleans. Our shipbuilders had constructed some excellent frigates, which made up the beginning of the United States Navy. These finally managed to triumph over the English vessels. A writer, Eloise Griffith, once said: "So, in 1812, we went to war again with England to make it plain we were a free, independent nation, and must be treated as such."

However, before the final victory, the summer of 1814 was a crucial period for us; the war with the British was not going well for our side: the invasion of Canada had "ended in humiliation"; the shores of Chesapeake Bay were ravaged by the British fleet under Admiral Sir George Cockburn; General Ross with four thousand troops had landed and captured Washington, D.C.

Ross's men set fire to the presidential mansion; they also burned the Capitol and other government buildings; the halls of Congress were in flames, as were the Arsenal and the Treasury Building. The enemy ruthlessly burned some of our vessels in the Washington Navy Yard. President James Madison and his wife, Dolley, escaped and made their way along country roads to Charlottesville, Virginia.

On a hot summer night, also along lonely roads, what was left of the American forces was making its way. That afternoon the British troops had beaten the Americans near Bladensburg, Maryland.

After this defeat, Dr. William Beanes, a prominent physician who had served with General Washington during the American Revolution and looked after Washington's men at Valley Forge, was captured by General Ross and held as a prisoner on Admiral Cockburn's flagship, the *Surprise.*

Dr. Beanes was an old settler who lived in Upper Marlborough. Some time before his imprisonment, when the British fleet sailed up the Potomac, it anchored off Alexandria, Virginia. General Ross and the admiral chose the Doctor's home in Upper Marlborough for their headquarters, as it was the finest one in town. Dr. Beanes had received them politely and treated them courteously during their stay in his home.

When the British officers left his place, they declared that the physician was honor bound not to take up arms against the British until all the men were safely back on their vessels.

But English stragglers on their way back to their ships went through Upper Marlborough and did some plundering in the town. Dr. Beanes and other vigilantes threw three of the offenders in jail. Because of this act, the doctor was dragged out of bed, taken from his home, and treated on the *Surprise* as a common criminal rather than as a prisoner of war. One British soldier swore that Dr. Beanes had injured him and had also tried to poison him and some of his comrades.

As soon as the prominent and influential young lawyer, Francis Scott Key, who was a personal friend of Dr. Beanes, heard of the latter's predicament, he asked for and received permission from President Madison to intervene with the British on Dr. Beanes's behalf.

With credentials from the President, Key set out at once on his dangerous mission. He galloped to Baltimore; there the thirty-four-year-old lawyer hired a small craft, the *Minden,* which was used as a flag-of-truce boat in the exchange of prisoners. It was in charge of Colonel J. S. Skinner, a government agent designated to carry out prisoner exchanges.

Key and Skinner sailed on the Chesapeake to the mouth of the Potomac, where the British fleet was preparing to attack the city of Baltimore, and Fort McHenry in particular. The two Americans were courteously received by Admiral Sir George Cockburn in his cabin, on his flagship, *Surprise,* where the physician was held prisoner.

Frances Scott Key showed his credentials and presented his case, requesting that Dr. Beanes be released. Colonel Skinner had with him some letters from wounded British officers, stating how well they had been treated by the Americans. After some discussion, the admiral and his officers consented to release the doctor.

However, since the fleet was ready to attack Baltimore, and the two Americans had heard their plans and also knew their fighting strength, Admiral Cockburn would not permit the three men to go ashore until the end of the attack, for fear they would reveal the details to their fellow Americans.

Under British guard the three were taken to the *Minden,* where they were forced to remain—back of the English fleet—until the attack on Fort McHenry was concluded.

This fort, constructed to defend Baltimore, was under the command of Major Armistead. The three Americans realized that it actually had little defensive power.

When part of the British troops—about three thousand strong—sailed up Chesapeake Bay on September 11, 1814, to attack Fort McHenry from behind, they ran into the major's "sunken barrier." (Major Armistead had sunk several small craft to prevent the enemy from reaching the city.) Bullets and cannon balls were fired at them from the fort; many were hit and killed; and General Ross lost his life that day. The troops finally gave up the idea of attacking by land, and returned to their ships to start the bombardment of Fort McHenry.

The first shot from the British fleet was fired at fourteen minutes before 6 A.M. on Tuesday, September 13, 1814. The English mortar shell landed in a hayfield just outside Fort McHenry. Then for twenty-five hours, without letup, the British pounded with rockets and bombs the little fort which "rocked and shook" under the continued attack. The bombardment continued all day, September 13, and on through the following night. Although between fifteen hundred and eighteen hundred shells were thrown, and about four hundred fell within the fortification it seemed a miracle that Major Armistead and his brave comrades held out against the fierce British onslaught. Only four men were killed and twenty-four wounded during the long bombardment.

Above the fort an enormous American flag, 42 feet long and 30 feet wide, was flying. It had fifteen stripes, thirteen for the original colonies and two for the additional states of Vermont and Kentucky. It had required four hundred yards of bunting to make this unusual banner. There was not much breeze on September 13, and it is said that the flag clung "sluggishly to the staff."

Key and his two companions were five miles away from the fort. Key had powerful field glasses with him, and although he peered anxiously up the Patapsco, the banner didn't really look like an actual battle flag. As long as daylight continued on September 13, the Americans could see the flag waving bravely over besieged Fort McHenry.

All through that terrible night, Key was in such anxiety and despair that all he could do was to pace the deck of the *Minden,* watch "the shells bursting in air," hear the noise of battle, and wait the coming of dawn. The shells dropped all night on the fort. Although at intervals Major Armistead's men sent shots in the direction of the British ships, their efforts were futile, for not one shot was able to reach the fleet.

The trio of Americans heard all around them the harsh sounds of the conflict during this "hot, persistent fight." One writer said of Key: "All through the flaming, thunderous night, Key sat between decks in an agony of fear for his beloved America."

Shortly before dawn the firing suddenly ceased. But the anxious watchers on the *Minden* could not tell who had won the battle—whether the fort had fallen or the British had stopped the attack—for the haze and smoke were too thick.

Luckily for the three Americans a break came at 7 A.M. when the mist cleared away for a short time. Then young Key was overjoyed to see "by the dawn's early light" that the flag they had seen the evening before "was still there." The shot-ridden ensign was flying high over the fort, despite the long-continued ordeal of bombardment. The three rejoiced together that the garrison had not surrendered, and Key declared it was glorious "to feel so proud of his flag."

They soon learned that the attack on Baltimore had been a failure, that the English forces were re-embarking, and that as soon as all had returned to their vessels, the American prisoners would be allowed to land from the *Minden.* They had watched Admiral Cockburn's flagship, the *Surprise,* go down the bay, past their American sloop; the Battle of Baltimore was over; and the discomfited British had to depart.

The young lawyer was so thrilled by the victory that he had to express his heartfelt feelings on the very spot. His patriotic fervor drove him to create an immortal poem which was inspired by the fury of battle and the joy of the American victory. His "song of confidence" was written under stirring circumstances, and according to one account, in a very few minutes.

He was filled with intense emotion as he composed the song, and fitted his words to the familiar melody of "To Anacreon in Heaven" which not long before he had heard the British officers singing in anticipation of their expected victory.

Various sources maintain that Key scribbled the words of "The Star-Spangled Banner" on the back of an old letter. Thus was written, during the War of 1812, the song that long after—in 1931—became by Congressional action our national anthem. It was composed by a man who might have been completely forgotten in his native land if he had not seen the American flag still proudly and defiantly waving in the morning breeze on September 14, 1814.

> Born under such auspicious circumstances, it seems very appropriate that this song should rank first in importance in our patriotic song lore.

Some authorities state that Francis Scott Key finished the four stanzas of his noted song on the sloop *Minden,* on the way to the shore, after being released by the British. Others say all the words were not yet written down, but that he held them in his memory.

When the craft docked at Baltimore, the three men all went to the Old Fountain Inn to spend the night. Dr. Beanes and Colonel Skinner went to bed early; but Key called for pen and ink and made "a fair copy" of his poem before retiring. It is said he did not regard this work as a song of victory, but as one of "courage in the midst of trouble."

(Some doubt that the poet made his first version on a letter; but they believe "the neat, original manuscript" was written following his release. For many years this was preserved in Annapolis by Key's wife's sister, Mrs. Nicholson, until her death in 1847. Then it was exhibited in the Walters Gallery in Baltimore; later, in 1953, the document was acquired by the Maryland Historical Society.)

According to a well-established report, the day after his return to Baltimore, Key went to the home of his brother-in-law, Captain Nicholson. Both the Nicholsons were delighted with the song and declared it should be printed at once.

Key's sister-in-law—so one version goes—took the poem that day to a printer, who struck off handbills, or broadsides, of it, with the title, *The Defense of Fort McHenry.* Later that same day, copies of the unsigned poem were circulated around Baltimore, where it met with instant popularity.

Another source gives this account of the first printing of what later was termed "The Star-Spangled Banner." A young boy named Samuel Sands was alone in a Baltimore printing shop, for all the men had gone to the defense of their town. Of course Samuel heard the cannon booming over Chesapeake Bay during the bombardment of Fort McHenry.

The youth was serving as an apprentice in the print shop. He had already learned some things, including how to handle the clumsy, old-fashioned printing press. Although he had watched the men at work very carefully, now that he was alone in the place he felt very incapable.

When someone came in and asked him to print the words of Francis Scott Key's poem as a broadside, Sam protested that he wasn't a printer yet. However, he decided to try and to do his very best to get out this work alone.

First he picked out the needed type; then he worked busily away, not even stopping for lunch. Toward evening he went home, ate a hurried supper, then borrowed a whale-oil lamp from his mother. Back at the print shop, young Sam worked all night; by late afternoon of the next day, he had printed seven hundred broadsides of *The Defense of Fort McHenry*.

On September 21, 1814, Key's poem was published in the Baltimore *American;* it was stated that it was to be sung to the melody of "To Anacreon in Heaven." This explanation was printed in connection with the poem:

> The annexed song was composed under the following circumstances. A gentleman had left Baltimore under a flag of truce, for the purpose of getting released from the British fleet a friend of his who had been captured at Marlborough. He went so far as the mouth of the Patuxent, and was not permitted to return lest the intended attack on Baltimore should be disclosed. He was, therefore, brought up the bay, to the mouth of the Patapsco, where the flag vessel was kept under the guns of a frigate, and he was compelled to witness the bombardment of Fort McHenry, which the Admiral had boasted he would carry [out] in a few hours, and that the city must fall.
>
> He watched the flag at the fort through the whole day with an anxiety that can better be felt than described, until the night prevented him from seeing it. In the night he watched the bomb shells, and at early dawn, his eye was again greeted by the proudly waving flag of his country.

Years later—in 1872—in the same newspaper which first published the poem, a writer made this comment about the history of the song: "The poet, Francis Scott Key, was too modest to announce himself, and it was some time after its appearance [in the *American*] that he became known as the author. . . ."

Just a few days after copies were circulated around the city, the song was first sung one morning on the sidewalk at a one-story tavern next door to the Holiday Theater. About twenty men— most of them soldiers—and including several actors, were gathered there, "all fortified by mint juleps."

Francis Scott Key was one of the assemblage; to them he read his new song two or three times and "electrified his audience." Then came a demand to hear the piece sung. At once, an actor named Ferdinand Durang got up on a rush-bottomed chair and ". . . sang the song with such voice and feeling as to throw his hearers into a state of excitement. All shouted and clapped and were thrilled by the new composition."

So it was that for the first time in our history the chorus of "The Star-Spangled Banner" led by the soloist, Ferdinand Durang, was re-echoed "with infinite harmony of voices" by the rest of the men in the crowd. They all liked the song so much that they sang it several times that morning.

Within a few days, it found its way to the stage, also all over Baltimore, in military camps and in homes. Everywhere Key's composition "went straight to the popular heart." It was hailed as "the finest patriotic song of the year."

To celebrate their victory over the British and the nonsurrender of Fort McHenry, the people of Baltimore in excited crowds roamed through the streets and gathered around great bonfires. They sang Key's new song, and it wasn't long before most of the populace knew the thrilling words. Three months later, the new piece was played at the Battle of New Orleans. (About a month after the first publication, Joseph Carr published a sheet music edition with a musical setting by his son, Thomas Carr. Other newspapers outside of Baltimore printed the poem; and before the year was over it had been included in three song books.)

In 1867—over half a century after Francis Scott Key had

written the poem—in a paper before the Pennsylvania Historical Society, Colonel John L. Warner described the events connected with its first singing by Ferdinand Durang:

> "The Star-Spangled Banner" was first sung, when fresh from the press, in a small, one-story frame house, long occupied as a tavern by Widow Berling, next to the Holiday Theater, but then kept by a Captain MacCauley, a house whose players "most did congregate" to prepare for the daily military drill, every man at that time being a soldier.
>
> There came also Captain Benjamin Edes of the 27th Regiment, Captains Long and Warner of the 39th Regiment and Major Frailet. Warner was a silversmith of good repute in the neighborhood. When a number of the young defenders of the monumental city were assembled, Captains Edes and Warner called the group to order to listen to the patriotic song which Captain Edes had just struck off at his press. He then read it aloud to the volunteers assembled, who greeted each verse with a hearty shout.

The tune of our national anthem, "To Anacreon in Heaven," is that of an old English drinking song. The air has had a long and interesting history.

During the latter part of the eighteenth century, and on to the present time, men's clubs were very popular in London and in other large British towns. Some of them were founded for political purposes, while others were simply get-togethers for eating, drinking, smoking, and conversation. Often such organizations indulged in singing "catches" and "glees" followed by "a cold collation." Some groups had their own special songs, with which they opened or closed their assemblies.

One of the most prominent and exclusive of these London clubs was the Anacreontic Society (termed by some critics as "a wild bacchanalian club"). The members—wealthy, high-class Londoners—met every two weeks at the Crown and Anchor on the corner of the Strand and Arundel streets. (The original meeting place burned in 1854.)

The name of this organization came from that of a celebrated

Greek poet, Anacreon, born in the year 560 B.C. He wrote many poems in honor of his patron, the tyrant Polycrates. He created five volumes of verse, and several other poets tried to imitate him. The type of poetry was called anacreontic verse. One writer has said: "Anacreon sang and wrote elegant poems about love, wine and revelry in a variety of lyric measures."

In his works, the Greek poet extolled the virtues of Venus, goddess of Love, and Bacchus, god of Wine. Lord Byron, in his poem "The Isles of Greece," referred to this Greek lyricist in the line, "It made Anacreon's song divine." Anacreon's works were translated into English, and one critic says that the best of these translations were done by the Irish poet Thomas Moore, in his "Odes of Anacreon," written in 1800.

This aristocratic society of music lovers met to enjoy long orchestral concerts, followed by elaborate banquets and informal singing by the members. At times, the latter provided outside entertainment; at others, they themselves furnished the numbers. Their evening meetings always ended with their singing of "To Anacreon in Heaven." According to one contemporary, this was indulged in "when the singers were feeling happy and spirits were high."

The words were written by Ralph Tomlinson, president of the Anacreontic Society, a lawyer at Lincoln's Inn. The members had requested him to write an original piece to be used as their theme song at all their gatherings. So he composed the lyrics "To Anacreon in Heaven," "a poem of six stanzas, in peculiar fashion."

John Stafford Smith, a young London organist and composer— also a member of the Anacreontic Society—was asked to write music for Ralph Tomlinson's lyrics. One source states that credit for the tune should be given the society's orchestra leader, Samuel Arnold; and that John Stafford Smith, in 1799, composed a musical setting for the composition, for three voices.

The poem was probably written between 1770 and 1775, and was first published in the *Vocal Magazine* in 1778. A sheet-music edition, with both words and music, was brought out in 1779 by Longman and Broderip.

The opening stanza of "To Anacreon in Heaven" was as follows:

> To Anacreon in heaven where he sat in full glee,
> A few sons of harmony sent a petition,
> That he, their inspirer and patron would be.
> When this answer arrived from the jolly old Grecian,
> "Voice, fiddle and flute, no longer be mute,
> I'll lend ye my name and inspire you to boot,
> And beside I'll instruct ye like me
> To entwine the myrtle of Venus with Bacchus's wine."

The air of "To Anacreon in Heaven" became very popular in England; several parodies were written to it. One was a Masonic ode, found in a collection compiled by Brother S. Holden. The melody was also used as a military march. When English settlers came to the American colonies, they brought the popular tune with them.

However, in the New World, it was not used as a drinking song, but to express patriotic feelings. The first of this kind of setting of the old air was made in June, 1798, by Robert Treat Paine, son of one of the signers of the Declaration of Independence, and it came about in this way.

The Massachusetts Charitable Fire Society of Boston commissioned Paine to write an original poem for their anniversary. In trying to find a good theme for this work, the poet decided to honor President Adams, who had successfully avoided conflicts with both England and France. Paine named his new composition "Adams and Liberty: The Boston Patriotic Song." It was greeted with much enthusiasm and was published immediately. The writer received $750 for the copyright, "an enormous sum for those days."

Since most Americans were familiar with the melody of "To Anacreon in Heaven," Paine fitted his poem to the air. It began with this stanza:

Ye sons of Columbia, who bravely have fought
For those rights, which unstained, from your sires have descended.
May you long taste the blessings your valor has bought,
And your sons reap the soil which their fathers defended.

Americans at once accepted this song and it gained widespread popularity. However, it was not considered universal enough for a permanent national hymn. Other poems to the same melody appeared from time to time, including "Jefferson and Liberty," published in *The Patriotic Songster* in Philadelphia. And among varied songs in the same meter and sung to the tune was one that celebrated the Russian victory over Napoleon. Such works were very popular for singing at banquets on such important occasions as Washington's birthday or the celebration of Independence Day.

In 1805 Francis Scott Key is said to have written his first poem to this air. It is related that he sang the piece himself at a dinner given in Georgetown, honoring the noted Stephen Decatur.

Therefore, it is not surprising that after his thrilling experience at Fort McHenry, he naturally expressed his feelings in words that could be sung to the familiar melody. And as *Collier's Encyclopedia* states: "It was not long before Key's words were recognized as the embodiment of the American ideas of patriotism, in song form, which the country had produced."

Although "The Star-Spangled Banner" was well received in the city of Baltimore, it took some time for it to make its way into song books around the country. Eventually it was accepted by the American people, but no official action on making it our national anthem was taken until over a century after it had been written.

And it really did not become generally popular until about the time of the Civil War. It survived this conflict and the Spanish-American War, while sharing honors with several other patriotic American songs. Admiral Dewey, an important figure in the last-mentioned conflict, preferred to use "The Star-Spangled Banner" rather than "Columbia, the Gem of the Ocean," which had been composed sixteen years before Key's song.

In 1889, Benjamin F. Tracy, Secretary of the Navy, ordered it to be played on all commissioned ships. And during the 1890's it became the authorized music at the Salute to the Colors, both in the United States Navy and the Army. It was specified that it must be played by military bands on all ceremonial occasions. President Woodrow Wilson approved the use of this music when he signed new regulations during World War I.

Although from time to time efforts were made to induce Congress to make "The Star-Spangled Banner" our official anthem, the members allowed a whole series of bills regarding the subject to die in committee.

Finally, the Seventy-first Congress had the honor of passing Public Law 823 (U.S. Code 36, Section 144) which officially recognized Francis Scott Key's composition as our national hymn. Herbert Hoover, thirty-first President of the United States, signed the act into law on March 3, 1931.

As soon as the news of the signing reached the House of Representatives, the song was sung in unique fashion. The Marine Band played it; one soloist was accompanied at the piano by the Speaker of the House, Nicholas Longworth; then everyone joined in singing, for the first time, "The Star-Spangled Banner" as our national anthem.

When Congress officially accepted this work, it termed the song simply as "the composition consisting of the words and music known as 'The Star-Spangled Banner,' the national anthem of the United States." However, there are varying versions of the piece.

Since there has been a decided growth in the popularity of community singing (also it is an important factor in army training), the need has been stressed of late years for an authorized version of the hymn. In an effort to bring about unity, a committee worked for almost a year on a service version which it hoped would come into universal use. But we still do not have an "official version."

In 1966, in an article in the *Saturday Review,* Mrs. Renée B.

Fisher stated that "The Star-Spangled Banner" should be scrapped as our national anthem: first because the song cannot be sung successfully by amateurs (with its range of almost two octaves); secondly, the lyrics are too warlike. (However, today we do not use the third stanza as it does not now represent our true attitude toward Great Britain.)

Gerald W. Johnson answered Mrs. Fisher's complaint about the song's warlike quality by saying that any national anthem "is essentially a battle cry."

Many citizens also think something should be done to make "The Star-Spangled Banner" more singable. Miss Lucy Monroe, who has sung the hymn at least five thousand times, believes it should undergo some minor changes, of the high and low notes, so that all may join in singing it; but she wants the basic melody to remain unchanged.

(When the tune was first created by John Stafford Smith, his air consisted of several different sections, to be sung by the tenors, baritones, and bases. This accounts for the great range of the tune, and makes it difficult for the average person to sing it today.)

For more than a decade, Congressman Joel Broyhill of Virginia promoted a Congressional resolution for "a definitive version of the anthem." But he was not successful in his project.

In answer to the statement which many make that "The Star-Spangled Banner" cannot be sung "beautifully," Cleave Jones (in the Long Beach, California, *Press-Telegram*) stated that it *can* be sung "beautifully," and as proof, cited the following example:

> Shortly after the Second Armored Division chased the Germans from the little city of Maastricht, Holland, the people paid honor to the United States Army. The local Symphony Orchestra and the Maastricht Men's Chorus gave a concert especially for the Americans.
>
> As the climax of the performance, the chorus sang "The Star-Spangled Banner" in English. The anthem rolled out with majesty and dignity and precision, and the troops responded with awe and reverence. It was wonderful and it was touching, and it was not surpassed anywhere as an expression of gratitude to our Army.

If Dutchmen can make "The Star-Spangled Banner" a thing of beauty and honor, certainly Americans can do the same.

And on July 4, 1968 (also in the Long Beach *Press-Telegram*) Vernon Scott quoted the opinions of Dwight Townsend, "a six-foot, four Yale-educated patriot, who 'bellows' the song at sporting events," in clubs and musical shows, and on other occasions. Here are Townsend's views on the subject of singing our national hymn:

> I don't find the anthem unsingable, although it does have a range of almost two octaves. . . .
> The only proper way to sing it is to really belt it out—like a Marine Corps band. You can't croon it.
> There are four stanzas in all, but most people don't even know the first verse, much less any of the others. I don't think it is taught in schools any more.
> Most Americans just mumble their way through the anthem. They sing "through the perilous *night*" instead of "through the perilous *fight*."

Mr. Townsend is opposed to those Americans who are trying to replace "The Star-Spangled Banner," as our national anthem, with "God Bless America" or "America." He firmly declares: "We should stay with 'The Star-Spangled Banner.' It still gives people goose bumps when it's played and sung correctly."

This hymn has played an important role in our history since its creation, and has been featured on various important occasions.

For instance, in April, 1861, on the Sunday after the stars and stripes had been fired upon at Fort Sumter, South Carolina, it was sung at many church services throughout the North; and just four years later, after the American flag had been hauled down at Fort Sumter, there was a notable gathering at the same place. This long-remembered historical event occurred on April 14, 1865, the day that President Abraham Lincoln was assassinated.

The identical shell-shattered flag which had flown during the bombardment in 1861 was raised again. The United States govern-

ment had invited the noted preacher and orator, Henry Ward
Beecher, to deliver the Oration of the Day.

Major Anderson, who exactly four years before had been forced
to capitulate, hoisted the stars and stripes; and again our national
ensign floated in the breeze. At once the band struck up "The Star-
Spangled Banner," and the great crowd, filled with patriotic emotions, joined in the singing.

On many occasions it has been proved that no other song stirs
the blood of Americans as this one does. Just a week after the
warship *Maine* was blown up in Havana Harbor, on February 15,
1898, the orchestra in Daly's Theater, New York, suddenly
changed its music to that of "The Star-Spangled Banner." The
audience almost went wild; all sprang to their feet and joined in
singing the anthem. Such a scene, one reporter declared, had not
occurred in a New York playhouse since the Civil War. It showed
the state of mind that Americans were in at that time of the Cuban
crisis.

In his book, *Stories of Great National Songs* (written in 1899)
Colonel Nicholas relates this happening:

> One of the most thrilling incidents in the annals of war, showing
> the power of a patriotic song, was that on the ramparts of Santiago
> on that memorable Friday, the first of July, 1898.
> I think it was in the Twenty-First Regulars, that man after man
> was fast falling in blood and death before a blazing fire of Mauser
> bullets, when the soldiers, catching a fresh gleam of the Flag at a
> critical moment, spontaneously began to sing "The Star-Spangled
> Banner," and its majestic strains so thrilled the souls of the men that
> they seemed to be nerved by some superhuman power to defy the
> storm of battle, and to win the victory that sealed the fate of
> Santiago.

There is also an interesting story connected with the famous
German singer, Madame Ernestine Schumann-Heink, and our national anthem. During World War I, she had sons fighting on both
sides of the conflict.

Here in the United States, the noted contralto visited many army camps and entertained the soldiers. One day she was asked to sing "The Star-Spangled Banner," of which she knew only the first few lines. A young newspaperman kindly wrote them down for her, and soon she had memorized them.

Just after the Armistice—November 11, 1918—Madame Schumann-Heink was singing in Kansas City when the news reached her of her son August's death in Germany. Even though she was grief-stricken, she consented to sing at the funeral of the buddy of the reporter who, some time before, had written down the words of "The Star-Spangled Banner" for her. And the great diva said simply, "I sang for him; it was all I could do."

In December, 1941, just after the United States had entered World War II, Sir Winston Churchill was a guest at the White House. Although it was a wartime holiday season, carols were sung as usual, along with "The Star-Spangled Banner" and "God Save the King."

The flag which had flown over Fort McHenry during the lengthy attack upon it in 1814 was presented to Major Armistead, who with his brave comrades had so gallantly defended the fort. During the long fight this ensign lost one star and part of its "broad stripes," and its length was reduced from forty feet to thirty-six. The distinctive flag had been made by Mrs. Mary Pickersgill of Baltimore and was returned to her for mending. (She was the daughter of Mrs. Rebecca Young, a well-known flagmaker of Revolutionary days, who fashioned the first banners carried by the American colonists in their struggle for independence.) The Fort McHenry flag was so large it could not be sewed together in the Pickersgill home; so it was spread out in Claggett's Brewery.

A descendant of Major Armistead presented the famous flag to the Smithsonian Institution in Washington, D.C., where it can still be seen "with its scars of battle carefully mended."

The Pickersgill home—now called Flag House—is open to the public. It was within its walls that the first stitches were taken in the banner that would inspire Francis Scott Key. When September 12 comes around each year, many citizens of Baltimore gather at the historic building. This event, on "Defenders' Day," is in reality "a re-dedication of the ideals expressed in Key's poem."

According to the rules for "The Proper Display of the Flag": "The Flag is customarily displayed from sunrise to sunset. . . ."

However, it *may* fly both day and night over the United States Capitol in Washington, D.C. The national emblem is flown continuously over the following places: the grave of Francis Scott Key (the ensign is never lowered there, except when being replaced); at Flag House Square, in Baltimore, the home of Mary Pickersgill; at Fort McHenry; and at the World War Memorial in Worcester, Massachusetts.

The story is told that once when a college professor was approaching Fort McHenry, he was surprised that the Stars and Stripes was not waving over it. At once he protested to the National Park Service; then this body gave the fort permission to fly the flag there both day and night. On July 3, 1948, President Harry S. Truman issued a proclamation for the twenty-four-hour display over the fortification.

In "Action Line," a column in the Long Beach *Press-Telegram,* the columnist, when asked at what places the American flag could be flown all twenty-four hours, added seven more to those mentioned above: the Marine Memorial at Arlington, Virginia; the birthplace—the Terra Rubra farm, at Keysville, Maryland—of Francis Scott Key; Betsy Ross's grave in Philadelphia; the grave of Captain William Driver, at Nashville, Tennessee (who first called our flag "Old Glory" in 1831); Pennsylvania Hall, at Gettysburg, Pennsylvania (used as a hospital at time of the battle); the grave of Jenny Wade, only civilian killed in that battle; and Taos, New Mexico.

The story is that in 1861, during the Civil War, Southern sympathizers kept tearing down the stars and stripes in front of the war office headquarters in Taos. Finally Kit Carson and several others went out of town, cut down the tallest tree they could find and set up the trunk in the middle of the plaza. Then they nailed the banner to the top of the pole; armed with guns, they defied anyone to haul it down. It is said a flag has flown there continuously since that happening in 1861.

Today Fort McHenry is an American shrine. Congress on March 8, 1925, created the site as a national park, in commemoration of its having inspired "The Star-Spangled Banner."

The fort is located on a small peninsula that juts out into busy Baltimore harbor; its grounds cover forty-seven acres. Along the driveway is a double row of markers, with bronze plaques, one for each of the fifty states. They are arranged chronologically in order of the entrance of the states into the Union.

One of the five brick buildings contains an officers' mess and a kitchen, where there is a display of utensils of the 1800 period. In one structure, now used as a museum, you can see early American furniture. Also there is a Flag Room; in another, the Bowie Collection of Firearms, with some rare old weapons, is housed. The fort also has a guardhouse and a powder magazine, and several cannon are mounted, pointing seaward.

Fort McHenry is maintained by a competent staff to look after the many visitors. Over half a million people visit this shrine each year. The Visitors' Register shows that thousands of foreigners have come to see the old fort.

When Alaska was admitted as the forty-ninth state, on July 4, 1959, an interesting flag ceremony took place here. The nation's new forty-nine-star flag was raised officially at 12:01 A.M. over Fort McHenry.

On this occasion, Interior Secretary Seaton hoisted the new ensign as the Marine Band played "The Star-Spangled Banner." Modern fireworks depicted "the rockets' red glare," while army and navy units re-enacted the bombardment that took place during the War of 1812.

Fort McHenry was chosen for the scene of these official rites honoring the flag with its new star for Alaska because this is one of the few places in our country where the stars and stripes can legally be flown at night.

Because of the impressive circumstances under which our national anthem was written, also because of the sincere fervor of its patriotic sentiments, "The Star-Spangled Banner" has received numerous tributes from both known and unnamed writers.

In 1899, Louis Elson paid homage to the song in these words:

> Its melody is by no means an ideal one for chorus singing, but its great associations and its lofty words have forever endeared it to the American heart, and until some native composer has given us a more practicable tune, "The Star-Spangled Banner" will justly remain the national air of our country, and every patriot's breast will throb responsive to its tones.

S. J. Adair Fitzgerald, in 1901, in his *Stories of Famous Songs* said:

> It was caught up in the camps, sung around bivouac fires, and whistled in the streets; and when peace was declared and we scattered to our houses, it was carried to thousands of firesides as the most precious relic of the War of 1812.

And another writer, Elias Nason, has stated:

> . . . it has unity of idea. . . . It is bold, warlike, and majestic, stirring the profoundest emotions of the soul, and echoing through its deepest chambers something of the prospective grandeur of a mighty Nation tramping toward the loftiest heights of intellectual dominion.

Gray J. Poole, in 1949, called "The Star-Spangled Banner" "the unconquerable song" and one of the finest documents of our American heritage.

> . . . the anthem of a nation that has become the guardian of freedom in the world, half slave, it takes on a social and historical significance that places it beside the Declaration of Independence and the Bill of Rights.

And a writer in *Collier's Encyclopedia* said: "No other patriotic song appears so regularly and over such a long period, and therefore its elevation to the position of national anthem seems to be justified by this extended popular acclamation."

In recent years someone, whose name was not given, wrote this tribute in the Long Beach *Press-Telegram,* July 4, 1959—one that no doubt would have pleased the poet, Francis Scott Key.

> The anthem, through all the years, transcends the man and the battle. It could have been written by a man at the Argonne.
>
> Or a man named Jones at Leyte. Because in "The Star-Spangled Banner" America found a song that suited herself.
>
> It's a big song, a song that's even hard to sing. But have you ever heard another with such great unshakeable strength? Another that ever sent out such an indomitable thunder of courage?
>
> Each time we hear it, we straighten our shoulders to the ringing reminder that the land we live in, the land we love, is "the land of the free and the home of the brave."

The Star-Spangled Banner

Francis Scott Key

1. O_____ say can you see by the dawn's ear - ly light, What so
2. On the shore, dim - ly seen thro' the mists of the deep, Where the
3. And_____ where is the band who so vaunt - ing - ly swore, 'Mid the
4. O_____ thus be it ev - er, when free men shall stand Be - -

proud - ly we hail'd at the twi - light's last gleam - ing? Whose broad
foe's haugh - ty host in dread si - lence re - pos - es, What is
hav - oc of war and the bat - tle's con - fu - sion, A_____
tween their loved homes and the war's des - o - la - tion; Blest with

stripes and bright stars, thro' the per - il - ous fight, O'er the
that which the breeze, o'er the tow - er - ing steep, As it
home and a coun - try they'd leave us no more? Their_____
vict' - ry and peace, may the heav'n res - cued land Praise the

ram - parts we watched were so gal - lant - ly stream - ing? And the
fit - ful - ly blows, half con - ceals, half dis - clos - es? Now it
blood has wash'd out their foul foot - step's pol - lu - tion. No_____
Pow'r that hath made and pre - served us a na - tion! Then_____

rock - et's red glare, the bombs burst - ing in air, Gave_____
catch - es the gleam of the morn - ing's first beam, In full
ref - uge could save the_____ hire - ling and slave From the
con - quer we must, when our cause it is just, And_____

proof thro' the night_____ that our flag was still there, O_____
glo - ry re - flect - ed now_____ shines on the stream, 'Tis the
ter - ror of flight_____ or the gloom of the grave; And the
this be our mot - to 'In_____ God is our trust!" And the

say, does that_____ Star - span - gled Ban - ner_____ yet_____ wave_____ O'er the
Star - span - gled_____ Ban - ner O long may_____ it_____ wave_____ O'er the
Star - span - gled_____ Ban - ner in tri - umph_____ doth_____ wave_____ O'er the
Star - span - gled_____ Ban - ner in tri - umph_____ shall_____ wave_____ O'er the

land_____ of the free and the home of the brave?
land_____ of the free and the home of the brave.
land_____ of the free and the home of the brave.
land_____ of the free and the home of the brave.

3

*

"Home, Sweet Home"

In his *Stories of Great National Songs,* in 1899, Colonel Nicholas Smith stated:

> There were hundreds of distinguished men in Washington, who were very conspicuous, and some of them performed great and memorable services. But no monument there will be visited by a greater throng of pilgrims, and no memory will appeal more tenderly to all of them, than that of the wandering actor who lived and died alone, and of whom nothing is remembered but that he wrote one song. . . .

The writer was referring to "Home, Sweet Home," the "loveliest song the world ever sang." Its composer was John Howard Payne, an actor, dramatist, editor, and diplomat.

He was born on June 9, 1791, the sixth in a family of nine children, whose parents were William and Sarah Isaacs Payne.

The father was a descendant of one of three brothers (Thomas Payne or Paine) who came to Massachusetts and settled at Yarmouth. One of the immigrants was a forefather of Dolley Payne Madison, at one time the charming First Lady of the White House. Another Payne brother was the ancestor of Robert Treat Payne, one of the signers of the Declaration of Independence in 1776.

John Howard Payne's family lived for some time in Boston, where William Payne was head of a school. While in this city, one of the boy's friends was Samuel Woodworth, who also is remembered for a noted song, "The Old Oaken Bucket."

A precocious, gifted child, young Payne from his early childhood showed an unusual talent for reading and reciting poetry and also for acting. His father taught him "declamation"—so popular in that era. Soon the boy was taking part in school programs and in private theatricals. This later led to his desire for a career on the stage. One source has said: "Howard, as the family called him, is said, at the early age of thirteen years to have foreseen his long association with stage life."

A well-known actor, after seeing the boy perform, offered to give him acting lessons and to get professional engagements for him. However Payne's father objected strenuously, for he firmly believed that "sin and the stage were synonymous."

In order to turn his son's interests in other directions, the elder Payne got the boy a job in the countinghouse of a large mercantile establishment in New York, owned by Grant and Bennett Forbes. He urged these men to keep his son at work for twelve hours each day. Also he wanted young Payne to be kept busy during the evenings so that he wouldn't have time to hang around theaters or to attend performances.

But no matter how much William Payne opposed his son's wishes for an acting career, he couldn't keep him from thinking about the theater; for this determined youth clung firmly to his heart's desire.

Even though he had so little leisure time, John Howard Payne, when he was fourteen, actually produced and published secretly the first numbers of the *Thespian Mirror,* from December 28, 1805 to May 31, 1806. This was an eight-page review of the New York theaters, issued every Saturday evening. In it he discussed what was going on at the various playhouses in the city; he also included literary and news items and some gossipy bits about the actors and actresses.

Payne was not only the editor but also the business manager and subscription manager. Stage-conscious citizens of the metropolis were delighted with the small weekly journal. But no one in town had the slightest idea about who the writer was.

William Coleman, editor of the New York *Evening Post,* made up his mind to ferret out the identity of the editor of the *Thespian Mirror.* He had been much impressed by one of the dramatic criticisms in the magazine, so he had reproduced it in his own newspaper, the *Post.* Coleman wrote and asked the unknown editor to come to his home on a certain evening.

He was astonished when young Payne appeared; he just couldn't believe the boy actually was the editor of the theatrical weekly. However, the youth finally managed to convince the older man of his identity. Later the New York editor remarked in regard to Payne's "polished conversation": "I found it required an effort on my part to keep up my conversation in so choice a style."

By this time, Payne had written his first play, a five-act comedy entitled *Julia,* or *The Wanderer.* It was produced for the first time on February 7, 1806, at the Park Theater in New York, and really proved his ability as a dramatist. One critic reported that the leading role was played by a Mrs. Jones and that "the comedy scored a real success."

Because of this unusual achievement Payne, who had an exceptional, attractive personality, soon was being feted by various prominent persons of the day in both the social and literary sets of New York. These included the noted American writers Washington Irving, Charles Brockden Brown, and James K. Paulding.

William Coleman was certain the youthful playwright would have a brilliant future. Soon he persuaded the boy's father to let the son leave his hated job at the countinghouse and to continue his education.

The editor solicited financial aid so that Payne could further his training. A wealthy New York merchant, John E. Seaman, agreed to send the youth to Union College at Schenectady. Payne was enrolled in 1806.

When settled in college, where he was very popular because of his "engaging disposition and pleasant manners," Payne at once started another weekly magazine, the *Pastime.* It was filled with essays, stories, and poems; it also stressed "the pleasures of home—of all pleasures the most delightful."

During his second year at Union College, Mrs. Payne died. After her passing it is said that the son never again knew what it was to have a real home.

Not long after the mother's death, John Howard Payne's father became bankrupt. Then the youth begged him for permission to quit college and try to make a career on the stage to help support the family. Finally William Payne consented, and the would-be actor's first stage part was that of young Norval in the tragedy *Douglas,* by John Home. The opening performance took place in February 1809, at the Park Theater in New York.

During the first six months of 1809, this young thespian of eighteen was an instantaneous and sensational success. His New York opening led to "a triumphal American tour." He played in several large cities, including Boston and Philadelphia, where he was billed as "The American Juvenile Wonder." People traveled long distances to see him perform, and several important critics praised his productions.

Young Payne not only had parts in the leading standard dramas, but also was seen in several plays by Shakespeare: *King Lear, Romeo and Juliet,* and *Hamlet.* One authority has said that he was the first American to play the title role in the last-mentioned tragedy. On April 17, 1809, in a Boston theater, Elizabeth Poe (mother of Edgar Allan Poe, then an infant) played Ophelia opposite Payne.

Unfortunately the young actor's success did not last very long. He encountered opposition from older, established players, including "the brilliant, but eccentric star," George Frederick Cooke. Payne rose—so it has been stated—as an actor, "with meteoric speed," but he fell almost as fast. Although he had been successful in several cities, he was not booked for any theatrical engagements during the theater season of 1810–1811.

He was a handsome young man whose eyes glowed "with animation and intelligence." In addition, Payne had a melodious voice. However he lacked the training and study that distinguished the older, experienced thespians. Also he had the misfortune to quarrel with the powerful theater manager Stephen Price.

In December, 1811, the magazine *Man of Talent* stated that the young actor had overcome some of his youthful defects, and that his work had improved. About this time Payne, who was "sensitive, petulant, and not yet aware of his gifts as a playwright," began to reveal a characteristic—instability—which would handicap him the rest of his days. Finally his father persuaded him to re-enter the business world as a bookseller. John Howard also decided he would like to start a literary exchange in New York. Although he had made money from his acting, he had no business ability; so this adventure was unsuccessful and "resulted in a complete financial debacle."

In 1812, after the death of William Payne, creditors kept pressing John Howard for the payment of his debts. He still had a dream of going to England, where he was certain he could make a successful career on the stage and later return to America as an accomplished tragedian.

Several of his American admirers, including Alexander Hansen, William Gwynn, and Jonathan Meredith, made up a purse of $2,000 so that the young man might spend a year in London. But as it turned out, he remained there for twenty years; and during this period abroad, his fortunes "were strangely interwoven with fame and poverty."

In January, 1813, he confidently set sail for Liverpool while the War of 1812 between Great Britain and the United States was at its height. With him Payne carried letters of introduction to Lord Byron, John Kemble, Samuel T. Coleridge, Shelley, Charles Lamb, and other current celebrities. Reaching London, he at once contacted Washington Irving, whom he had known in New York; while in England he roomed for a time with Irving.

Soon after his arrival there, Payne was sent to prison for two weeks as a national enemy and possibly a spy. But he was released, perhaps through the influence of Irving and other important friends.

A few months later (after he had become acquainted with the celebrated actor, John Kemble), Payne was given a part at the renowned Drury Lane Theatre. His debut, again as young Norval in *Douglas,* took place on June 4, 1813. During the months that followed, he played other characters and traveled through the provinces, acting in *Romeo and Juliet* and other dramas. He was popular with many British theater-goers and was greeted with "audible" applause, but it was not "overwhelming." One critic once said of Payne that he "just missed greatness as an actor." But the young American did "enter actively into the field of the British theater, both as an actor and a dramatist." He was noted as the first American to attract the attention of people there, in these two fields.

When Payne returned from his acting tour through the provinces, in 1814, he was without funds and had no more immediate prospects for further stage roles. Now that he realized he would never be able to duplicate his early youthful success, he decided to try writing and adapting plays to support himself.

After a rather brief stay in London, he went to Paris where he became acquainted with the well-known actor Talma, who introduced the young American to the French drama. In this city he lived in a garret at the top of an old house.

After seeing the French play, *La Pie Voleuse* ("The Maiden and the Magpie") by Caigniez and Baudouin, he was intrigued by it. At once he translated it into English and sold it, for £150, to the manager of the Drury Lane Theatre, where it was performed twenty-seven times. This is said to have been the beginning of Payne's career as a dramatist.

However, his first real success—and many consider it his best drama—was *Brutus*. Once in a while—so one writer has stated—in the midst of the drudgery of translating and adapting theatrical productions, the playwright did "strike it rich." This happened in the case of *Brutus,* or *The Fall of Tarquin*. It was a five-act tragedy that had its initial performance at Drury Lane on December 3, 1818, when the dramatist was just twenty-seven-years old. The outstanding British actor Edmund Kean played the title role, while Julia Glover was the feminine lead, Tullia.

Brutus was not an original drama, but an adaptation from, and a combination of, the works of seven other writers, as the author himself admitted. But it revealed Payne's unusual skill in handling dramatic scenes. Although it was produced fifty-two times during its first season in London, the unfortunate author received only £183 for his work.

For more than seventy years *Brutus* was played on the British and American stages. Some of the greatest tragedians of all times acted the title role, including Edmund Kean, Edwin Forrest, and Edwin Booth. Payne had actually written it for Kean, and its distinctive success was due—so several critics declared—to this incomparable actor's playing of the lead. "Kean"—one unnamed source stated—"made *Brutus,* a tragedy by Payne, a success by the fire of his subtle and powerful acting." Arthur H. Quinn once suggested that Payne's *Brutus* might have been responsible for "the emergence of the remarkable drama in France under Hugo."

During two theatrical seasons, 1818–1819, Payne worked at various jobs connected with theaters. For instance, he took care of the correspondence for the Harris playhouse, distributed orders on this theater, and in several other ways helped promote plays and players.

In 1820, following the success of his *Brutus,* he leased the Sadler's Wells Theatre, where he planned to put on his own plays. But after only one season, Payne found himself deeply in debt—in fact, to the amount of $7,000, as one of his own melodramas had suffered a collapse. Although it has been asserted that his productions at Sadler's Wells were "artistically noteworthy," his one season as its manager was "financially disastrous." The result was that the budding dramatist was sent to Fleet Street debtors' prison.

In an interesting but rather strange way, Payne was released from this predicament. One day, someone left a package of work at the prison for him with no name on it. During the next two days, the playwright worked continually on the contents of the package and completed the translation of *Therese,* or *The Orphan of Geneva.* At once it was accepted by the Drury Lane manager.

Fortunately he was able to get permission to direct the actors and to see the first performance; one writer said the guards allowed him to slip past them to attend rehearsals. This melodrama, *Therese,* which had its London première on February 2, 1821, was a financial success; and the dramatist was able to make a deal with his creditors.

After this, Payne had a long career of doing dramatic hack work. At times he would try to get back to acting; but he continued to quarrel with theater managers, especially with Douglass Kinnaird of Drury Lane.

During the summer of 1823, he wrote plays with his close friend, Washington Irving. The latter had long been intrigued by Payne's varied theatrical adventures. When Irving returned from Dresden with some unfinished operas, the playwright persuaded him to collaborate with him.

Together they wrote ten plays, seven of which were produced with some success. But it is affirmed that none was really outstanding. The combined works of these two friends reveal Payne's "erratic brilliance" and his "lovable nature." And Irving showed his true friendship in allowing himself to be continually bothered by Payne's creditors.

One of the two best dramas was the three-act comedy, *Charles II* or *The Merry Monarch,* first performed at Covent Garden on May 27, 1824, with Charles Kemble as the King and Faucett as Captain Copp. This play was distinguished by its "unity of structure, rapidity of action, and brilliance of dialogue. . . . It very nearly achieved the quality of high comedy . . . and bolstered the tottering fortunes of England's greatest theaters."

The second drama was *Richelieu, A Domestic Tragedy,* which opened at Covent Garden on February 11, 1826. It ran only six nights, even though Charles Kemble and Mrs. Glover had the leading roles. In the introduction, this play was dedicated to Washington Irving; thus, for the first time the collaboration of the two writers—Payne, the dramatist, and Irving, the essayist—was revealed.

The slight financial returns from these plays caused Irving to discontinue his close association with Payne. But he still aided his friend by criticizing his manuscripts and by protecting him from continual dunnings. From time to time, Payne went to Paris to escape these financial demands. From that city he would send adaptations to London, which Irving—or perhaps another friend, William Hazlitt—would succeed in selling to a stage manager. From the fall of 1823 to the summer of 1825, the dramatist was in London; sometimes he went under the name of "J. Hayward."

Between October 2, 1826, and March 24, 1827, Payne produced in London twenty-six numbers of *The Opera Glass,* a weekly magazine "for peeps into the microcosm of the fine arts, and more especially the drama." For five more years (a period during which not much is known of his activities), he remained in England.

Payne's love for the theater dated from his early boyhood and continued all his life, "although he never attained lasting success or financial security in this field." Because of weak copyright laws, he received little monetary return from his most successful works.

He is said to have translated and adapted more than sixty French plays, melodramas, and operettas, besides doing some original works. His prolific productions were used for many decades on the stage, both in Great Britain and the United States.

As a playwright, Payne has been rated rather highly by various critics. A writer in the *Encyclopaedia Britannica* states that he was:

> . . . one of the most notable of the school of American playwrights that followed the techniques and themes of the European blank verse dramatists. . . . Although Payne was no innovator, his plays were strong, both in language and structure.

In *Yankee Doodle Doo* (a compilation of songs of the early American stage) Grenville Vernon states:

> Though John Howard Payne is remembered by the modern world only as the author of "Home, Sweet Home," he was in his day an important figure in the dramatic world, both of England and America. He was the first American to secure for himself a firm position on the London stage, and most of his mature works were produced in London before they were seen in New York.

It is a strange fact that while so many of Payne's dramas were doomed to oblivion he gained "a slender immortality" from the single song "Home, Sweet Home" which he had inserted in his operetta, *Clari, the Maid of Milan.*

In 1823 the playwright had sold a number of play adaptations to Charles Kemble of the Theatre Royale, Covent Garden, for £230; £50 was paid him for *Clari.* Kemble had requested that the dramatist change the drama to an operetta and write several songs for it. Payne did so, and included in the score the song, "Home, Sweet Home," which he had written some time before. In London the production was advertised as:

CLARI, THE MAID OF MILAN, a musical by
John Howard Payne, author of BRUTUS, THE LANCERS,
LOVE IN HUMBLE LIFE, CHARLES II, ALI PACHA, etc.

There are varying accounts as to the circumstances under which "Home, Sweet Home" was created. One source (Bennie Bengsten) says that the haunting words were composed while Payne, "discouraged and downcast in spirit" was in prison, jailed as a possible spy, soon after his arrival in Great Britain during the War of 1812.

Another writer (S. J. Fitzgerald) claims that Payne wrote the lyrics that were to make his name immortal on a dreary day in Paris in 1822. At that time he was still heavily in debt, unhappy about his work, and thinking of his faraway land of America. From his attic window Payne looked down on the busy street below, where people were hurrying home to their loved ones; but he had no such place to go to. It is said that since the playwright had left his childhood home in East Hampton, New York, he had never known a real home, for his parents had moved frequently.

Now in his early thirties, in a foreign city, he was longing for the love and feeling of security that had been his in the "lowly thatched cottage" which was surrounded by the fragrance of woodbine. He also recalled the birds that had come at his call, and he thought longingly of his mother who had been so dear to him.

Although Payne had tasted some success, and had roamed "mid pleasures and palaces," the great desire of his heart was to see his homeland again. For he had become convinced that in spite of his foreign travels and unusual experiences, there truly was "no place like home," "be it ever so humble."

In his song, the composer wanted to convey the thought that one's home is his greatest blessing, "the most hallowed, the dearest place in the world." And he believed that, through the heroine's singing of this simple lyric in *Clari,* he could perhaps make people realize this.

Like other aspects of John Howard Payne's life, there has been uncertainty as to which "home" he was referring when he wrote "Home, Sweet Home."

At East Hampton, on Long Island, New York, there is a weather-beaten shingled farmhouse, built in 1660, where the dramatist is said to have lived as a child with his parents. Some years ago, when the owner, a Mr. Buck, died, the villagers bought the house for $60,000 to preserve it as a fitting memorial to Payne and his song.

However, some persons assert that the boy really never lived there, but had visited an aunt residing there. Another story is that the Payne home was actually a house across the street. Despite these conflicting tales, the people of East Hampton carried out their plan and bought the cottage. For they believed that it was of just such a home the composer was thinking when he wrote the familiar words. It is said that Payne once made this statement: "I should so much like to settle down in old East Hampton and have a comfortable cottage and a comfortable little better half all to myself." But his wish did not come true, for he never married.

Today the place is preserved and is much the same as it was during Payne's boyhood. Woodbine still twines around the building and the interior remains as it was many decades ago. The home has become an American shrine. Numerous visitors come from far and near to enter the memorial to a composer and his song, written while he was in a foreign country, homesick for his native land.

There has long been a controversy as to how the tune of "Home, Sweet Home" originated. Sir Henry Rowley Bishop (1786–1855), director of the Covent Garden Orchestra, composed the musical score of *Clari,* but whether he created the famous air has never been definitely decided.

The claim has been made that when Sir Henry was editing a collection of national airs of various countries, he made the discovery that Sicily did not have one that he considered worthy of being included. Therefore he invented one. This resulted in the melody of "Home, Sweet Home." Sir Henry said he had created it to go with the words of Payne's poem about home. Another source states that it was taken from the old French song, "Ranz des Vaches."

One story has often been told that Payne had heard an Italian peasant girl singing the air; that he took down the notes and then shaped the meter of his poem to suit the melody. However, this legend has been refuted; for it is asserted that Payne did not read or write music. So the mystery remains unsolved as to how the origin of the music for "Home, Sweet Home" actually got its start.

The operetta *Clari* was first heard at Theatre Royale, Covent Garden, on May 8, 1823; It was performed for several decades thereafter, both in Great Britain and in the United States. That opening night the house was filled with a brilliant first-night audience. Miss Maria Tree sang the title role, and the melodrama got off "to a fast and tearful start."

In the first scene it is revealed that Clari, the farmer's daughter, had believed the Duke's promises of marriage and had eloped with him to his handsome chateau. There she lived in luxurious surroundings, but no plans for a wedding had been made. So the young heroine began to long for her humble home, as she recalled her happy, carefree life there.

When lovely Maria Tree began to sing the song, opening with "Mid pleasures and palaces though we may roam, . . ." the audience was silent as she tried to keep her emotion from choking her voice. At the conclusion of "Home, Sweet Home," there were many tear-filled eyes among the listeners. For those who heard the song for the first time had realized its great impact. S. J. Fitzgerald remarked: "Miss Tree created quite a furor by her singing of the touching melody, the words going straight to the hearts of her audience."

This young actress was noted for her beauty, charm, and melodious voice. It is said that her singing on this opening and never-to-be-forgotten evening won her a wealthy merchant as a husband, and a London mansion. Also her excellent rendition made *Clari* a popular success.

Immediately the critics proclaimed "Home, Sweet Home" as "the loveliest song the world ever knew"; and soon all London was singing it. John Howard Payne's song was so popular it was played by bands and by barrel organs on the streets. Even though the radio, phonograph, and television had not been heard of, the first year 100,000 (one source says 300,000) copies of the sheet music were sold; later the figures ran into the millions. By the end of its second year, the music publisher had made over $10,000 from it—a large sum at that time.

That night, at the opening of the operetta neither the composer, Payne, nor the people in that distinguished audience had any idea that "Home, Sweet Home" would be sung for countless years to come and that it "would penetrate to the farthermost parts of the world." It has been translated into various languages, and has been sung in such far-off places as China, Arabia, and the South Pacific. It has become part of the folklore of the entire world and is found in many song books and hymnals. The original manuscript is the property of the Eastman School of Music in Rochester, New York. The secret of its popularity is its universality. Of it, Colonel Nicholas Smith once said:

> It was in this opera that one song was found that melted the heart of London and the world, and the plaintive melody is everywhere familiar, and everywhere its tender pathos invests with affectionate regard the memory of John Howard Payne.

There has been some doubt as to which singer actually presented "Home, Sweet Home" for the first time to an American audience. The initial production of *Clari* was given in New York at the Park Theater on November 11, 1823, about six months after its opening in London. A Miss Johnson played the title role.

However an early edition of the sheet music carried a picture of a Mrs. Holman, who had sung the part of Vespina. It is thought that she may have introduced "Home, Sweet Home" here; for in Ireland's *History of the New York Stage*, the author states that the musical roles of *Clari* were "sustained" by Mr. Pearman and Mrs. Holman.

In London—where it was given only twelve times at its first presentation—*Clari* was a great success financially for everyone except the unlucky American playwright. He had sold this production for the sum of £50, and he never received any royalties for the numerous later performances. It is claimed that he had been promised £25 more after the twentieth production, but it seems that he was cheated out of this sum. He did not receive a penny—so the story goes—for his song, "Home, Sweet Home"; also his name as the composer did not appear on early editions of the sheet music. The publishers didn't even compliment him by sending him a copy.

One authority asserts that if Payne had been given royalties for the sheet music and the performing rights for this one composition, he could have lived in comfort. But "the writer of the song was in a lonely and almost hopeless struggle with pining want."

Finally Payne ended his long exile of about twenty years abroad; on June 16, 1832, he started back across the Atlantic. The money for his homeward passage was furnished by some friends. At this time he was forty-one years old; he had had many unusual experiences, but he was then disillusioned and as poverty-stricken as ever. Although, not long after his arrival in the United States, friends arranged benefits for him, both in New York and Boston, his financial condition remained unsettled. As the author of "Home, Sweet Home," he was received with much acclaim, and treated almost like a national hero. Excerpts from Payne's works were given all over the country, and his undying song was always featured.

On November 29, 1832, an important benefit was staged for him in New York at the Park Theater to help get him on his feet again. This was one of "the most brilliant and successful dramatic entertainments ever given in New York."

Parts of *Brutus,* his best work, were given with the eminent Edwin Forrest in the chief role. Charles Kemble and his daughter, the famous actress, Fanny Kemble, were in the United States on their first visit here; this distinctive British theatrical pair contributed to the outstanding program by appearing in selections from *Katherine and Petruchio.* Another well-known actor, James W. Wallack, played Captain Copp in *Charles II.*

There was an address of welcome to Payne, between acts "Home, Sweet Home" was sung, and the last act of *Clari* was staged. In addition a public dinner was given to honor the dramatist. Of course the exile was pleased by such attentions, but as usual his creditors were on his trail. Before long the income from the benefit had been taken over by them.

Payne soon was making some grandiose plans, which included

the establishment of a magazine to be published in London and devoted to the advancement of art, science, and literature. This proposed adventure almost cost him his life, but it revealed how considerate and unselfish he really was.

In 1835 he championed the cause of the Cherokee Indians who were at odds with the government of the state of Georgia. Looking for material for his magazine, Payne became interested in some original data owned by John Ross, head of the Cherokee nation. The latter gave the material to the writer for a series of articles for his proposed magazine. But while Payne was engaged in this research, the Georgia Guards arrested the two men. Payne was accused of being an abolitionist and in league with the French. After a time he was released and warned never to return to the state.

But on his way back to the North, he had the courage to publish two pieces in the Knoxville, Tennessee, *Register,* entitled "John Howard Payne to His Countrymen" and "The Cherokee Nation to the People of the United States." These articles were good accounts both of his own predicament, and of the wrongs inflicted upon the Cherokee Indians. When he was back in New York City, he began to write the history of this native tribe. The work can still be seen in manuscript, along with an unpublished drama, *Romulus, the Shepherd King,* written in 1839.

The last part of his life continued to be clouded by disappointments and debts. In 1841, Payne went to Washington, D. C., where he applied for a position in the Consular Service while President John Tyler was in office. The Chief Executive sent him to Tunis as American consul.

There Payne was well liked by the natives; he was responsible for changing their hostile attitude toward the United States into friendliness. While engaged in writing the history of Tunis, the consul was recalled in 1845 by the new President, James K. Polk.

He returned to America via Rome, Paris, and London; and by the summer of 1847 he was back in New York. Here again his creditors swooped down upon him. During the next few years, the dramatist existed mostly on the hospitality of his friends, although he did write some pieces for various newspapers.

Then in March, 1851, after a struggle against the strong opposition of Thomas Hart Benton, Payne was returned to the consular post in Tunis by President Fillmore. But he held the office only a short time as his death occurred on April 10, 1852.

During the preceding winter, the consul's health had failed rapidly. "An exile from home," attended by two faithful nuns and a devoted Moorish servant, Payne, after a lingering illness, succumbed to pneumonia. At the time of his passing he was "still beset by unfinished plans and unpaid debts." He was buried in the Cemetery of St. George in Tunis, under a stone bearing this inscription:

> IN MEMORY OF COLONEL JOHN
> HOWARD PAYNE, TWICE CONSUL OF THE
> UNITED STATES OF AMERICA, FOR THE
> CITY AND KINGDOM OF TUNIS, THIS STONE
> HERE IS PLACED BY A GRATEFUL COUNTRY.

William J. Corcoran, of Washington, D.C., had seen John Howard Payne on the stage when the actor was only seventeen years old. He had long been a great admirer of the dramatist, and declared he was a distinctive credit to the American stage. Three decades after Payne's death, Corcoran thought that it was not right that the body of the creator of "Home, Sweet Home" was still interred in that far-off land of Tunis on the African continent. Therefore he declared that the poet who had written the immortal classic should be buried in his native American soil. The philanthropist stated that he would bear the entire expense of transferring the remains to this country. First, the consent of the governments concerned had to be obtained. Then the body was disinterred and placed in a new casket in Tunis on January 5, 1883. At the Cemetery of St. George a service was held honoring him, and "Home, Sweet Home" was sung by a choir.

A French vessel, the *Burgundia,* brought Payne's body to New

York on March 22, 1883. A band of sixty-five pieces played his masterpiece. The body lay in state in the city, and thousands of mourners passed by the bier.

The casket was reburied at Oak Hill Cemetery just outside the national capital. At last the wanderer had found a final resting place. His bust stands at the grave and these words are inscribed on the shaft:

SURE, WHEN THY GENTLE SPIRIT FLED,
TO REALMS BEYOND THE AZURE DOME,
WITH ARMS OUTSTRETCHED, GOD'S ANGEL SAID,
"WELCOME TO HEAVEN'S HOME, SWEET HOME."

At the funeral service, held on June 10, 1883, President Chester A. Arthur, members of his Cabinet, representatives of both houses of Congress, the diplomatic corps, and other important personages were present. Dr. J. C. Welling, president of Columbia University, was the master of ceremonies; there were eulogies, and music was furnished by the Marine Band and the Philharmonic Society. "The benediction of the ceremony was the blending of one thousand voices and instruments in 'Home, Sweet Home.' Never was a dead poet, famous only for a single song, so honored."

During his last years, when Payne was experiencing another period of depression, he "witnessed one of the most brilliant and soul-stirring scenes in all the course of his checkered life."

Jenny Lind, "the Swedish Nightingale," was making her triumphal tour through the United States. She gave three concerts in Washington, D.C. One occurred in the Hall of the House of Representatives before a distinguished audience in which were President Millard Fillmore and his family, his Cabinet members including the noted Secretary of State, Daniel Webster, the judges of the Supreme Court, senators and representatives, foreign diplomats and other celebrities.

The Philadelphia *Record* gave this account of the event:

No common poet ever received a more enviable compliment than was paid to John Howard Payne by Jenny Lind on her last visit to his native land. It was in the great national hall of the city of Washington, where the most distinguished audience that was ever seen in the Capitol of the republic was assembled.

The matchless singer entranced the vast throng with her most exquisite melodies, "Casta Diva," the "Flute Song," the "Bird Song," and "Greeting to America." But the great feature of the occasion seemed to be an act of inspiration.

The singer suddenly turned her face to that part of the auditorium where Payne was sitting, and sang "Home, Sweet Home" with such pathos and power that a whirlwind of excitement swept through the vast audience. Daniel Webster himself almost lost his self-control; and one might readily imagine that Payne thrilled with rapture at this unexpected and magnificent rendition of his own immortal lyric.

Then applause swept through the house, while many eyes were filled with tears. Daniel Webster was filled with emotion and rose and bowed to the composer. At once the audience stood and gave John Howard Payne the greatest ovation of his life; and his heart was filled with joy at this outstanding tribute, not only from a great diva, but from the audience.

"Home, Sweet Home" was sung under several unusual circumstances during the Civil War. Mark Twain told of an incident that happened when the gray- and blue-clad soldiers were encamped on the banks of the Rapidan River, just across from each other.

Early that evening, the Yankees played and sang "Yankee Doodle," and then the Rebs replied defiantly with "Dixie." But after the clear rich tones of a cornet played "Home, Sweet Home," there was a moment of silence. At once men in both armies joined in singing the universal song; and for a time, at least, sectional differences were forgotten.

On another memorable occasion, during the same long conflict, two great forces were resting in the northern part of Georgia before the next day's battle. At eight o'clock that evening a federal band played the "Star-Spangled Banner" as loud cheers went up from their side. The Confederate musicians at once countered with "Dixie," which was welcomed with "a vigorous Rebel yell." The Northerners then played "Hail, Columbia," followed by a Southern rendition of "Maryland, My Maryland." Next the Union soldiers came out strongly on "Yankee Doodle," after which the "Bonnie

Blue Flag" was heard from the Southern army. Soon the hills rocked with the stirring sounds of "The Battle Hymn of the Republic."

After a short period of impressive silence, the gray-clad Confederates broke the spell by playing the soft, sweet strains of "Home, Sweet Home." Without any hesitation, Union musicians and soldiers joined with their enemies in singing "the world's greatest refrain":

> Home! Home! Sweet Home!
> There's no place like home; there's no place like home,

At the conclusion of the song both sides applauded loudly and with all their hearts. And Colonel Nicholas Smith has well expressed their reactions:

> . . . and for once their hearts beat in unison, and the voices of the two armies rose in sweet concord in that deathless song, which goes to the human heart wherever love and home are known. There was no other power outside of the realm of the miraculous but "Home, Sweet Home" that could have united the hearts and voices of those two hostile armies.

Besides Jenny Lind, another great diva was closely associated with Payne's masterpiece. It is related that in 1862 Adelina Patti, the famous Italian coloratura, was invited by President Abraham Lincoln to sing at the White House.

After singing several of her noted florid arias, she sang "The Last Rose of Summer." The Lincolns had recently lost their son, Willie, and at the conclusion of the last number, Mrs. Lincoln was in tears. Madame Patti wondered what she could do to dispel the gloom. When she asked the President what song he would like to hear, he replied, "Home, Sweet Home." As she wasn't sure of the words, Lincoln placed the music on the piano for her. When she finished singing the song, Patti realized it was just the right one for this occasion and the sorrowing Lincoln family.

During the following forty years, the singer ended nearly every one of her concerts with Payne's masterpiece. For she, like several other great artists, realized the impact this simple piece could have upon an audience. Adelina Patti always made her public love her, because she at once established a friendly relationship with her hearers. And by her impressive singing of "Home, Sweet Home," she showed her extraordinary power over audiences. It is said that she could play upon the emotions of her listeners to a degree that very few other singers could achieve.

For almost all of her long musical career, Patti was closely associated with this Payne composition; and no doubt on at least two occasions her singing of it saved many lives.

Once when she was giving a concert in the city of Bucharest, a man climbed up on some irons at the side of the stage so he could see her better. He slipped and fell, hitting a woman who was standing in the wings. She was badly hurt, and her cries caused the audience to panic. Then some one added to the terror by calling out "Fire!" Adelina Patti stepped to the front of the stage, told the audience there was no fire, and began to sing "Home, Sweet Home" with no accompaniment. Soon the frightened crowd calmed down, and her brave act without doubt saved lives that evening.

When the artist was performing one night in the New Orleans Opera House, she looked up at the overcrowded balcony. To her great horror, she realized the structure was beginning to sag. She was afraid that there would be a stampede and that many persons might be crushed to death.

The frightened musicians had stopped playing, so without waiting for music, Patti began to sing "Home, Sweet Home," and succeeded in calming the attendants and preventing a panic. There might have been a terrible catastrophe if it hadn't been for her courage. Later when people talked to her about this incident and how she calmed the audience with her singing of the beloved, familiar melody, the diva replied simply, "It was the only thing to do."

Countless tributes have been paid this composition and its creator during the many years (almost a century and a half) since it was created. Colonel Nicholas Smith said of it:

. . . the tender pathos of the song invests with affectionate regard the memory of John Howard Payne. . . . A many-sided genius, handsome, buoyant, affable, he made an impact on his time as actor, playwright, dramatic critic, editor.

In his article, "The Story of 'Home, Sweet Home,' " Bennie Bengsten declared that although many other compositions had been written about the magic word "home" no other song is

. . . so secure in the hearts of people everywhere, so deeply loved and cherished as John Howard Payne's "Home, Sweet Home." . . . There is something about this beautiful song, which, no matter where it is played or sung, evokes feeling of a universal brotherhood. . . . It preserves and increases an appreciation for our own homes.

And Dr. Clarence Mackey made this statement about the song:

It has done more than statesmanship or legislation to keep alive in the hearts of the people the virtues that flourish at the fireside, and to recall to its hallowed circle the wanderers who stray from it.

Home, Sweet Home

4

*

"America"

On July 4, 1832, Edward Everett Hale, the noted American orator, was just ten years old. Many years later, on November 19, 1863, he gave a long speech—the main oration—at the dedication of the National Cemetery in Pennsylvania. On that occasion President Abraham Lincoln delivered his brief but immortal Gettysburg Address.

But back in 1832, young Hale attended an unusual Independence Day celebration. He had gone to Boston Common that morning; then after spending all his pennies for oysters, ginger snaps, and root beer, the boy decided to start for home.

However, he was surprised to see a large crowd of boys and girls going into the Park Avenue Congregational Church near Boston Common. To satisfy his youthful curiosity, Edward marched in with them. This is how he came to take part in a memorable event—the first public singing of "My Country, 'Tis of Thee"—or "America," as it is often called—by five hundred young voices. The writer of the words of this song, Samuel Francis Smith, did not know beforehand that the poem he had written some months previously was to be presented to the public on that Fourth of July.

Dr. Smith was a Baptist minister, poet, and editor. He was born in Boston, on October 21, 1808, under the chimes of Old North Church. His parents were Samuel and Sarah Bryant Smith. The young Bostonian attended the Eliot School and also the Boston Latin School. At the latter institution, he won the Franklin Medal, and a prize for a poem. He was graduated from Harvard University in 1829, in one of its most distinguished classes, whose memory was perpetuated by one of the other famous members, Oliver Wendell Holmes. In his long-remembered poem, "The Boys," Holmes wrote of Samuel F. Smith:

> And there's a nice youngster of excellent pith—
> Fate tried to conceal him by naming him Smith;
> But he shouted a song for the brave and the free—
> Just read on his medal, "My country" "of thee."

(Although Holmes mentioned several class members in this noted poem, he identified only the author of "America" by name.)

Samuel Smith, after his graduation from Harvard, studied for the ministry at Andover Theological Seminary in Massachusetts, and during the following year did editorial work in Boston. After his ordination as a Baptist minister, he married Mary White of Haverhill on February 12, 1834. They had six children, one of whom, Daniel, went in 1863 as a missionary to Burma, and was president of Karen Baptist Theological Seminary for forty years.

As a clergyman, Dr. Smith served at two important educational centers. While engaged in this occupation, he was also a teacher and editor. This versatile man apparently enjoyed having more than one job at a time.

While at the First Baptist Church in Waterville, Maine, he acted as professor of modern languages at Waterville College (now Colby College). All his life he had been interested in the study of various languages, and when he was in college he had earned part of his expenses by doing translations for the *Encyclopedia Americana*. It is stated that Dr. Smith could read books in fifteen different languages; also that he took up the study of the Russian language at the advanced age of eighty-seven.

His second church was at Newton Center, Massachusetts, where he served from 1842 to 1854. At both places he was the editor of the *Christian Review*. From 1854 to 1869, Smith edited the publications of the Baptist Missionary Union.

On May 4, 1877, at the Old South Church in Boston, there was a meeting at which such notables as Ralph Waldo Emerson, Oliver Wendell Holmes, and Julia Ward Howe took part. Dr. Smith was asked to read "My Country, 'Tis of Thee" and to recount the story of how he had written this masterpiece.

Before reading his hymn, he answered a question asked him by some friends: whether, after his year in Europe, that continent had supplanted in his affections his own native land of America. He read some verses in which he had praised several European lands; however he concluded with these lines:

> We own them rich and fair—but not
> More grand, more fair than ours.

His last years were spent as secretary for the American Baptist Missionary Union. He spent the years 1875–1876 in Europe, visiting the chief missionary stations on that continent. During the two years from 1880 to 1882, Dr. Smith continued such visitations in Asia.

In April, 1895, just a few months before his death, a great celebration was held in Boston in recognition of his authorship of "America." Today a tower and chime of bells at the First Baptist Church in Newton Center are a memorial to him.

On November 16, 1895, Dr. Smith got on the 5:40 train for a Boston suburb, where he was to speak on the following day. After greeting a friend he gasped, and died immediately. As Amos R. Wells has said: "And so passed from earth the Christian patriot, whose love for his country widened out into a mission of love for the whole world." And another writer declared: "The simplicity of his life is one secret of its strength and beauty."

From his early youth Samuel Smith had enjoyed writing verse. So it was not surprising that, while attending Andover Theological School, he wrote the poem that was destined to bring him enduring fame.

It was on a chilly day in February, in a sparsely furnished room of "a drab-looking frame house" that the young student was "carelessly sprawled in a tattered arm chair," sitting with his feet up on the woodbox near the stove. He was glad he did not have to attend any classes that afternoon on the Andover campus so that he could sit comfortably in his warm study. Outside his windows "the leafless trees shivered, forsaken in the icy wind."

Smith had always been a great lover of music. Because he was so proficient in German, a friend of his named Lowell Mason had just lent him a book of songs recently brought from Germany. (Mason was a composer of hymn tunes and with George Webb had been the cofounder of the Boston Academy of Music.) A well-known American educator, William C. Woodbridge, had given Lowell Mason several music books used in the schools of Germany. As Mason did not read this language, he suggested to his friend Samuel that he look through the books and translate some of the pieces into English. Or if he should find some tunes especially to his liking, he could compose his own lyrics to go with them. Lowell Mason was planning to publish a song book for use in the local schools.

That dreary afternoon, as Smith was looking through this German music, one tune suddenly attracted his attention. He was "pleased with its simple and easy movement." Besides, he felt so strongly the urge to express his inmost feelings about his native land of America that he at once began to write the immortal words.

In this poem, Samuel F. Smith first addresses his country and praises it as "the sweet land of liberty," the home of his forefathers and the Pilgrims. His great desire is for freedom to ring from every part of the land. He also speaks of the varied characteristics of terrain and scenery. The poet shows his great love for music in the lines beginning, "Let music swell the breeze." He wanted all America to join in the hymn of praise. Finally Dr. Smith ends his poem with a sincere prayer that God would protect and preserve our native land, thus summing up "all he hoped and felt for his beloved America"; and in this final stanza "he made a prayer to the God of all nations."

(Dr. Smith's son bequeathed to Harvard University the original manuscript written on "a scrap of paper." This precious manuscript is now preserved where the author received his classical education.)

On June 5,1887, in answer to an inquiry, Samuel Smith wrote to J. H. Johnson that "My Country, 'Tis of Thee" was not written with reference to any special occasion, adding these words:

> On a dismal day in February, turning over the leaves of some music books, I fell in with a tune, which pleased me—and observing that the words were patriotic, without attempting to imitate them, or even read them, I was moved at once to write a song adapted to the music—and "America" is the result.

Later on, in his book of collected poems, *Poems of Home and Country,* published in 1895, the poet wrote in similar fashion:

> I glanced at the German words and seeing that they were patriotic, instantly felt the impulse to write a patriotic hymn of my own. Seizing a scrap of paper, I put upon it, within half an hour, the verses, substantially as they stand today.

It is reported that the author didn't have the slightest idea of the importance of the words he had dashed off, nor of the mighty impact they would have on future generations. As a young seminary student, Samuel Smith was moved to express "his prayerful appreciation of our freedom and of God's abundance in our land."

Dr. Smith declared later that if he had foreseen how popular his work would become he would have written it more carefully. But he added, "Such as it is, I am glad to have contributed this mite to the cause of American freedom." And not long before his passing, the author wrote: "I pray that the spirit of the simple verses may be the spirit of our people evermore."

The origin of the tune which Dr. Smith chose for his "My Country, 'Tis of Thee" has long been the subject of much debate, and probably this question will never be solved. It is said that the same melody, or one quite similar to it, had been popular centuries before in several European countries, including Finland, Scotland, and France; also that the Germans used this tune long before the British attached it to their "God Save the King" (or the Queen). One source claims the melody can be traced back to the time of Cromwell in England, where it was used as a dance measure. The music was first published with the words, "God Save the King," in a song collection entitled *Thesaurus Musicus,* published in 1744. This air, adapted for the Prussian national anthem in 1790, is the one that inspired Dr. Smith. It is stated that when he wrote "America," he did not know it was the tune used for the British hymn.

The music has been credited to Dr. John Bull (1563–1628), a well-known English organist. It is claimed that this was written for a banquet, in 1607, honoring James I. Others maintain it was the work of Captain Henry Carey (1690–1743) who helped write the British national anthem. He was the author of several witty poems and songs including "Sally in Our Alley." This is said to have been created for a London celebration in 1740 after the capture of Porto Bello in Panama.

Before Samuel F. Smith wrote "America," we had such songs as "God Save America" and "God Save Washington." After "My Country, 'Tis of Thee" was composed, some Americans are said to have objected to the fact that it had the same melody as "God Save the King." However, Dr. Smith did not agree with this contention, for he felt that the air formed a tie between the two nations.

This "splendid, dignified tune" has been a popular one, not only for national anthems, but for several other musical compositions. For instance, Von Weber used the melody in an overture; Beethoven wrote variations on it; and Haydn used it as the theme in one of his compositions. Therefore, no matter what its origin, we must admit it is an excellent tune which impressed the Boston poet as fitting and highly suitable for an American patriotic anthem. As one critic has stated: "There certainly must be something more than ordinarily inspiring in an air that has struck the popular heart of the four greatest nations on earth."

After Dr. Smith had completed writing "My Country, 'Tis of Thee," he gave a copy to Lowell Mason, placed the original in a portfolio, and did not look at it again for several months.

Mason was "unstinting in his admiration" of the song. Without consulting his friend Smith, Mason decided to publish the poem and to present it to the world at a children's Fourth of July observance at the Park Street Congregational Church in Boston, just off the Common. And he certainly did surprise the author that day of July 4, 1832 when the words were heard in public for the very first time.

(Two sources seem to differ about the year in which "America" was composed. John Tasher Howard stated, in 1846, that the hymn was first sung in 1831—instead of 1832—and that an account of this happening had appeared in the magazine, *The Christian Watchman* on July 8, 1831. Another person has also asserted that the verses actually were composed in 1831, instead of 1832, as stated by Dr. Smith, himself.)

It is reported that upon its publication, the song was greeted with great enthusiasm all over the country. Soon afterward it appeared in several hymn books, the first one being Lowell Mason's *The Choir* in 1832. "America" was being heard at various patriotic gatherings. It seemed to invoke popular acclaim, for it was composed at a period when there was rapid development in our country. "The West was being settled, and the young nation was becoming conscious of its magnificent destiny."

After Fort Sumter was fired upon, "My Country, 'Tis of Thee" became more popular than ever. People seemed to consider it our national anthem, even though it had never been legally made so. And Samuel Francis Smith became famous as its composer.

Although he will always have a firm place in American history and literature as the composer of one of our distinctive national songs, Dr. Smith also was the author of more than one hundred other hymns including the well-known "The Morning Light Is Breaking," which is still today one of the most inspiring and widely sung of all our missionary songs. His poem "The Lone Star," created in 1863, is generally conceded to have saved the Telegu Mission, at Nellore, India, from being closed out. A dramatic reference to it in the midst of crisis in 1925 led to the strengthening of the Baptist missionary efforts in the Orient. Samuel Smith's poems are said to be "the outpouring of a simple, wholesome idealism," as suggested by the name of his volume of collected verse, *Poems of Home and Country,* published in 1895.

He felt that he had written many things of more importance than "My Country, 'Tis of Thee." These included historical writings and various translations of foreign books. They are: *The Life of the Rev. Joseph Grafton* (1849); *Missionary Sketches* (1879); *History of Newton Center, Massachusetts* (1880); and *Rambles in Mission Fields* (1883), based on his tour of the Baptist mission fields in Europe and Asia. Also, along with Baron Stow, Smith edited *The Psalmist* (1843), which for more than thirty years was the hymn book most widely used by members of Baptist congregations.

The composer was fortunate in that he lived long enough to hear "America" sung not only in various parts of the United States, but in large European and Asiatic cities, and on the Atlantic Ocean and the Baltic and Mediterranean seas.

In 1889 Dr. Smith was invited to visit the Board of Trade in Chicago. On that unusual occasion, the men all stopped their important work and stood with uncovered heads while they joined together to sing "My Country, 'Tis of Thee." When the Pope asked the poet for an autographed copy of the hymn for the Vatican Library, Samuel Smith presented it to him on New Year's Day, 1895.

The following month, at a patriotic gathering in celebration of George Washington's birthday in Old South Church in Boston, the author was honored when Edward Everett Hale recited the words of "America." In his address he included the comment made about Dr. Smith by Oliver Wendell Holmes: "What is fame? To write a hymn which sixty million people sing; that is fame." Not long before this meeting, the same writer had declared: "Now there's Smith. His name will be honored by every school child in the land when I have been forgotten a hundred years."

Since Smith's death in 1895, "My Country, 'Tis of Thee" has been heard widely, both in times of peace and war, and has been sung on battlefields in far-flung plarts of the globe. On October 21, 1908, thousands of persons joined together on Boston Common to celebrate the centennial anniversary of Smith's birth. Five boy cornetists played this national anthem from the belfry of Park Street Congregational Church, where it was first sung more than seventy years before.

Near the Lincoln Memorial in Washington, D.C., on Easter Sunday, 1939, 75,000 people stood and listened to a program. It opened with the singing of "My Country, 'Tis of Thee" by the noted artist, Marian Anderson. And on January 2, 1942, a National Day of Prayer just after we entered World War II, President Franklin D. Roosevelt and Sir Winston Churchill sat in George Washington's old pew in the ancient church in Alexandria, Virginia, and together sang the words of "America."

After World War II, a young soldier named Richard Raksin told of hearing this patriotic song during the war, and of his reactions to it. On a hot afternoon, on an island in the South Pacific, he stood near a long row of newly made graves. Each of the chaplains gave a short talk and prayed for the dead; then one chaplain announced: "Gentlemen, the National Hymn."

As the young marines sang "America," Richard Raksin recalled an old schoolhouse with a picture of Abraham Lincoln on the wall and a large wood stove. It was here that he had first learned the words. He thought of the many and varied circumstances under which he had heard the impressive song since then. But on this day, when he and his fellow marines, "hot, exhausted and lonesome," sang it over the resting place of their fallen comrades, he was more inspired than ever before by the real meaning of the words. Richard Raksin declared that he and his living comrades had really become aware of the significance of its message, and that "from every mountain side" . . . they wanted with all their young hearts to "let freedom ring."

In 1931 by an act of Congress, as we have seen, "The Star-Spangled Banner" was officially designated the national anthem of the United States of America. Up to that date, Americans could choose the one they preferred as the official national hymn or anthem. Such songs as "Hail Columbia," "Yankee Doodle," "My Country, 'Tis of Thee," "The Star-Spangled Banner," etc., appealed to different members of our society.

Even though "America" was not chosen, it was really considered our national hymn by millions of Americans for many years. "It well expresses the loyalty, love and devotion" which true citizens of our great republic feel for their native country. Thus today it shares honors with "The Star-Spangled Banner" because of the sentiment connected with it and for its widespread popular approval. So, "for most informal occasions 'America' will continue to be our most commonly used patriotic song."

Some efforts have been made to revise the words, and also to create a new song to take its place. But no amount of prize money was sufficient to create another composition of comparable merit, or to replace it, because of the devoted affection of the American people for it. For "My Country, 'Tis of Thee" is filled with the true spirit of patriotism, and of our hopes for and faith in our beloved land.

A writer, Herbert D. Bard, once asserted that the hymn would not have become immortal if Dr. Smith had used the expression, "our country" instead of "my country." Each one who sings it feels that it is an expression of his own personal feelings.

Covert and Lawfer, compilers of a hymnal, wrote of "America" in their preface: "It may be said of this hymn that it is at once the most devotedly patriotic and the most universally beloved of our patriotic songs."

And E. Leigh Mudge, in an article, "Fate Named Him Smith," paid the poet this tribute:

> Could Samuel Francis Smith return to this life, now that his song has been sung for a century, he would find it published in almost every popular song book in our land—school books, books for community singing, church hymnals of all sorts. Doubtless, this song can be repeated from memory by more Americans than any other.

On August 28, 1963, Dr. Martin Luther King, Jr., delivered his famous "I have a dream" speech at the Lincoln Memorial in Washington. It included the following paragraphs:

> I have a dream that one day this nation will rise up and live out the true meaning of its creed: We hold these truths to be self-evident; that all men are created equal.
>
> I have a dream today. I have a dream that my four little children will one day live in a nation where they will not be judged by the color of their skin, but by the content of their character. . . .
>
> This is our hope. This is the faith with which I return to the South. . . . With this faith, we will be able to transform the

jangling discords of our nation into a beautiful symphony of brotherhood. With this faith we will be able to work together . . . knowing we will be free some day. This will be the day when all of God's children will be able to sing with new meaning, "My Country, 'Tis of Thee, Sweet land of Liberty, Of Thee I sing. . . ."

America

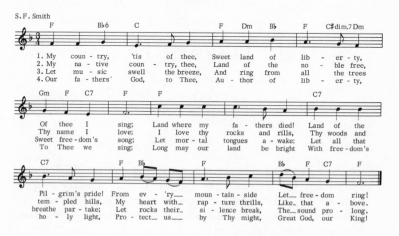

S.F. Smith

1. My coun - try, 'tis of thee, Sweet land of lib - er - ty,
2. My na - tive coun - try, thee, Land of the no - ble free,
3. Let mu - sic swell the breeze, And ring from all the trees
4. Our fa - thers' God, to Thee, Au - thor of lib - er - ty,

Of thee I sing; Land where my fa - thers died! Land of the
Thy name I love; I love thy rocks and rills, Thy woods and
Sweet free - dom's song; Let mor - tal tongues a - wake; Let all that
To Thee we sing; Long may our land be bright With free - dom's

Pil - grim's pride! From ev - 'ry moun - tain - side Let free - dom ring!
tem - pled hills, My heart with rap - ture thrills, Like that a - bove.
breathe par - take; Let rocks their si - lence break, The sound pro - long.
ho - ly light, Pro - tect us by Thy might, Great God, our King!

5

*

"Old Folks at Home"

To write one song that seventy years after you are dead is sung everywhere, and recognized by everybody, is an amazing thing; to write half a dozen, is all but incredible; yet this miracle was performed by a man who died during the Civil War, at thirty-seven, believing himself a failure.

—FREDERICK HALL

Stephen Collins Foster, American composer, was born on Independence Day, 1826. This was an important date in American history. Our American republic was exactly fifty years old; and on that very day two of our presidents, Thomas Jefferson and John Adams, died just a few hours apart.

"The best American folk-song writer," Stephen Foster, was born on the family farm at Lawrenceville, Pennsylvania (now part of the city of Pittsburgh). He was mainly of Scottish-Irish stock. His great-grandfather had arrived in the New World from Londonderry, Ireland, and settled in Lancaster County in 1728. Stephen Foster was "of prosperous middle-class parentage," his father being William B. Foster, a merchant of Pittsburgh and "a tasteful player on the violin."

His mother was Elizabeth Clayton Tomlinson, a descendant of an old Maryland family, "a woman of high culture and poetic attainment." Stephen is said to have resembled and adored her. He was the tenth child in a family of eleven boys and girls. It is reported that, while the other members loved him and were proud of him, they really didn't understand him. As a boy, he was modest, timid, and not at all inclined to be self-assertive.

Love of music was inherent in Stephen Foster, and at the age of only two years he lay on the floor, strumming his sister's guitar. When he was six he had mastered the clarinet, and could play almost any tune on it by ear. A year later he was also performing on the flute. About this time the boy wrote his first letter to his father and said: "I wish you would send me a comic songster; you promised it."

Although the youth received little formal musical training, his great talent for music was evidenced by these early achievements. For he had a most unusual gift of melody. In 1841, when Stephen was fifteen, his father declared, in a family letter, that the boy had "no evil propensities," but that "his leisure hours were devoted to music, for which he had a strange talent."

He also learned to play on the piano at their home, and he enjoyed picking out his own tunes on it. Then, after harmonizing the melodies, he would write them down as best he could. At the age of only fourteen, Stephen Foster wrote "The Tioga Waltz" for a flute ensemble of four members. This composition was played at the commencement exercises of Athens Academy.

As a youth, he was lighthearted, "generous, sociable, and lovable." For two years he received some education at Athens Academy in Pennsylvania. After enrolling at Jefferson College at Cannonsburg, he stayed only a few weeks. He was a "desultory student," mostly self-taught. However he did become acquainted with French and German; also he could paint fairly good pictures.

The boy was fourteen when he wrote his father that he did not want to go back to his school, calling it "that lonesome place." He added, that if he could remain where he was

> I will promise not to be seen out of doors between the hours of nine and twelve, and one and four, which hours I will attribute to study. . . . I will also promise to pay no attention to my music until after eight.

Following his brief stay at Jefferson College, he was tutored at home. William Foster once stated that his son was "uncommonly studious at home," but that the lad disliked going to school, declaring there was too much confusion there.

Stephen Foster headed a group of teen-agers who staged amateur productions and sang the minstrel songs so popular at that time. Often in the evening, they would go out with their instruments and serenade some young ladies in the town.

After he had concluded his formal education, Stephen wanted to take up music as his career, but the family made serious objections, for at that period, American music was not on a very high level: "The most popular songs of the day dwelt on bereavement and unrequited love, and were soggy with sentiment."

Despite the family's objections, Stephen did not give up his great interest in music. He went to hear good concerts whenever he could, and spent all his leisure time playing and singing. Sometimes he wrote poems, which he set to music and made manuscript copies for interested young friends. Although he played the piano, he often used his guitar when composing the songs.

Young Stephen's studies had included bookkeeping; therefore, since music was denied him, he left Pittsburgh at the age of twenty, in 1846, and went to Cincinnati. There he kept books for his brother, Dunning Foster. It is said that Stephen Foster was good at this subject, and that his letters were always "accurate and business-like."

While employed by his brother, Stephen began his ballad writing in earnest. He sold a few songs and received some royalty contracts from New York publishers. After living four years in Cincinnati, the musician decided to leave the bookkeeping job and make music his life career. He went back to Pittsburgh and settled there.

During the height of his song writing, the decade of the 1850's, he married Jane McDowell, a member of a prominent Pittsburgh family. One of her sisters, in writing an account of the wedding, said that both the bride and groom were frightened, and that Stephen looked quite pale. But she added that "the bride looked sweet, and her wedding dress fitted her perfectly."

The Fosters had one child, a girl named Marion. At the time of her birth, the couple paid four dollars a week rent at their boarding house. After the child arrived, the price was raised to five dollars.

Unfortunately the marriage of Stephen Foster and Jane McDowell did not endure. During the decade of the 1850's, he had an annual average income of about $1,400, which was not bad for that era. Even though Foster had simple tastes and was not extravagant, song writers and theater people generally had some hard times. For about two and a half years before the success of his "Old Black Joe," the composer had received, in all, only about $700.

By July of 1860, Stephen Foster had overdrawn his account with his New York publishers by $1,400. Desperate, the composer sold—for only $1,600—all the future rights of his compositions to his publishers, Firth and Pond. They deducted his overdraft, and with the remaining $200, he paid some of his bills "to square up his affairs" in Allegheny and decided to move to New York. He wanted to be nearer his publishers, and also to the headquarters of the minstrel companies that featured his songs.

However, after his move there, things did not improve for Foster; he was unfortunate in his business arrangements. Then the appetite for strong drink grew on the harassed composer, and he became quite dissipated. His uncontrollable habit, together with his inability to support his wife and daughter, compelled them to leave him and go back to Allegheny. It is maintained that while Jane was devoted to him, she could not stand his profligate habits. Stephen Foster grieved much over the failure of his marriage and tried to lose himself in his work and drink. He also developed tuberculosis, which was to plague him for the rest of his life.

His final years were tragic ones; he lived a sad and precarious existence. Until the beginning of the Civil War, in 1861, Foster had been popular all over the United States. But the Southerners refused to use many of his pieces because he was from the North; and some Northerners resented his having written songs about the Southern states.

In spite of all this, the composer worked hard, "struggling alone against illness, poverty and alcholism." He lived in a dismal basement room in a small hotel. Even though he made continual efforts to create salable songs, he had little success during his last years. He really "drove himself"; he wrote constantly, but his inspiration had waned. Although he produced many pieces, none were successful except "Old Black Joe" and "Beautiful Dreamer." Only these two had "the spark and vitality" of the works he had produced during his best years. By this time his finest work had been done; now he was willing to take any sum from anyone who would buy one of his compositions.

On the morning of January 10, 1864, weak from ague and fever, Foster fainted while trying to wash himself. He fell and cut his neck and face badly on the wash basin. A Mr. Cooper, his only friend in New York, called later and found him unconscious. At once Cooper got him to Bellevue Hospital and under a doctor's care. But by the time he reached there, Foster had lost much blood and was quite weak.

There is a story that it was snowing heavily on January 13, the day Stephen Foster died at the early age of thirty-seven. The dying song writer heard a melody being played by a musician who was wandering along the street, and he recognized it as one of his own compositions.

As America's greatest composer closed his eyes in his long and peaceful sleep, the last music he heard on earth was that strain of his song, "Beautiful Dreamer."

At his death, Foster's pocketbook contained thirty-eight cents and a scrap of paper on which he had scribbled the words, "Dear Friends and Gentle People," perhaps the idea for another composition.

When notice of his death appeared in a New York paper, one of his brothers arrived, paid the hospital bill, and arranged for the casket to be shipped to Pittsburgh. It was carried there by the Pennsylvania Railroad Company, which refused to take any payment for the transportation.

The body of Stephen Collins Foster was laid to rest beside that of his father, William B. Foster. At the burial, the Citizens-Press Band played two Foster songs, "Old Folks at Home" and "Come Where My Love Lies Dreaming." One spectator at the cemetery declared the scene was so affecting that several of the musicians "all but broke down."

Stephen Foster, often called the "Great American Folk Song Writer," was the composer of about two hundred songs. For most of them he wrote both the lyrics and tunes. His words, it is said, usually came to him with the melodies; so when he had completed the stanzas, his new song was finished. Although he died over a century ago, at least twenty-five of his works are still universally sung. The reason for the continued popularity of his compositions is that Stephen Foster expressed fundamental human emotions "with straight-forwardness and sincerity."

During his formative years, many things were combining to mold his life and his incomparable talent for writing sentimental ballads and Negro (or Ethiopian) numbers. They included his home and family life, and the groups of musicians that traveled about the country singing nostalgic, appealing pieces. He also saw Negroes dancing and heard their songs at minstrel shows. All these varied influences combined to prepare Stephen Foster for his life's work.

His compositions were mainly of two types: the drawing room ballads—then "high·fashion"—sentimental songs such as "Come, Where My Love Lies Dreaming" and "Jeanie with the Light Brown Hair," and the so-called Ethiopian songs, including "Massa's in de Cold, Cold Ground," "Old Black Joe," and "My Old Kentucky Home." Such pieces usually followed a simple formula; first, a refrain was played on the banjo, then the singing of the stanzas revealed the story behind the song.

In writing his compositions, Stephen Foster considered the tastes of ordinary people. The range of his tunes was usually kept to the first six notes of the scale; however, he sometimes added a high note for dramatic effect. Most of his pieces he wrote in popular march or polka time. Therefore it is no wonder that the "common people" loved his music. Some critics of his era did not consider Foster's works too highly; they listened "with lifted eyebrows" when such outstanding singers as Madame Adelina Patti included "Old Folks at Home" in the same program at which she performed arias from famous operas. One writer (whose name was not given) wrote:

> The popularity of Foster songs is in their true melody, sung within the range of the human voice, and in the quality of the verse which is simple, sincere, dealing with the fundamental emotions of all mankind, giving to them lasting popularity, echoing as they do the folk voice of the nation.

Although Foster wrote nostalgically of the South, he really had had little contact with that part of our country. Probably he made only one trip there—in 1852—and this was after his "Old Folks at Home" had been published. He had never lived in the Southern states, or had extended opportunities to study the southern ways of life.

However, Foster did come in contact with many Negroes. It is stated that he first became acquainted with their music when his colored nurse took him to her small church in Pittsburgh. There he heard Negro spirituals and other types of their music. Later on, Foster often attended their camp meetings, and at every opportunity, he seriously studied their music.

In Pittsburgh the young man went to minstrel shows and listened carefully to the so-called Ethiopian numbers. He also spent much of his leisure time on the Ohio River front—both at Pittsburgh and Cincinnati—where he obtained much firsthand knowledge of the Negro way of life. Early in his song-writing career, Foster decided to write musical numbers for the blackface minstrel performers, in order to improve the quality of their songs. In 1852, he wrote the noted minstrel showman, E. P. Christy, that he had concluded ". . . to pursue the Ethiopian business without fear or shame . . . and to establish my name as the best Ethiopian song writer."

Foster wrote his lyrics in imitation of the Southern Negro dialect, or as someone has said, "of the minstrel singer's idea of the way the Negro talked English." Since his pieces did catch the spirit of Southern plantation life, today they are a valuable part of our American folk music.

He wrote sentimental plantation melodies, "deeply moving in their sincerity and simplicity," such as "Old Folks at Home," "My Old Kentucky Home" and "Massa's in de Cold, Cold Ground." Or some of a more rollicking nature, as "Camptown Races."

According to his biographer, H. V. Milligan, Foster's best Negro songs contain something that is vitally distinctive: "The Negro ceases to be a caricature, and becomes a human being. . . . In this type of song, universal in the appeal of its native pathos, he has never had an equal."

At first the composer (who was a poor businessman in regard to the sale of his musical compositions) often sold his works for only a few dollars. Then they were printed under the names of the performers, as was the custom at that period. In this way Stephen Foster sacrificed all future royalties. He arranged with E. P. Christy to have his works performed by Christy's noted minstrel troupe, in manuscript, before they were published. Perhaps it was a good move, for this company made his songs popular all over the country.

His earliest printed works were "La Belle Louisiana," "Oh Susanna" and "Down South"; they were published in *Songs of the Sable Harmonisers* in 1848. A year later, his "Nelly Was a Lady" appeared in Christy's *Ethiopian Melodies*.

It is strange that Foster did not seem to resent the fact that his publishers were making good money, while he was receiving little profit from his works. His most successful songs were produced between 1850 and 1860. It is true that during this period he did receive considerable money, but he soon made it disappear and "was always poor."

During his last days Stephen Foster tried to recapture his early successes, but luck was not with him. He wrote incessantly, and in the year before he died (1863), Foster turned out about forty pieces. He also collaborated with other lyric writers and produced some potboilers, not remembered today. "They lacked vibrancy, warmth and folksiness, and, as a result, were not well received by the general public."

In addition to his many songs, the composer produced a dozen or more instrumental works, including a descriptive number entitled "Santa Anna's Retreat from Buena Vista." A few of his compositions were published after his death; they included melodies written to pieces by Shakespeare and Charles Dickens. Two of these were "This Rose Will Remind You" (from *Romeo and Juliet*) and "Wilt Thou Be Gone, Love."

Despite his drinking, Foster became deeply religious and created several hymns, including "There Is a Land of Love," "Tears Bring Thoughts of Heaven," "We'll All Meet Our Saviour," and "Give Us This Day Our Daily Bread."

He resented, it is said, his downfall through drink, and he showed this feeling in such songs as "Mine Is the Mourning Heart" and "None Shall Weep for Me." As a professional song writer,

Foster was ready to write for any group or desired occasion. Therefore, for a temperance society, he composed "Comrades, Fill No Glass for Me to Drink My Soul in Liquid Flame."

Foster didn't dream that any of his works would live beyond his own time. But according to many critics, the following songs possess the power and functions of imperishable American folk music: "Uncle Ned," "Nelly Bly," "Old Folks at Home," "Massa's in de Cold, Cold Ground," "My Old Kentucky Home," "Old Dog Tray," "Old Black Joe," "Come Where My Love Lies Dreaming," and "Jeanie with the Light Brown Hair."

Both the melody and words of "Old Folks at Home" (better known by its initial line, "Way down upon the Swanee River"), were written by Foster. It is a song the world refuses to forget, and some rate it as the most popular folk song in the world.

Several years ago a symposium was conducted by the National Music Week Association, a group of 150 professional musicians. The idea was to discover which American works represent our native music at its best and are most liked by Americans. In the voting, the melodies of Foster ranked highest, and "Old Folks at Home" got first place. This has long been considered a masterpiece; one critic has declared: "A more tender lyric of home and its memories has never been written."

"Old Folks at Home" has a universal appeal, "transcending nationalism, race and time." It has been translated into various languages around the globe. In 1931, the Florida state legislature adopted it as the state's official song.

E. P. Christy of the minstrel shows had asked Foster to compose for his troupe a "home" ballad with the name of a river in it. The composer did so; at first he wrote "Way down upon the Yazoo River." However, he didn't like this name, or the name Pedee; one source says he asked his brother Morrison for some help. The latter studied the atlas and looked for names of rivers with two syllables. Finally, he came across the name "Suwannee,"—a modest stream that flows from Georgia through Florida and into the Gulf of Mexico. For the sake of rhythm, this word was shortened to "Swanee."

Foster sold "Old Folks at Home" to Christy for the small sum of $15. His name did not appear on the sheet music when the song was first published. But in 1879, fifteen years after the composer's death, his authorship was acknowledged when it was reprinted along with other songs under the general title of *Foster's Plantation Melodies as Sung by Christy's Minstrels*. During the first five years after its original publication, 1851–1856, 200,000 copies of "Old Folks at Home" were sold; but Stephen Foster received less than $1,700. Within a few years, sales had reached half a million, and the composition had been sung by various minstrel troupes all over the Northern states. By the opening of the present century, "Old Folks at Home" had become firmly established "as one of the unquestioned classics in our song literature."

Many assert that the musician never saw the "Swanee" River; however one source thinks he visited it in 1860. But whether he did or didn't is not of too much importance, for as someone has said:

> The real Swanee River does not rise in any part of Georgia, but in the highest mountains of the human heart.
>
> And it is "Old Folks at Home," greatest of all Stephen Foster songs, universal in appeal to home and family, enduring as life, which arouses an emotion, elemental in the human race. Its words bring back memory of loved ones. It is one of the most widely known and best loved songs ever written and has been translated into many languages and sung by millions all over the world.

"Open Thy Lattice, Love" is a beautiful, sentimental song which Foster composed in 1844 and had published in Philadelphia. The story is that he had read a poem in the New York *Mirror* and at once created a melody for it, dedicating it to Miss Susan Pentland of Pittsburgh. Although it was his first published song— written when he was only eighteen years old—"Open Thy Lattice,

Love," is considered one of Foster's most appealing compositions. He was "a star performer in a boyish thespian group." Often he and other members went around serenading local young ladies, and they would sing "Open Thy Lattice, Love."

"Massa's in de Cold, Cold Ground" expresses the love of Negro slaves for their master:

> Massa made de darkeys lub him,
> Cayse he was so kind.

It also shows their deep emotions at his death. One says

> I try to drive away my sorrow,
> Pickin' on de old banjo . . .

According to one writer (no by-line given) "Massa's in de Cold, Cold Ground"

> . . . is one of the most graceful of the Stephen Foster melodies. It has the same simple harmonic structure which is characteristic of all of his compositions. The words voice the love of the servants for their kind master.

"Camptown Races" is one of Foster's gayest, most "rollicking" pieces. At first it was published as "Gwine to Run All Night," and it was written soon after his marriage to Jane McDowell. It ranks in popularity with "Oh Susanna," and gives a vivid description of horse-racing in ante-bellum days.

The dog has long been considered "man's best friend." Foster's composition, "Old Dog Tray" exemplifies this. In the song, the devoted companion is watching near his master, whose old friends have all gone on before him. Only his faithful dog, Tray, is still with him to comfort him. The master relates that his dog once saved him from drowning; and declares that grief cannot drive him away.

He's gentle, he is kind,
I shall never, never find
A better friend than Old Dog Tray.

This Foster piece was quite popular for its universality. The composition was so well received by the public that within eighteen months after its publication, 125,000 copies had been sold.

Stephen Foster's most successful and lasting pieces were mainly his earliest ones; according to one writer, the only one of his non-Ethiopian songs that achieved greatness was "Jeanie with the Light Brown Hair." It has the feeling of a sentimental ballad—the type that was so well liked by the general public during the middle decades of the nineteenth century.

When "Jeanie with the Light Brown Hair" came out, in 1854, it was advertised as "a song with a beautiful vignette." This lovely melody, with its haunting lyrics, was inspired—so most critics believe—by his wife, Jane McDowell. In the composition, Stephen Foster "dreams," "longs," and "sighs" for Jeanie. But "her smiles have vanished and her sweet songs flown."

This composition is reported to be the only one that "ever made the Hit Parade eighty-seven years after it was written." It has a plaintive air, and its words express "a wistful longing." Lauritz Melchior, the noted opera singer, gave "a strong rendition" of it which pleased American listeners. So in our time, "Jeanie with the Light Brown Hair" again came alive.

Today it is sung as a song, an aria, a chorus, a fantasy. It has survived through the years to become the most popular melody of our time.

—*N.R.T.A. JOURNAL*

Although Stephen Collins Foster was a genius in his field, it is asserted that, of the last hundred of his songs created during his final years, only one—"Old Black Joe"—was a real success. The others were potboilers, composed for minstrel shows, and as a result attained only temporary popularity.

In 1860, when Foster wrote "Old Black Joe," Abraham Lincoln was a candidate for the presidency of the United States. During the campaign there were many heated debates on the subject of slavery. The long-remembered Lincoln-Douglas debates were the talk of that period. At the time Foster was living in an area which was in sympathy with Lincoln's views. Foster was in bad financial condition and also in poor health. Therefore, in a desperate effort to make a financial comeback, he thought out the idea for his classic lyric, "Old Black Joe."

One authority states that the composer wrote this song to honor Joe, the Negro houseman, at the McDowell home in Pittsburgh. Here he had courted and won his wife, Jane. The story is that Joe saw to it that the songwriter was able to make his marriage proposal to Jane McDowell ahead of another suitor, a rich young lawyer of the city.

After Foster had completed this song, he carried it in person to his publishers. At once they recognized its true worth; in it they found "all the tenderness and warmth" that had characterized the composer's earlier hit songs. At once "Old Black Joe" was a tremendous success. Although the publishers made large sums of money from the piece, Foster did not benefit from the sales. Soon afterward he was again in a terrible condition—friendless, in bad health, and poverty-stricken.

In this classic, Foster pictures the elderly slave as worn out from his years of toiling long hours daily in the cotton fields. Now he is looking forward to the end of his earthly life. But he also looks back to the time when his "heart was young and gay." His slave friends have already "gone from earth." Alone, the old man lives with his memories of earlier, happier times; now he hears "gentle voices" calling him to join his long-gone comrades. Foster, it is said, was trying in "Old Black Joe," to put into words the feelings of a Negro slave, so that others could understand his reactions. Someone once stated that while various distinctive monuments of stone, etc., have been erected to honor Foster, his most enduring memorial will always be the words of "Old Black Joe"; for they embody "the great spirit of Stephen Collins Foster, the Yankee who sang of the South."

"Oh Susanna!" one of his earlier songs, was published in 1848. At that time the minstrel-show business was in its heyday. Foster is said to have written it as a kind of stunt, for it is really a "nonsense" piece. It begins with these words:

> It rained all night the day I left,
> The weather it was dry,
> The sun so hot I froze to death,
> Susanna, don't you cry . . .

It was sung for the first time, it is believed, at Andrew's Eagle Ice Cream Parlor in a song contest on September 11, 1847.

The composer let a friend in the publishing business have the song as the latter had very little material to publish. Foster had no idea of making any money from it and as with many of his other compositions, the song writer did not receive much in return for it—although the publisher did. But there was one good result, the instant and wide success of "Oh Susanna!" encouraged Stephen Foster to make a decision to take up composing in earnest, and really make it his life work.

This was the period of the Gold Rush in California, and men eager to make their fortunes were heading west by the thousands, taking several different routes. The would-be miners who made their way across the continent in covered wagons took up this gay song. Many a night it was heard around their campfires; and soon it was a popular number from Maine to California. This was perhaps the favorite song of the gold miners, for it was a good marching song with a decidedly catchy tune.

The songs of Stephen Foster have become so well known everywhere, that it is said some other countries look upon them as their own. For years "Oh Susanna!" was the theme song of the Voice of America, broadcast to Germany. The Germans had sung, "Ich komm von Alabama mit der Banjo auf dem Knie." Finally the song was taken off the program because the people complained that they didn't want to hear a German folk song, but an American one!

"My Old Kentucky Home," the official song of the state of Kentucky, was written by Foster at the height of his most creative period and "out of the joys of his marriage to Jane McDowell." (Up to this time he had composed "Oh Susanna!," "Nelly Bly," "Old Uncle Ned," "Come Where My Love Lies Dreaming," and "Louisiana Belle.")

One account tells that in February, 1852, just two years after his marriage, Stephen and his wife were able to take a trip to New Orleans on the steamer *James Milligan,* owned by one of his brothers, who was taking a cargo of goods to New Orleans to sell there.

En route, they stopped off and visited Federal Hall, the home of Judge Rowan, a cousin of Stephen's father at Bardstown, Kentucky. The Pittsburgh *Press,* in February, 1852, reported that the song writer had visited there; the result of this stopover was the creation of the composer's beloved "My Old Kentucky Home."

Federal Hall, a stately old Southern home, is maintained today as a shrine. Annually it is visited by thousands of persons, many of whom come long distances to see it. The mansion is owned by the state of Kentucky. It was built in 1795 by John Rowan of Louisville, and according to one account he imported the bricks from England; they were brought overland, during the winter months, from Newport News, Virginia, on ox-drawn sledges. The owner also purchased elegant furnishings for this fine home to which he brought his bride. It has high-ceilinged rooms, and still contains many rare antiques, with furniture styled by Chippendale, Sheraton, Hepplewhite, and Duncan Phyfe. There are also paintings of members of the Rowan family, executed by well-known artists.

One of the chief reasons modern Americans enjoy visiting the old mansion is because of its association with Foster. Many celebrities have "slept" at Federal Hall, including Henry Clay, the

Marquis de Lafayette, and President James Monroe. Members of the Rowan family owned and occupied the mansion until 1922, when Kentucky acquired it and all its furnishings.

Mrs. Harriet Rowan Harshbarger of Long Beach, California, a great-great-grandaughter of the builder, said of it when the state bought it: "It became known as 'My Old Kentucky Home' and it is maintained as a perpetual shrine." Each year Mrs. Harshbarger is invited to Federal Hall to the birthday celebration on July 4 of Stephen Foster. She stated that the memory of Judge Rowan's grave on the federal estate was the incentive for Foster's song, "Massa's in de Cold, Cold Ground."

When young Foster stopped off at the home, he at once fell in love with it and its fine hospitality; he especially enjoyed meeting the Rowan children. As he was so sensitive to beauty, the scenes on his cousin's plantation impressed him strongly. So the song, "My Old Kentucky Home" is said to have been written there, or at least inspired by his enjoyable visit to the plantation. (It was during the same year that Harriet Beecher Stowe wrote *Uncle Tom's Cabin.*)

While at Federal Hall, the composer watched the slaves toiling long hours each day in the fields. Then, after their work was over, they would sit on the steps of their cabins in the evening and sing.

One story about the creation of this immortal song is that when Foster arose one morning he heard the mockingbirds and wood thrushes singing. He saw the Negroes at work while the children played nearby. All these scenes so impressed him that he at once put down on paper his thoughts about them in the stanzas of "My Old Kentucky Home."

The separating of families, when some of the members were "sold down the river," is brought out in this song; then the carefree, joyful life on a Kentucky plantation would yield to the grief of parting. In some unexplainable way Foster had already "drawn deeply from the wellspring of Negro melody, and had caught the beauty of the African soul."

No author or composer has touched the sympathetic chord of the home-love of the colored race as surely as Foster did in this song. It embodies some of the best characteristics of American Negro music and is in truth fitted to rank with the best legendary folk songs of any land.

—From *55 Songs and Choruses for Community Singing*

There are deeply expressed emotions in this well-known song; and in it, Foster shows his deep sympathy for Negroes as he depicts their yearning for the former happy days—days now only remembered.

Whether "My Old Kentucky Home" actually was written at Bardstown is not known, although it is said that members of the Rowan family used to point out to visitors the spring house where the composer created the lyrics, also the desk in the front hall where he is said to have written them down as soon as he came into the house.

One old Kentucky gentleman, many years ago, claimed he had been present at Federal Hall and had heard the first singing of "My Old Kentucky Home." He said that among the gay house party of young people was a girl with a beautiful voice. Stephen Foster taught her his new song; then she performed for the guests "the song the world has been singing ever since."

(Frith, Pond and Company published it in 1854; soon they had sold 90,000 copies.)

Kentucky calls Federal Hall "My Old Kentucky Home" and stages a celebration there each Independence Day, the composer's birthday. On July 4, 1958—the 132nd anniversary of Foster's birth—the cornerstone was laid for an amphitheater. Fletcher Hodges, Jr. curator of the Stephen Foster Collection at the University of Pittsburgh, and Mrs. Hodges unveiled a painting of Federal Hall.

The Louisville *Courier-Journal* of July 4, 1958, stated that Mrs. Evelyn Foster Morneweck of Stuart, Florida, was present for the yearly observance. She had done much research and had written a two-volume history of the Foster family. She is the daughter of Stephen's brother, Morrison Foster; but she never saw her famous uncle. Mrs. Morneweck is the last living member of her generation of the family.

She stated that Stephen did visit Bardstown in 1852 while on a river trip, and that when the steamboat docked at Louisville on its way from Pittsburgh to New Orleans, the song writer stopped at the Rowan home, but that his visit must have been a very short one.

When Mrs. Morneweck was ten years old, she visited Federal Hall. She told of other songs written by her uncle. She declared that her father's favorites were "Jeanie with the Light Brown Hair" and "Laura Lee" while hers was "Wilt Thou Be True?" This, she said, is not sung any more; and she wondered why such a beautiful composition was neglected.

For some time, there has been some debate about the wording of some of the Foster songs.

> While appreciating the songs of this great American composer, we should not forget that many cultured Negroes resent being typed in dialect or mannerisms. Certainly the ante-bellum language and customs reflected in the Foster songs have little or no relevance to the lives of today's Negroes.

However, Mrs. Morneweck in 1858 expressed herself as being against making changes in her uncle's songs. (When Paul Robeson sang "Old Folks at Home," he used the word "children" instead of "darkies.") She believes that ultimately people will retain the original terms, for she thinks the changes would take away part of the Negro history. Frank Chelf, a Kentucky Representative, agrees with Mrs. Morneweck, and advised Dinah Shore to sing the Foster songs as they were written or not at all.

The niece of Stephen Foster declared that his songs belong to everybody and should be kept intact. She said the radio networks in some instances had altered the lyrics as they feared they might offend some listeners.

One of the most striking statements that Mrs. Morneweck made in her interview (when she attended the Foster birthday observance in 1958 at Bardstown) was that "My Old Kentucky Home" was *not* written about the mansion—Federal Hall—but about a slave cabin on the plantation. Also that the person who was being told "Weep no more, my lady," was not the mistress of the big house but a Negro woman living in her humble cabin.

(About ten years after Mrs. Morneweck's interview, some Negro leaders in Frankfurt, Kentucky, objected to "possible racial overtones" in Kentucky's official song, which is played each year before the start of the famous Kentucky Derby. As some resented the use of the term "darkies," officials of the National Association for the Advancement of Colored People asked that the word be omitted.)

Although Foster died alone and in poverty, today he is highly honored by various memorials in different parts of the United States. As someone has said, it is doubtful whether "any monument of brick or stone" would last longer than the heritage of songs he gave us.

In 1941, the composer was elected to the New York Hall of Fame; countless schools all over our country bear his name; and in Rochester, New York, at the Eastman School of Music, a dormitory, Foster Hall, honors his memory. James H. Park presented to the city of Pittsburgh "the probable site" of his birth; now it is visited annually by many lovers of his immortal compositions.

A wealthy manufacturer of Indiana, Josiah K. Lilly, gathered together as many available mementos as possible—"original Fosteriana"—and enshrined them in Foster Hall in Indianapolis for the public to enjoy.

The auditorium at the University of Pittsburgh is named for the song writer. Foster Hall has a valuable collection of music and relics, including his piano, which is on display in one of the main galleries. This building is the mecca each year for thousands of

Foster song lovers from all over the United States and from many foreign lands.

On January 13, 1932, the sixty-eighth anniversary of Foster's death, the University of Pittsburgh joined with the South in paying tribute to his genius. Chimes rang out from various churches, and such favorite Foster compositions as "Old Black Joe," "My Old Kentucky Home," "Old Uncle Ned," and "Old Folks at Home" were heard throughout the city of Pittsburgh.

For some time after the composer's death in 1864, most musicians paid little attention to his works. But in 1932 the National Association of Composers, Authors, and Publishers sent a representative to Pittsburgh to place a wreath on Foster's grave. Ministers in various churches honored him in their sermons, and choirs featured his songs on that anniversary day.

One of the most beautiful places in the entire state of Florida is the Stephen C. Foster Memorial on the Suwannee River at White Springs. This is a truly fitting shrine to the memory of America's beloved composer. Josiah K. Lilly is given credit for suggesting this memorial in Florida. Each year on January 13 Stephen C. Foster Day is observed there.

The Florida Federation of Music Clubs started the movement. A Stephen Foster Memorial Corporation was formed, and land was purchased for a suitable monument to his memory. Soon afterward the holdings were ceded to the state, and in 1939, the Stephen Foster Memorial Commission was established by the state legislature. The shrine was opened to the public in 1950. At the formal dedication in 1951, distinguished guests came long distances to take part in the ceremonies. One of them was Mrs. Jessie Welsh Rose, Foster's granddaughter.

The "stately ante-bellum type building," with its great white colonial columns is surrounded by rolling woodlands and is located in a 245-acre state park. There are shady paths and places where visitors may picnic. Also they can ride on paved roads around the attractive grounds in a motorized Conestoga wagon, reminiscent of the time of Stephen Foster. On the nearby Suwannee River is a steamboat, the *Belle of Suwannee,* which carries passengers.

There is no admission charge to the building, for the state of Florida set up a fund of half a million dollars years ago for the erection and maintenance of this outstanding museum.

Blanche S. McKnight (writing some years ago in *Classmate*) gave this reaction to her visit to the distinctive memorial:

> In the $200,000 imposing red brick and white pillared building, set like a gem in the forest fastnesses of the park, and surrounded by tangible reminders of "the beloved bard," the visitor may also capture a bit of the spirit of the Old South.

As one climbs the broad steps of the museum, his ears are greeted by Foster music which follows him throughout the building. There are hundreds of authentic relics of the composer to be seen in this structure, including original manuscripts and first editions of his many works. The furnishings of the building are those of Stephen Foster's period (1826–1864).

For visitors the most impressive attractions are the large animated three-dimensional dioramas, constructed at a cost of $50,000. They illustrate several Foster songs, and as one writer has said, they really transport viewers back to ante-bellum days in the Old South, ". . . for their life-likeness, movement, and depth and lighting combine to bring back the Stephen Foster songs to life." These amazing and fascinating dioramas are set into the walls, and beautifully illustrate some of his masterpieces.

The curator of the museum believes that the "Old Folks at Home" presentation is the most popular one with visitors. A distinctive animated scene depicts this composition, beginning with the words, "Way down upon the Swanee River." The diorama reveals an ante-bellum plantation picture. Children are playing around a cabin (surrounded by live oak trees); Negro mothers are seen with their youngsters; at the right slaves are toiling in a cotton field. On the Suwannee is an old stern-wheeler. And across the stream, in the distance, is the master's home. The picture is made more realistic as it is synchronized with the music of a Negro quartet singing "Old Folks at Home."

In the diorama "Old Dog Tray," an old man is sitting in his library in front of a fireplace with his faithful dog nearby. In the fire the master sees visions of loved ones and friends who have passed away. These change as visitors study the scene and realize that only Old Dog Tray alone remains to comfort his master.

"Jeanie with the Light Brown Hair" is another "vision" picture. At the left in this diorama, the writer himself is shown composing the song. While he is at work, a picture of Jeanie flashes on and off at the far right ("perhaps a bit too realistically"). Many believe this work was written about Jane McDowell Foster, the wife of the composer, who was separated from her husband when he wrote this touching ballad (first published in 1854).

Stephen Foster's first published song was "Open Thy Lattice, Love." In the diorama illustrating this song we see a male singer and two companions serenading his love, who stands above them on a balcony of an old colonial home with beautiful, lacy grillwork, painted white. At one side is a great tree hung with Spanish moss, while a river boat is seen in the distance.

The diorama showing "Old Black Joe" contains an aged white-haired Negro, leaning on his cane, and accompanied by his dog. He realizes he has not long to live and sees a vision in the clouds, the faces of friends "gone from the earth to a better place I know." As he looks upward, he seems to hear "gentle voices" calling to him from Heaven. Some consider "Old Black Joe" the most spiritual of all of Stephen Foster's many works.

The representation of "My Old Kentucky Home" shows the home life of the slaves. It reflects the tragic grief of family separation when slaves were sold and shipped to the South, far from their dear ones at home. (One critic says this diorama fails to bring out the tragedy in the song itself, but it does make the home life of these workers come alive.) Smoke is coming from a cabin, before which a young man is playing his harmonica—a gay contrast to the sad mood of the song. In the background some mule-drawn carts move along a dusty road.

"Camptown Races" features an actual ante-bellum horse race, with spectators in the foreground. The horses are seen "flying on a ten-mile heat" and the "bob-tailed nag" really passes the bay.

The diorama of "Oh Susanna!" shows a camp at night. The would-be miners, who are heading westward to seek gold, are resting after their hard day's journey. Some are sitting around a campfire singing "Oh Susanna!" their favorite Gold Rush days' song. At the left, in front of a covered wagon, a woman is standing, clutching her shawl around her and listening to the gay singing of the men.

On the extensive grounds of the Florida memorial to Foster, there is an amphitheater where Foster Song Festivals are held. From a two-hundred-foot carillon tower one hears the beloved melodies, often played by well-known musicians. Once an unnamed writer gave this reaction to his visit: "To browse through this peaceful memorial is a never-to-be-forgotten experience, that brings to life the Stephen Foster that all America—and all the world—knows and loves."

Stephen Collins Foster's life was a tragic one, marked by strange contrasts. A Northerner, he received high acclaim for his Southern plantation songs. Although he probably never saw the Suwannee River, he made it famous. While in many compositions he speaks tenderly of family and home, he died homeless in the charity ward of a New York hospital.

In his songs the composer expressed his deep yearnings for relatives, friends, home, freedom, love, and other strong emotions common to the hearts of all people. These compositions have all the characteristics of American folk songs; "he wrote into his songs the traits of our people, simply, truly; for he was one of us." It has been stated that Foster left us one of the richest legacies imaginable, and the "most important group of sounds of the people" ever written by one person.

The writer Frederick Hall once said of Foster that the world today is imbued with a stronger love of home because of the songs he wrote about it. And Louis C. Elson in 1899 stated that while Foster's music was "primitive, limited and uneven,"

> . . . his best songs gave permanent expression to one phase of American life—the nostalgic melancholy of the Negro—and remain a valuable contribution to the folk-literature of American music.

> It was the diversity of mood in the lyrics and the peculiar American twang of melodic inflection that saved Foster's songs from monotony.
>
> —Nicholas Slonimsky

> He was of that imperial race of melodists. . . . Beautiful melodies came to him as naturally as breathing. . . . Though he was not a trained musician, his best songs reveal qualities of the great musician: taste, refinement, directness of speech.
>
> —David Ewen

Several years ago in the *National Retired Teachers' Journal* this tribute appeared under Foster's picture (no by-line):

> Stephen Foster was a boy with a far-away look, listening to something nobody else could hear.
>
> Other kids saved marbles, he collected sounds. The pockets of his memory were stuffed with the sounds of American living.
>
> There were the soft sounds of his mother telling about the old days, and the hard sound of his father chuckling at the children's games.
>
> There were field sounds, school sounds, church sounds and train sounds; the sounds of old folks remembering and young ones hoping.
>
> And there were the haunting sounds of the levee, the banjos and the Negro voices, singing of hard work and simple pleasures.
>
> Stephen Foster took them all and gave back to the people the music they had made themselves.
>
> He gave them bouncy songs full of their own kind of fun, and

wistful songs full of their own kind of longing. He caught their sense
of the sweetness of life, its sadness and goodness. And most of all,
he caught their feeling about home—that American sense of home
as a haven of security and peace . . . worth working for, worth
saving for, worth protecting.

Old Folks at Home

Stephen C. Foster

Stephen C. Foster

6

*

"Dixie"

Over a century ago (1859) Daniel Decatur Emmett, an Amercian minstrel performer and composer, wrote both the words and music for "Dixie," a typical American song with a gay and catchy tune. Although he was a Northerner, his song won immediate popularity.

It is a strange fact that several of the best Southern songs were written in the North, including "Swanee River," "Nellie Gray," "Listen to the Mocking Bird," "Maryland, My Maryland," and "Dixie," which is considered the South's most popular song.

At the beginning of the Civil War, "Dixie" was taken over by the Southerners as their Confederate battle song. But today all sections of our great country sing "Dixie," termed one of "the most rollicking of our national songs," known and loved throughout the world.

Daniel Emmett, one of the originators of the "Negro minstrel troupe," was born in Mount Vernon, Ohio, on October 29, 1815. He was of Irish descent. His ancestors, Virginia pioneers, migrated from that colony beyond the Blue Ridge Mountains. Then they crossed the Alleghenies, finally settling in Ohio.

Emmett's grandfather fought in the American Revolution and

was at the Battle of Cowpens. His father, Abraham Emmett, was apprenticed to a blacksmith, but during the War of 1812 he volunteered and served in the regiment commanded by the noted Lewis Cass. He helped in the defense of Fort Meigs, and was present when the British General Hull surrendered at Detroit.

On his return from the War of 1812, Abraham Emmett took up his interrupted trade at Mount Vernon, Ohio, and married Sarah Zerick in Clinton, Ohio. Daniel was the oldest of their four children. He had little formal education, and at an early age was working in his father's blacksmith shop. However, after learning to read and write, the boy became an apprentice in a print shop where his real education began.

At the youthful age of thirteen years, he was working in the office of the Huron *Reflector* in Norwalk, Ohio, and later was employed by the *Western Aurora* in Mount Vernon. Daniel remained there until he was seventeen, when he enlisted in the army as a fifer. His first military service was at Newport, Kentucky. Later during his leisure time, when stationed at Jefferson Barracks near St. Louis, the young soldier studied music. He played both the violin and flute. Emmett had learned many familiar melodies from his mother, who it is said was quite musical. As the youth was underage, his father secured his release from army service on July 8, 1835 "on account of minority."

Emmett liked to compose verses to be sung to popular tunes—a pastime that was indulged in by other young people in his day. "In this way," one source states, "Mr. Emmett formed a taste for verse-making and singing which later led him into minstrelsy." Before he was seventeen years old, in 1830 or 1831, he had composed one of his best-known pieces, "Old Dan Tucker."

At twenty, he again left home and played the drums in a circus band; he toured with this company for a year or more. He was good at composing songs in Negro dialect, and his voice was well suited for singing this type of music. After several tries, Emmett launched himself into the career of a minstrel performer, and in the theater found the life for which his talents were well suited.

The minstrel show was a purely American form of entertainment, consisting of varied vaudeville numbers. The white performers, in blackface, sat on the stage in a semi-circle, while the musicians performed behind them. A "straight man," or "interlocutor," acted as master of ceremonies. The star performers were two end men; "Mr. Bones" and "Mr. Tambo," so called because of the instruments they played—the ivory bones, or clappers, and the tambourine.

These shows started in the United States in the decade of the 1840's and were popular all over the country until about the end of the century. Originally the idea began with the singing and dancing of the Negro slaves. Stephen Foster wrote several of his best compositions, including "My Old Kentucky Home," "Old Black Joe," and others for the minstrel groups.

In 1842 there was a depression in the United States and many actors found themselves without work. Emmett decided to get together a company of his own which would perform Negro songs and dances. During the winter of 1842–1843, he organized the Virginia Minstrels. At their first performance, on February 9, 1843, at the Bowery Amphitheater, Emmett gave the public its first experience of an entirely different kind of theatrical fare. His blackfaced minstrels sang, danced, and told jokes. Because Emmett started this form of entertainment, he had a strong influence for several decades upon the development of the American theater.

For his troupe, he designed what one writer termed their "ludicrous" costumes. These included white trousers, striped calico shirts, and long blue swallowtail coats. Emmett had some exceptionally good entertainers in his company, including the stars Frank Brown, Billy Whitlock, and Dick Phelan. From February 9, 1843, to the first of March, his men, playing such instruments as the violin, banjo, bones, and tambourine, were a great success. They "firmly fixed themselves as among the inaugurators of a half-century institution," according to G. H. Odell in his *Annals of the New York Stage*.

The group also performed in Boston and in other American cities, where they were enthusiastically received. Emmett himself as a minstrel was a great favorite with the public. "His understanding of the Negro dialect was perfect, as was likewise his rendering. . . . His love of minstrelsy is still visible" (Edward Bok, 1895).

Because of the overwhelming success of the Virginia Minstrels in this country, they decided to make a tour through Great Britain. But overseas they were not received too well, and on their return to the United States found some competition. For E. P. Christy and others had also organized such troupes and were making a great hit with the general public

It was in 1857 that Emmett joined the Bryant Minstrels. In his contract with Jerry Bryant, he was "to hold himself in readiness to compose for them a new 'walk-around,' whenever called upon to do so, and to sing the same at the close of their performance." He was their chief songwriter; and at about this time he was writing various Negro songs. Emmett was with Bryant's Minstrels from 1857 to 1861.

The details of how the composer wrote his famous work "Dixie" have fortunately been preserved. One of his fellow minstrels, Charley White, wrote about it in his diary; and Emmett, too, has left us an account of its creation.

It was the custom for each performance of a minstrel show to end with a "walk-around," during which all the members of the company joined in songs and dances. Such pieces, too, were often used as "hooray songs" and were sung on the streets by various members to advertise their productions. These compositions had very catchy tunes that could be sung or whistled on the street after people had heard them in a theater.

One Saturday night, when Bryant's Minstrels were performing at Mechanics Hall in New York City, Jerry Bryant told Emmett he needed a new walk-around for the show on the following Monday, and that it must be ready for that morning's rehearsal. This struck Emmett as entirely too short a time in which to compose the words and music for a completely new piece.

However, he told Bryant he'd do his very best to get something together. And the song writer was true to his word. For Emmett not only wrote a gay and unforgettable song (with words exactly as we sing them today), but it was a piece that "he scratched off in a few hours, but which will keep his name alive forever."

Emmett started in early the next day; it was a dark, dreary, rainy and chilly Sunday morning, not very conducive to inspiring him to do the task. At first he wasn't successful. He wanted to concoct an entirely different kind of composition, but good ideas just failed to come to his mind. His wife urged him on; she tried to encourage him and said she'd be his audience.

As he sat shivering in the drab boardinghouse, trying to concentrate on the job, Daniel grumbled and declared, "I wish I was in Dixie." He had traveled through the South, and when he and other showmen were back in the cold North, they would often say, "Oh, I wish I was in Dixie." Later, after writing his masterpiece, "Dixie," the composer asserted: "The words, 'I wish I was in Dixie' haunted me until I put them on paper."

Hoping that this phrase would stimulate an idea for the walk-around, Daniel took up his violin and began to improvise a tune to go with the expression that he made the first line of his new lyrics. Then the rest of the words came easily to mind, and it wasn't long until the work was complete. In later life, he was always amazed by the popularity of "Dixie" which he had dashed off so casually and quickly—written, as he said, because "it had to be done."

Next morning, when the Bryant Minstrel Company met for rehearsal, Daniel Emmett presented the new walk-around. The company tried it out, and Jerry Bryant and all his troupe were delighted with its tune and gay words. That evening, September 9, 1859, at Mechanics Hall, the audience, too, was thrilled, and many went home singing or whistling the pleasing air. At first its title was "I Wish I Was in Dixie," followed by "Dixieland"; finally it became just "Dixie." Someone declared, "It was one of those war songs that came into martial use by accident."

Soon it became a favorite all over the United States, as fast as minstrel troupes could bring it before the people. Immediately, other theatrical companies asked Emmett for copies of his new hit, and for permission to use "Dixie" on their programs. Several just took over the composition and had it published without even giving the composer any credit for his work. The result was that Emmett not only was robbed of his copyright, but some unscrupulous individuals even questioned his authorship.

Others had their own versions printed, but here is the original first stanza of "Dixie" just as Daniel Emmett wrote it:

> I wish I was in de land of cotton,
> Old times dar am not forgotten,
> Look away! Look away! Look away! Dixieland!

At the beginning of the Civil War, "Dixie" was arranged as a quickstep for the Washington Artillery. Soon the tune was heard everywhere—on the streets, in saloons, and in homes. The contagious nature of its melody helped to bring about its rapid spread and popularity.

There has long been much controversy about the meaning and obscure origin of the word "Dixie." The term is associated with the Negro, with minstrelsy, and with the Southern states. Some maintain it is a diminutive for the South, used before the Civil War, and that the term was applied especially to those states that formed the Confederate States of America. In the years from 1763 to 1767, Charles Mason and Jeremiah Dixon established the famous Mason-Dixon Line, the boundary between the free and slave states. Certain authorities believe the word is a derivation, or corruption, of Mason and Dixon Line. The word is said to have come into use after Texas entered the Union.

Some say that "Dixie" was first used by circus men in the North. When a member of a circus company was wintering in that part of the country (and not enjoying the freezing weather), he would think of the warmer climate down South and wish to be there again. It is said that Daniel Emmett himself gave this explanation of the term, "Dixie."

Perhaps the most popular and believable explanation of its origin is that it had its start in ten-dollar notes issued by the Citizens Bank of New Orleans some time before 1860. Because many French people were living in Louisiana, these notes had *dix* ("ten") on the reverse side. Louisiana and the entire South became known as the "Land of Dixies," or "Dixieland," finally shortened to "Dixie."

Another theory arises from the story that Dixie was the name of a kindly, paternal farmer who lived on Long Island in the last half of the eighteenth century, and sheltered runaway slaves. When word trickled through to Southern Negroes about this refuge up north, they called it "Dixie's Land." When they ran away they tried to make their way to this farm, where they knew they would receive good treatment. The Negroes regarded the spot, so it is said, really as paradise—"a place of unalloyed happiness," and "Dixie" became synonymous with an ideal locality.

Another version of this New York story is that when the Abolition movement became strong there, and the sentiment against slavery increased, the New York State Assembly planned to outlaw it. So Mr. Dixie had to sell some of his slaves down south. The Negroes lamented their new, harsh treatment in the South, and wanted to go back to Mr. Dixie's land, meaning his New York farm. They were continually talking and singing of its joys, and longed to return there.

Although Emmett, a Northerner, had written "Dixie" in the North, it is interesting to note how the Southerners simply "took over" the song. It soon became the Confederate rallying piece and inspired the Southern troops to deeds of great courage, sending them into battle bent on victory. One source states that "Dixie" may have been responsible for the South's long-continued resistance against its stronger Northern foes.

Late in the fall of 1860, a spectacular burlesque production was staged in New Orleans by John Brougham. It was entitled *Pocahontas, or The New Orleans Varieties.* The musical director, Carlo Patti (a brother of the celebrated soprano, Madame Adelina Patti), needed a lively marching song for the grand chorus, composed of a drill team of forty females in Zouave costumes. Director Patti simply tried out the tune of "Dixie" and appropriated it by writing new words to go with the air.

He chose Mrs. John Wood to sing the new number, which was used at the close of the performance. The audience went wild; all applauded it vigorously and soon all New Orleans was ringing with the outstanding melody. When Jefferson Davis was inaugurated in Montgomery, Alabama, as president of the new Confederate republic on February 18, 1861, "Dixie" was heard all over the city. And it soon was used throughout the Southern states as the most popular marching song.

When it was first published in the South, there was no mention whatsoever of the Northern composer's name—Daniel D. Emmett. There was a notation to the effect that it had been sung by Mrs. John Wood. And a rumor spread in New Orleans that "Dixie" was the work of a Negro who was expressing his love for his Southern home and master.

Confederate soldiers who heard it sung in New Orleans took the song with them to their camps and then to the battlefields. The tune swept through their ranks and was accepted as *their* song. General Pickett ordered his musicians to play "Dixie" just before the noted charge at the Battle of Gettysburg.

After the South had taken over "Dixie" and it had become the distinctive Confederate song, other words were soon written by various writers in the South. For example, on May 30, 1861, the Natchez *Courier* printed a poem by Albert Pike of Arkansas, which was sung to the "Dixie" tune. Pike was a poet, a veteran of the Mexican War, and a brigadier general in the Confederate Army. His version began in this way:

> Southrons, hear your country call you!
> Up, lest worse than death befall you!
> To arms, to arms, in Dixie . . .

Also Mrs. M. B. Moore of North Carolina began in 1863 to write a "Dixie" series of school books, which included primers, readers, histories, and arithmetics.

In the North, after Emmett's composition had been adopted by Southerners as their own stirring marching song, it was branded as a "Rebel" number. Some newspapers even attacked the composer and accused him of being a Southern sympathizer. Born in the North, and sincerely dedicated to the Union cause, Emmett was both amazed and appalled at the use to which his minstrel number had been put, and at finding himself idolized by the Confederates.

Hoping the North would adopt them, he accordingly wrote some entirely new words to his tune of "Dixie," including these lines:

> Go meet those Southern traitors with iron,
> And should your courage falter, boy,
> Remember Bunker Hill.

The noted blind hymn writer, Fanny Crosby, also penned words suitable for Northern use. A third version associated with the Union cause was the work of T. M. V. Cooley. Although the term "Dixie" became synonymous with the Southern states, Daniel Emmett's words are the only ones that have survived. Now "Dixie" is the song "beloved by the entire nation."

"Dixie," like other important American patriotic numbers, has been heard on historic occasions. During the lively political campaign when Abraham Lincoln was a presidential candidate for the first time, some Republicans composed words to the melody and used them as a campaign song. "Dixie" was a great favorite with President Lincoln, and five years later when many people gathered on the White House lawn to celebrate the surrender of General

Robert E. Lee at Appomattox, Lincoln asked the Marine Band to play "Dixie," and jokingly added: "As we have captured the Confederate Army, we have also captured the Confederate tune, and both belong to us."

Several years ago, Archibald Rutledge told of a poignant experience that happened earlier when he was just out of college and teaching at a boys' school between Antietam and Gettysburg. In an old nearby cemetery he found three graves. One was marked "Unknown"; the others bore the names "J. W. Alban" and "W. H. Quintance." The "Unknown" was said to have been a Confederate raider killed by a Union sniper. The others, wounded, had made their way to a nearby schoolhouse where they were cared for.

Since Rutledge recognized the name "Quintance" as of Virginia origin, he sent the story to a Richmond paper. Soon he received a letter from the widow, saying she would like to visit her husband's grave. He consulted his minister, who urged him to invite her to come.

She arrived, "a gentle and beautiful lady with snowy hair." Everyone was at the station to meet her. There was an honor guard of the Grand Army of the Republic, along with a reception committee. The local band played "The Bonnie Blue Banner" and "Dixie" in her honor. At the cemetery all gathered in a circle around the three Confederate graves. Rutledge concluded his reminiscences with these words:

> As I considered the lovely reception accorded her, I thought, "That buries the guns for me. As far as I am concerned, the Civil War is over! This moving spectacle of human tender-heartedness at its best spoke to me of human understanding and friendliness."

Emmett traveled with his own minstrel company from 1865 until 1888. During those years, he made his home in the city of Chicago. But in 1888, he returned to a little farm in Ohio, just outside of Mount Vernon. His first wife, Catherine Rives, died on May 3, 1875, and four years later, Emmett married Mary Louise (Brower) Bird, who survived him.

Although he is remembered mainly for "Dixie" and "Old Dan Tucker," the composer created many other songs, including "The Boatman's Dance," "The Road to Richmond," and "Walk Along, John."

In his last years he received little or no money for his works, and was often in financial need at his home in Ohio. For some persons still were critical of his having written "Dixie." In reality, few knew that Emmett was still alive until 1895, when Edward Bok, the outstanding editor of the *Ladies' Home Journal,* called attention to the fact. Bok stated in an editorial that "the venerable and retired minstrel," the author of "Dixie," was alive, but poor, and almost forsaken. He declared: "Thousands who know the words of his famous song, know not the name of the composer." That same year—1895—Daniel Decatur Emmett, at the advanced age of eighty years, traveled with Al G. Fields's Minstrels on a "Farewell Tour" through both the North and the South and sang his most famous lyric, "Dixie."

Fortunately the songwriter lived long enough to see "Dixie" win "universal acclaim" all over the United States. Also many people made his last years more comfortable, and gave him the recognition he so truly deserved for his musical achievements.

When Emmett died, in 1904, at his farm near Mount Vernon, Ohio, he was buried in Mound View Cemetery. Many gathered to honor him; and as his casket was lowered into its grave, a band played his well-known composition.

Emmett's masterpiece has been given much praise by various writers. Louis C. Elson, in *The National Music of America,* stated that "Dixie," "a rollicking picture of plantation life, bears its charm in its music rather than its words," and added that it was "a great influence on the battlefield, and remains a favorite in days of peace." Elson also emphasized that "Dixie" was a great favorite of the Civil War President, Abraham Lincoln, as well as of the Northern soldiers, pointing out that "it was one of the most characteristic melodies that sprang from the epoch of the war, although written as a picture of peace and happiness." In *Patriotic Songs of America* a booklet published by the John Hancock Insurance Company) an unnamed writer says: "This was the most popular war song of the Confederate soldiers, and is, among the people of all sections of the country. It is typically American."

Another comment, made by one whose name was not given, was that the beloved song "Dixie" was not a product of the Civil War, but

> . . . a peculiar and fortuitous circumstance led to its adoption by the Confederate Army in 1861, and it soon carried the people into a state of impassioned emotion; and today its popularity is so great that in reality it has become one of the songs of the Union.

In *Songs and Choruses for Community Singing* is this paragraph about "Dixie":

> This, the most rollicking of our national songs, was written and composed for a Negro minstrel show, by Daniel Decatur Emmett. . . . The song as originally written, was instantaneously successful and became a Confederate war song. Since then it has become a favorite throughout the country, and as a band composition is played all over the world.

Arthur Farwell and W. D. Darby, in their volume *Music in America,* paid this tribute to Emmett's song:

> The music of "Dixie" is so pleasing to the people that it has become almost a universal tune without words.
>
> Its beginning was in the minstrel show; it was dedicated as a battle song in the great uprising of the South; and in its last estate it has a place among the enduring music of the Union.

Dixie

Daniel Emmett

Dan. Emmett

1. I___ wish I was___ in the land ob cot - ton,___ Old time dar___ am
2. Old Mis - sus mar - ry___ Will, de wea - ber,___ Wil - lium was___ a
3. His___ face was sharp___ as a butch - er's clea - ber, But dat did___ not
4. Now___ here's a health___ to the next old Mis - sus,And all de gals___ dat
5. Dar's buck - wheat cakes___ an'___ In - gen' bat - ter, Makes you fat or a

not for - got - ten, Look a - way! Look a - way! Look a - way! Dix - ie Land. In___
gay de - ceab - er; Look a - way! Look a - way! Look a - way! Dix - ie Land. But___
seem to greab-'er; Look a - way! Look a - way! Look a - way! Dix - ie Land. Old___
want to kiss us; Look a - way! Look a - way! Look a - way! Dix - ie Land. But___
lit - tle fat - ter; Look a - way! Look a - way! Look a - way! Dix - ie Land. Den___

Dix - ie Land, whar'___ I was born in,___ Ear - ly___ on___ one
when he put___ his___ arm a - round 'er He smiled as___ fierce as a
Mis - sus act - ed the fool - ish part, And___ died for a man___ dat
if you want to___ drive 'way sor - row,___ Come and___ hear___ dis
hoe it down___ an'___ scratch your grab - ble, To Dix - ie's___ land___ I'm

frost - y morn-in' Look a - way! Look a - way! Look a - way! Dix - ie Land.
for - ty pound - er, Look a - way! Look a - way! Look a - way! Dix - ie Land.
broke her heart,___ Look a - way! Look a - way! Look a - way! Dix - ie Land.
to - mor - row, Look a - way! Look a - way! Look a - way! Dix - ie Land.
bound to trab - ble, Look a - way! Look a - way! Look a - way! Dix - ie Land.

Chorus

Den___ I wish I was in Dix - ie, Hoo - ray! Hoo - ray! In___

Dix - ie Land, I'll take my stand to lib and die in Dix - ie; A - -

way, A - way, A - way down south in Dix - ie; A - -

way, A - way, A - way down south in Dix - ie.

7

*

"The Battle Hymn of the Republic"

Julia Ward Howe, the creator of that poetic masterpiece, "one of the noblest patriotic lyrics ever published," was born in New York City, on May 27, 1819 (just three days after the birth of Queen Victoria) and died on October 17, 1910.

During her lifetime the composer of "The Battle Hymn of the Republic" became one of our most famous American women. She came from distinguished lineage on both sides of her family, and was descended from John Ward of Gloucester, an Englishman who served as an officer under Oliver Cromwell in the 1600's. After the Restoration, when Charles II ascended the British throne, John Ward emigrated to America, settling in the colony of Rhode Island. One of Mrs. Howe's ancestors, Richard Ward (1689–1763), served as royal governor of that colony, and his son, Samuel, headed the state after the American Revolution.

Julia Ward Howe's father, Samuel Ward III (1786–1839), was a wealthy banker who founded the family fortune and gave its members "solidarity and respectability." In addition to his wealth,

Samuel Ward was a man of much culture and influence. He was a strong advocate of temperance and reared his children in a religious atmosphere. It is said that his famous daughter, Julia, always "retained her simple girlhood faith in the might of Divine Providence."

Mrs. Howe was born to this prominent family in their luxurious home facing the Battery, then the most fashionable section of New York City. Since her parents had abundant means, she received an excellent education as a young girl, both under governesses in her home, and also in good private schools.

From her mother, Julia Cutler Ward, the daughter is said to have received much of her personal charm and creative ability. Early in life, Mrs. Howe revealed her talent for writing by producing poems and romances. It is stated that all the children born to Samuel and Julia Ward were persons of talent and genius, and that they also married persons of equal ability. One writer has reported that Julia Ward Howe was "a ravishing belle in New York, and a bluestocking in Boston."

One summer, while visiting Boston—often termed the "Hub of the Universe"—she met her future husband, Dr. Samuel Gridley Howe, who was twenty years older than she. He, like the English poet, Lord Byron, had helped the Greeks gain their independence from Turkey. The doctor had served with them both as a soldier and as a surgeon.

In 1832, he founded in Boston what later became the Perkins Institute for the Blind; he continued to direct it until his death on January 9, 1876. He attracted worldwide attention by his outstanding work with the deaf, dumb, and blind. He was especially successful in teaching the noted deaf mute Laura Bridgeman.

The couple married in 1843, and spent their first two years together in Europe; their first child was born in Rome. During those years Julia Ward Howe developed an international outlook; she and Dr. Howe made many friends among foreign literary celebrities. After this stay abroad, Mrs. Howe spent the rest of her life mostly in Boston.

At their rambling home, Green Peace, in South Boston, Lord Byron's hunting helmet hung in the hallway. This house was the center of Boston's intellectual life, and refugees from various lands visited there.

Dr. Ward was not happy unless he was crusading against some social wrong. He aided Horace Mann in his educational reforms, and Dorothea Dix in her work with the mentally ill. The couple also became deeply involved in the Abolitionist movement and were close friends of William Lloyd Garrison and Wendell Phillips. The renowned preacher and reformer Theodore Parker (who also was strongly against slavery) often visited Green Peace, as did many of New England's most distinguished poets, writers, and philosophers.

Although Mrs. Howe had six children to look after, she managed to help Dr. Howe (nicknamed the "Chevalier") to edit a paper called the *Boston Commonwealth,* one of the most important antislavery journals. In addition, the Howes aided in rescuing fugitive slaves. They gave money and raised more to help keep Kansas a free state. Dr. Howe helped organize the New England Aid Company, an organization formed to assist settlers to get to Kansas Territory. On two brief occasions they met John Brown. While the Howes did not fully approve of his "revolutionary act," his "great-hearted attempt" strongly enlisted their sympathies.

John Brown, "a man of burning zeal and highest motives," was a native of Connecticut and a strong Abolitionist. He sincerely believed that slavery was "a barbarous and unprovoked warfare of one portion of the citizens upon another portion, in utter disregard of and in violation of those eternal and self-evident truths set forth in the Declaration of Independence."

When guerilla warfare broke out in Kansas over the slavery question, John Brown, together with his sons and neighbors, went out against the "slavers"; and at once his name struck terror to their hearts. Finally federal troops drove Brown and his band out of the Territory.

Soon the stern reformer hit upon a plan that he was sure would bring the burning issue squarely before the American people. He decided to attack and capture the United States Arsenal at Harper's Ferry, Virginia, with his small force. He also called upon the Negro slaves to rise against their masters and join him.

On October 16, 1859, John Brown calmly took the law in his own hands. There followed a short period of hopeless fighting. Finally, the aroused townspeople besieged him, but there was no slave uprising as he had expected. Some blood was shed on each side; then he and his few surviving followers were taken prisoners.

At the trial John Brown declared he had acted "to free the slaves, by the authority of God Almighty." He was sentenced to be hanged on December 2, 1859, and stood by calmly as the rope was put around his neck. His body hung from a gibbet in Charlestown, Virginia. Colonel Preston of the Virginia Militia was in charge of the execution, which was witnessed by a large crowd, including Robert E. Lee, Stonewall Jackson, and John Wilkes Booth.

After his death, John Brown was regarded by many as a hero, a martyred saint. As a result, although his body "mouldered in the grave," many people did not forget him.

The tune of "John Brown's Body" and of "The Battle Hymn of the Republic" has had a long and unusual history; not all sources agree as to its origin. However some say it began about 1856 in the South as a humble Methodist camp-meeting song, often sung by Negroes with religious words.

It is reported that William Steffe, of Richmond, Virginia, a composer of Sunday-school songs, was asked, in the 1850's, to go to Georgia to lead the singing at a camp meeting. The young man was much surprised on his arrival to find there were no song books for the gatherings. Steffe asked how he could get the participants to sing. He was told just to make up words as he went along. He had discovered that Negro spirituals were popular because of their repetition which made them easy to learn. This is what he tried in his first song:

Say, brothers, will you meet us?
Say, brothers, will you meet us?
Say, brothers, will you meet us?
On Canaan's happy shore?

CHORUS

Glory, glory, hallelujah,
Glory, glory, hallelujah,
Glory, glory, hallelujah,
Forever, ever more.

Within a short time, this song was sung in many places. It was especially popular in Charleston, South Carolina, where many Negroes were familiar with it. It is said that two soldiers carried the tune and words to the North. One source states that Steffe also was asked by a fire company in Charleston to write a song for them beginning "Say, Bummers, will you meet us?" So this version also was known before the Civil War.

Before the air of the old camp meeting song composed by Steffe was used by Julia Ward Howe in "Battle Hymn of the Republic," it first served as the music for the song "John Brown's Body." And this "thundering old hymn tune" is still heard round the globe, "wherever men march and fight for their freedom."

But strange to say, the words were *not* inspired by John Brown, the zealous reformer who tried to solve our slave problem by attacking the Harper's Ferry Arsenal. Irwin Silber tells us:

> By a strange quirk of history . . . "John Brown's Body" was not composed originally about the fiery Abolitionist at all. The name-sake for the song, it turns out, was Sergeant John Brown, a Scots-man, a member of the Second Battalion, Boston Light Infantry Volunteer Militia.

This group was known as the "Tigers." Since the government would not accept their services as an independent battalion, many of the members enlisted in Colonel Fletcher Webster's Twelfth Massachusetts Regiment. (He was the son of the noted statesman Daniel Webster; later he was killed at the Second Battle of Bull

Run on August 30, 1862. It is said that after his death, his men never sang their favorite marching song, "John Brown's Body," again.)

At first these soldiers were stationed at Fort Warren in Boston Harbor, with orders to put it into as good condition as possible. These men liked to sing; they formed a glee club in which they sang many popular songs, including the camp-meeting number, "Say, brothers, will you meet us?" Often as they toiled away with their picks and shovels, they would sing it. It was just the sort of song to lessen their hard labors.

The Scotsman John Brown was second tenor in their quartet. He was so good-natured that the other soldiers loved to play jokes on him. So it wasn't long before they were improvising a stanza really about him rather than the Abolitionist of Ossawatomie, Kansas. It went as follows:

> John Brown's body lies a-mould'ring in the grave,
> John Brown's body lies a-mould'ring in the grave,
> John Brown's body lies a-mould'ring in the grave,
> His soul goes marching on.

CHORUS

> Glory, glory, hallelujah,
> Glory, glory, hallelujah,
> Glory, glory, hallelujah,
> His soul is marching on.

This was called the "John Brown Song"; at Fort Warren it had only this one stanza. Later others were added including the words:

> We'll hang Jeff Davis to a sour apple tree.

But the original stanza continued as the first one of the song.

It was to this melody that the soldiers of John Brown's company began to improvise verses. Of course everyone in the company got a big kick out of the fact that most listeners thought the song was inspired by the martyr of Harper's Ferry.

—Irwin Silber

The tune adapted as a marching song by the Webster Regiment bandmaster was revised soon afterward by Dodsworth's Military Band, reputed at that time to be the best in the entire United States.

On July 18, 1861, the famous orator Edward Everett presented a flag to Webster's Regiment. His men—on that long-remembered occasion, 1,040 strong—marched past the Old State House in Boston. A quartet first sang the song, while boys were busy on the streets selling broadsides with the printed words of the song. Many persons in Boston and elsewhere who had not known the old Methodist camp-meeting air, "Brothers, Will You Meet Us?" thought this was an original composition inspired by the life of the famed "Apostle of Freedom," John Brown of Kansas. Thus the Scotsman John Brown of Massachusetts became immortal as his fellow soldiers sang "John Brown's Body" from place to place. Finally, he made the "supreme sacrifice," during a Union retreat.

Later on, other stanzas were added to the first one, stanzas that related to the life and death of the Abolitionist. These words have been credited to various persons.

In a letter to the Boston *Transcript* in 1874, Charles S. Hall of Charleston, Massachusetts, claimed to have written most of them. The Grand Army of the Republic adapted, for their own use, some of Hall's words. Henry H. Brownell is said to have composed five stanzas, sung to this melody, while Edna Dean Proctor created an abolitionist hymn to be used with the same air. Her poem, honoring the American reformer, "the more celebrated John Brown," began with this line:

John Brown died on the scaffold for the slave . . .

Several critics agreed that *her* version rather than Hall's should have been "the song of the people."

When the Twelfth Massachusetts Regiment was ordered to Washington, D.C., they stopped in New York City en route. As they marched together down Broadway, they halted and sang

"John Brown's body lies a-mould'ring in the grave. . . ." They took the city by storm, and it "created the wildest enthusiasm among the assembled multitude." That incident is reported to have started the song's great popularity with the Union forces. Civilians, too, took it up, many believing it was a new song written to help them conquer the rebellious Southerners.

The soldiers of the Twelfth Massachusetts Regiment also sang the song in Baltimore, and in the national capital. It was this martial music that Julia Ward Howe heard on her memorable visit to Washington late in 1861.

(When the enlistment of this regiment expired in July, 1864, only 85 of the original 1,040 returned to their homes and families. In Boston immense crowds cheered the survivors. Loud calls were heard for them to sing "John Brown's Body" but ". . . the brave heroes marched silently to their barracks and the 'Websters' passed into history.")

However, the popularity of the song soon spread from one Union regiment to another. The Northerners sang it on their way to the South, and their rendition helped spread its use among civilians. Thus "John Brown's Body" became the greatest marching song of the Union forces, for "it sprang from the very soil of conflict in the midst of the Civil War."

It was sung with real feeling by General Sherman's forces as they made their way through Georgia in 1864, on that famous march to the sea. An officer, Lt. Chandler, wrote of an incident that occurred when some of the troops stopped at a town named Shady Dale. A Georgia band played "John Brown's Body" and several Negro girls came out and danced to the music in dignified fashion. Some older Negroes told the Northern soldiers that the air was called "The Wedding Tune"; also that whenever Negro girls heard it they must dance to it or they would never get married.

Louis Elson once said of this composition that it was

. . . the rhythmic swing of the tune that caused the song to spread so rapidly; it is one of the best marching songs in existence. It has taken root in England, and it is said that even in faraway Soudan, General Kitchener's men sometimes made the route less wearisome by singing "John Brown's Body."

Colonel Nicholas Smith, in 1899, declared the song

. . . became the battle cry of hundreds of thousands and the Marseillaise of Emancipation . . . the explanation of its power is the sublime truth that the man whom it celebrates died for men and performed a service for human liberty as he saw it.

In August, 1870, a noted journalist, Murat Halstead, reported that when he was in eastern France, he had heard some German troops singing "John Brown's Body." Also during the Spanish-American War, Admiral Schley, in describing the destruction of the Spanish fleet off Santiago on July 3, 1898, said that the firemen and coal heavers on the flagship *Brooklyn* shoveled coal into the great furnaces while singing this same Civil War song.

At the outbreak of the Civil War, the United States had no generally accepted national anthem. Therefore, many Northerners felt a new one was needed "that would inspire [them] to patriotism and military ardor."

So in 1861, some important Union men set up a committee of thirteen members to select a proper and fitting anthem. A prize of $500—or a medal of equal value—was offered to the winner for the words and music for an acceptable national song. On May 17, 1861, they sent out the call for such a composition. By the end of three months they had received more than 1,200 manuscripts; some came from New England and others from California; they arrived even from several foreign countries, including Italy.

The "dejected" committee worked hard, but after several months decided that none contained any real "soul feeling." Louis Elson once made the statement that no person ever sat down deliberately to create a patriotic hymn and succeeded in the attempt; for

A national anthem comes by inspiration and sometimes by accident; sometimes a piece of very worthy music is a failure as a national song; sometimes a work which may strictly be classed as trash becomes a nation's war cry.

When the Civil War began, Dr. Samuel Howe was too old for field service; therefore, he took a position with the Sanitary Commission. This was a bureau of the War Department designed to supplement the work of the Medical Bureau and the Commissariat, both of which at the beginning of the conflict were deficient. (There was no Red Cross until years later.)

Since Dr. Howe's duties as a member of this commission often took him to Washington, his wife was able to visit the national capital in the fall of 1861. There she saw the Union Army "lying like a steel girdle around Washington to protect it." Mrs. Howe at this time met Abraham Lincoln and long remembered "the sad expression of Mr. Lincoln's deep blue eyes. . . . The President at this time was laboring under a terrible pressure of doubt and anxiety." When the Howes made this trip to the national capital, a visit that was destined to have long-lasting results, they had with them Governor Andrews of Massachusetts and their minister, Dr. James Freeman Clark. The group drove out several miles to an army camp and saw a "Grand Review" of General McClellan's Army of the Potomac. It was on this day that Julia Ward Howe heard soldiers singing "John Brown's Body" for the first time. She was much impressed by the rousing tune, but after studying the words, Mrs. Howe realized they were "inadequate for a lasting hymn."

On the way back to Washington, she and her friends sang several patriotic songs, including "John Brown's Body," to encourage the weary soldiers. Mrs. Howe discussed the words with her minister. Then Dr. Clark challenged her by asking, "Why don't you write more suitable words for this tune?" The poet decided to think it over, and the result of her stay in Washington was one of our finest patriotic songs.

Julia Ward Howe was tired after all the excitement of the day and went to bed early. The appealing melody kept haunting her. That night at her Washington hotel she reviewed the varied events of the day and came to the conclusion that the war was a conflict between God and His adversary. She was quite depressed and discouraged, feeling that she could not do much to help.

In her *Reminiscences,* Mrs. Howe related that she slept as usual that night, but awoke early "in the gray dawn." The lines of the poem came easily to her as she planned the different stanzas. Then she decided to get up and write the words down before they were forgotten.

Mrs. Howe found "an old stump of a pen" and scribbled her poem almost without looking at the paper. (It is said that she had been used to doing this at home, writing without lighting a lamp, in order not to disturb her baby's sleep.) The preceding day she had experienced "the grim reality" and significance of this war between the states and was driven by an intensely patriotic feeling to express her deep emotions on this subject.

She completed her stanzas on a piece of Sanitary Commission paper. (Later the bureau was to be proud that she had used their stationery for the first draft of her immortal "Battle Hymn of the Republic.") Then Mrs. Howe went back to bed; afterward she declared that she had experienced the feeling "that something of importance had happened to her that morning." She read the poem—to be sung to the air of "John Brown's Body"—to her husband that day.

Back in Boston, Mrs. Howe showed the poem to James T. Field, editor of the *Atlantic Monthly,* who suggested the title. He accepted the poem and published it in the February, 1862, issue of his magazine. It is said that Field recognized its merits, but neither he nor the author realized what its impact on the nation would be. According to one source, Mrs. Howe was paid only $4 for it. (Another writer has said $5.) On its first appearance in print her name was not given as the author.

At once the new words were accepted as the most favored Union battle song. To its "strongly accented beats," the troops marched in high spirits as they sang the words at the tops of their voices. Mrs. Howe received nationwide fame for creating the hymn that has long been considered one of our most beloved patriotic songs and "one of the gems of American verse."

Magazines and newspapers all over the United States copied the poem; it soon became widely known and was often distributed on broadsides. It was printed, too, in the army song books. (Later some new tunes were composed for it; but Mrs. Howe always preferred the air of "John Brown's Body.")

The immense popularity of "The Battle Hymn of the Republic" all over our country was due to a large extent to its enthusiastic singing by a Civil War chaplain, later a Methodist bishop.

Charles Cardwell McCabe, a native of Ohio and chaplain of the 122d Ohio Volunteer Infantry was later known far and wide as the "Singing Chaplain," and also as a preacher and lecturer.

When he read Mrs. Howe's poem in the *Atlantic Monthly* in February 1862, he at once wrote the author that it had impressed him so strongly he learned all the stanzas by heart before he rose from his chair.

On June 16, 1863, the chaplain with other Union men was captured by the Confederates at Winchester, Virginia, and sent to the notorious Libby Prison at Richmond. While a prisoner there, he almost died of typhoid fever. During his confinement of five months, Chaplain McCabe took care of wounded men and tried to cheer up his comrades under those terrible prison conditions.

Deeply religious, and of a happy, cheerful disposition, he did much to keep up the imprisoned men's spirits. He also managed to secure three bathtubs for them, along with books and other reading materials. Whenever the men were especially depressed, they would call out, "Chaplain, give us a song!" Although he was not a professional singer, he later made quite a name for himself as a vocalist. One contemporary spoke of him in these words: "The charm in his voice went beyond the technique of training; a baritone voice of strange, plaintive sweetness, yet possessing a thrilling spiritually-moving power of a rare sort."

On July 6, 1863, the Union prisoners were especially low in

spirit. For on that day two Northern captains were to be executed. The men had also heard of disasters to their forces, including Grant's repulse; all these things increased the feelings of depression.

However on that day a friendly Negro, Old Ben, managed to "sneak into" Libby Prison a Richmond newspaper containing the exciting news that General Robert E. Lee had been defeated at the Battle of Gettysburg. The men all jumped to their feet and almost went wild with joy. At once Chaplain McCabe got up on a box and started his favorite song, "The Battle Hymn of the Republic." Then his fellow prisoners joined with him and all sang "Mine eyes have seen the coming . . ." as they had never sung it before.

After the chaplain was released from Libby Prison, he resumed his work on behalf of the Union Army and continued to sing Mrs. Howe's song. He was a delegate to the United States Christian Commission. On February 2, 1864, there was a meeting held for the benefit of this commission in the Hall of the House of Representatives. It was presided over by Vice-President Hannibal Hamlin, and the audience contained many other notables.

On that important occasion Chaplain McCabe gave the prayer; he was also asked to tell of his experiences at Libby Prison. So he related how the Union men had reacted to the news—first of the defeat at Gettysburg, then of the victory. After his talk the chaplain thrilled the audience with his inspired rendition of "The Battle Hymn of the Republic." It is said there was "a tumult of applause," and the people all jumped to their feet. This was the first time—so the account goes—that President Lincoln had heard the words penned by Mrs. Howe. Tears were running down his face after the last stanza. He called out, "Sing it again!" and Chaplain McCabe complied.

(In recent years, in a letter to the editor of *Together* magazine, a somewhat different version was given as to when and where Abraham Lincoln first heard the song. Mrs. James Colonna of Wilmington, Delaware, whose father was a Methodist minister belonging to the Wilmington Conference—also a Civil War soldier

—stated that he was present one evening during the war in Ford's Theater in Washington where the President first heard the song. She wrote:

The audience went wild with cheers and enthusiasm over the great hymn and the rich baritone voice of the young Chaplain. President Abraham Lincoln was seated in his box in the theater, and was so greatly stirred that he sent a note to the stage which read: "Ask that young man to sing it again," which the Chaplain did.)

After President Lincoln's assassination, Chaplain McCabe sang the hymn at several memorial services for the martyred President, including those at Chicago and at Springfield, Illinois, in May, 1865.

While lecturing on "The Bright Side of Life in Libby Prison," the "Singing Chaplain" continued all the rest of his life to popularize Julia Ward Howe's hymn. He once declared: "No hymn has stirred the nation's heart like this."

During the years 1868 to 1884, Bishop McCabe gave all the proceeds from his famous address to further the cause of church extension. It is said that he raised more than $50,000 for new churches, parsonages, and needy preachers.

The story is told that in 1882, the noted infidel and lecturer, Robert Ingersoll, foretold the early collapse of Christianity, declaring that "the churches were struck with death." At once Chaplain McCabe wired him that the Methodists were building a church a day and would make it two a day!

Julia Ward Howe often expressed her great appreciation for the way Bishop McCabe had sung her composition for so many years and had made it popular all over our country, "sending its moving message to the far corners of the United States." The hymn was sung at her funeral. Also when the beloved "Singing Chaplain" was laid to rest, his friends sang his favorite, which ends with the stirring admonition:

. . . As he died to make men holy,
Let us die to make men free,
While God is marching on.

After the publication of her masterpiece, Mrs. Howe continued her philanthropic work in Boston. Dr. Howe, who had held positions with the federal government both during and after the Civil War, died in 1876. Julia Ward Howe survived her husband by about thirty-five years—"years of incessant activity and of great fame."

She gave most of her time and energy to various reform movements both at home and abroad; she was an ardent crusader in several lines. After the end of the war, she helped organize the New England Women's Club, the first of its kind in this country, and for several years served as its president. She was an active champion for women's suffrage, and was the first head of the New England Women's Suffrage Association. "Moved by the economic plight of Civil War widows, Mrs. Howe worked for equal education, professional and business rights for women."

She was not only for more education for her sex, but was active in other good causes. She was a very strong believer in world peace and founded the Women's International Peace Association. In 1872 she was a delegate to the World's Prison Reform Congress in London. Someone once said of her:

> Her courage, her incisiveness, and quickness of repartee, her constructive power, the completeness of her conviction, accompanied by a balance of mind, and a sense of humor . . . made her the greatest of women organizers.

It is said that Mrs. Howe made the first known suggestion for Mother's Day in the United States, in 1872. She believed that June 2 should be celebrated as such a day; also that this same date be dedicated to peace. And for several years she promoted a Mother's Day program in Boston.

This remarkable woman had a command of such languages as Latin, Greek, French, Hebrew, and Italian. In addition she had read enough to grasp the philosophy of Kant, Fichte, Hegel, and Spinoza and to be able to lecture on these men and their beliefs. Mrs. Howe was much sought after as a lecturer on other literary and cultural subjects as well as on women's rights and varied social problems. At times she also preached at Unitarian churches. She was president of the Boston Authors' Club and the first woman member of the Academy of Arts and Sciences.

As a writer, she was quite versatile, too. Mrs. Howe wrote extensively—articles, poems, essays, etc.—which were published in newspapers and magazines, including the New York *Herald-Tribune* and antislavery publications. She served, also, as the editor of the *Women's Journal*.

In 1854 she published two volumes of verse, one entitled *Passion Flowers*. Oliver Wendell Holmes asked her how so "quiet a blend" as herself had "such tropical flashes of passion" running through her veins.

Other published works were: The *World's Own,* a play (1857); *Words for the Hour* (1859); *A Trip to Cuba* (1860); *An Appeal to Womanhood Throughout the World* (1870); *Sex and Education* (1874); *Memoirs of Dr. Samuel Gridley Howe* (1876); *Modern Society* (1881); *Margaret Fuller* (1883); *Is Polite Society Polite?* (1895); *Poems Old and New* (1898); *Reminiscences* (1899); and *At Sunset* (1910).

Mrs. Howe not only had a play *Hippolytus,* produced on Broadway, but she had the satisfaction "of being a legend in her own time." Although she was always working for women's causes, she was best known for her "Battle Hymn of the Republic."

In Boston Common and facing the State House is a well-known monument by the renowned sculptor St. Gaudens, which honors Robert Gould Shaw and his Negro soldiers, the heroes of Fort Wagner. At its dedication, addresses were given by the writer William James and by Booker T. Washington; and Mrs. Howe's composition was featured.

In the winter of 1884–1885, at a reception in New Orleans, the composer was asked—to her great surprise—to recite the poem. She was pleased, for this revealed how much the old ill feeling between the North and South had died out.

On Memorial Day, 1888, Julia Ward Howe was in San Francisco at the Opera House where every seat was filled. The Grand Army of the Republic gave her an ovation when attention was called to the fact that she was in the house. After three cheers had been given for her, she arose and bowed. Then J. C. Hughes sang "The Battle Hymn of the Republic," and the great crowd joined in the chorus. Flowers were presented to her; she walked to the footlights and spoke a few words, including these: "I remember those campfires. I remember those dreadful battles. . . . Let us thank God who has given us these victories."

Mrs. Howe was especially loved by the members of the Grand Army of the Republic—the Union soldiers who survived the conflict. In 1888 there were interesting ceremonies in Boston; she rode to the hall in an open carriage with the two daughters of Major-General Joseph Walker, a Confederate officer, who had been invited to give the chief address of the day.

She was sitting in a box with the Misses Wheeler when a performer, Myron T. Whitney, started to sing her song and bowed toward the box where she was seated. At once the audience arose and joined with the soloist in singing "The Battle Hymn of the Republic" "at the top of their lungs," as one reporter stated.

Ten years later—in May, 1899—in the same Boston theater, the G.A.R. and their friends gave her another tremendous welcome. And in 1909, at the Metropolitan Opera House in New York, when the Hudson-Fulton Celebration was in progress, Mrs. Howe was asked to read a poem about Robert Fulton. This was followed by a round of applause.

Several important educational institutions gave her the degree of doctor of laws. When Brown University in Rhode Island paid her the honor, there was this summary of her achievements: "Julia Ward Howe, Boston, Massachusetts, author, philanthropist, mother, friend of the slave, prisoners and all who suffer, singer of 'The Battle Hymn of the Republic.' . . ." This event occurred on June 16, 1909; when she walked up to receive her degree, she heard the organ pealing out her famous hymn.

On October 5, 1910, when she was ninety-one years old, Smith

College conferred on her the degree of doctor of literature. At that time she was in a wheel chair. A noted British editor remarked: "It was for this that Julia Ward Howe was born into the world."

Mrs. Howe enjoyed to the full the affection and honors heaped upon her, and she loved to recite the immortal words of her hymn. She "toured the nation, giving lectures in her eighties, and enjoyed every moment of every ovation she received." Thus all over our great country thousands of Americans had the privilege of hearing her personally recite the famous lines. Death came to her just twelve days after she had been honored at Smith College.

Two of her daughters, Laura E. Richards and Maude Howe Elliott, wrote a two-volume biography of their noted mother named simply *Julia Ward Howe*. They received a Pulitzer prize for it in 1917.

In their biography they trace her life as she grew up in the young republic; also as she lived into the next century when her country had become a world power. Although Mrs. Howe was wealthy and could have lived a life of pleasure and leisure, she followed the call of duty. ". . . Out of her own experience . . . she had written 'Be swift, my soul, to answer Him. . . .' "

Countless tributes have been paid to Julia Ward Howe and to "The Battle Hymn of the Republic." Henry Steele Commager has declared that Mrs. Howe was the author of "the one great song to come out of the Civil War, the one great song ever written in America."

J. A. Lomax and Alan Lomax state that the melody longest remembered from the Civil War is the one that rolls through both "John Brown's Body" and "The Battle Hymn of the Republic."

In 1899 Colonel Nicholas Smith described her composition as "the spontaneous generation of the uprising of the North . . . a grim, uncouth melody and a commanding refrain."

An unnamed writer (in *Patriotic Songs of America,* a pamphlet published by the John Hancock Insurance Company) terms it:

. . . a vigorous, energetic melody, its even rhythm lending itself particularly well to marching . . . a war song, with scarcely an equal. It sounds of marching feet and of heart throbs of moving, excited masses. It is one of the mysterious tunes whose rhythm urges one on and on.

Florence Howe Hall wrote of her mother's hymn that it contained nothing sectional, nothing of a temporary character, and declared it was composed "with intense feeling."

The lyrics of "The Battle Hymn of the Republic" lend themselves easily to world use. It is reported that not long before World War I started, Sir Arthur Conan Doyle cabled his report to the United States in the first two lines of the hymn.

A well-known journalist, Murat Halstead, some years ago called Mrs. Howe's work "the incarnation of patriotism and martial feeling . . . simple, but dignified, full of vigor and worthy of being the imperishable war song of a Christian nation."

The British writer Rudyard Kipling once alluded to this composition as "the terrible 'Battle Hymn of the Republic.' " In his novel *The Light That Failed* he has a group of Englishmen and others of different nationalities singing this piece together.

This song was very popular during World War I and was heard on the battlefields of France. In large churches and cathedrals in England, such as Westminster Abbey, the British, "with great gusto," sang it alongside their American allies.

Although "The Battle Hymn of the Republic" has generally been considered a patriotic song, rather than a hymn, the work is included in church hymnals of many different religious denominations.

While its belligerent message may affect its universal acceptance, and thus limit the use of "The Battle Hymn of the Republic," this in no way will detract from the majesty of Julia Ward Howe's five stanzas, and the fact that they have earned for themselves a permanent place in the archives of patriotic hymnody.

—Ernest K. Emurian

Another author, whose name was not given, said of this composition:

There are many who consider "The Battle Hymn of the Republic," with its fine fanatic fervor, its vivid symbolism, its visions of a vengeful Puritan Deity tramping out the grapes of wrath, sifting out the hearts of men, and extending His grace only to foes of secessionists and slaveholders, the best of our patriotic songs. . . . Senator Hoar believed it equal in power to the "Marseillaise"; and Rudyard Kipling found it the greatest of all martial anthems.

The Battle Hymn of the Republic

Julia Ward Howe   Air: "John Brown's Body"

1. Mine_ eyes have seen the glo - ry of the com - ing of the Lord; He is
2. I have seen Him in the watch-fires of a hun-dred cir-cling camps; They have
3. I have read a fier - y gos-pel writ in bur-nished rows of steel: "As ye
4. He has sound-ed forth the trump-et that shall nev-er call re-treat; He is
5. In the beau-ty of the lil - ies Christ was born a-cross the sea, With a

tram - pling out the vint - age where the grapes of wrath are stored; He hath
build - ed Him an al - tar in the eve-ning dews and damp; I can
deal with My con-tem - ners, so with you My grace shall deal." Let the
sift - ing out the hearts of men be-fore His judg-ment seat; Oh, be
glo - ry in His bos - om that trans-fig - ures you and me; As He

loosed the fate - ful light - ning of His ter - ri - ble swift sword, His
read His right - eous sen - tence by the dim and flar - ing lamps, His
He - ro, born of wom - an, crush the ser - pent with His heel, Since
swift, my soul, to an - swer Him! be ju - bi - lant, my feet! Our
died to make men ho - ly, let us die to make men free, While

Chorus

truth is march - ing on.
day is march - ing on.
God is march - ing on. Glo - ry glo - ry! Hal - le -
God is march - ing on.
God is march - ing on.

lu - jah! Glo - ry! glo - ry! Hal - le - lu - jah!

Glo - ry! glo - ry! Hal - le - lu - jah! His truth is march-ing on.

8

*

"The Bonnie Blue Flag"

According to Richard B. Harwell, music was highly favored by the Southern forces: "For the Confederate soldiers music was a sustaining reminder of home, and a promise of peace. . . ." Many of them sang their favorites from memory. Others had written copies of the words. Also, numerous broadsides were printed and distributed, and some soldiers even carried copies of sheet music with them. Then too there were "songsters," small pocket-sized books with just the words of standard old favorites and patriotic songs.

Southerners who lived in border states or in Northern ones enjoyed singing "Dixie," "Maryland, My Maryland," or "The Bonnie Blue Flag" on the streets of Washington, D.C. It is reported that often from windows in the national capital came the sounds of these Rebel pieces, sung by young ladies from the Southern states especially for the benefit of the "damned Yankees." And the story goes that one night at eleven o'clock, loyal Washington citizens were outraged when a bunch of rowdies loudly sang "The Bonnie Blue Flag." Also in Baltimore, Southern sympathizers cheered Jefferson Davis and sang Confederate songs.

Southern music did not die out with the end of the war. But it "passed into the nation, a heritage of the South and North. . . ." At Confederate reunions there was vigorous singing of the old Southern war songs which were thus handed down to succeeding generations. And "the songs of the Confederacy echoed the spirit of the times."

When the War Between the States broke out, there was need for a new banner to represent the seceding Southern states. Since many considered that our national flag belonged to the South as well as to the North, some Southerners wrote new words to go to the tune of "The Star-Spangled Banner." Others in the South thought they should claim the song as their own as it had been written by a Southerner, Francis Scott Key. In that case, the North would have to find a new song to represent them.

In the South a committee was chosen, consisting of the Messrs. Miles of South Carolina, Morton of Florida, Shorter of Alabama, Harris of Mississippi, and Sparrow of Louisiana. However, these men could not agree as to whether they should discard the old flag. Here is a portion of their report:

> Whatever attachment may be felt, from association, for the Stars and Stripes (an attachment which your committee may be permitted to say they do not *all* share) it is manifest that, in inaugurating a new government, we cannot retain the flag of the government from which we have withdrawn, with any propriety, or without encountering very obvious practical difficulties.

A Confederate general, William C. Wickham, and Admiral Symmes of the *Alabama* openly expressed their regret about abandoning the historic flag, the star-spangled banner. But soon in the South there was a new song, "The Bonnie Blue Flag," with its stirring refrain:

> Hurrah! Hurrah! For Southern rights, Hurrah!
> Hurrah for the Bonnie Blue Flag that bears a single star!

South Carolina was the first Southern state to leave the Union. On December 20, 1860, her representatives voted to withdraw from the United States. For her flag she used a simple blue one with a single white star in the center. This remained South Carolina's official ensign until, as a member of the Southern Confederacy, she adopted another on January 28, 1861. This too was blue, but it had on it a palmetto tree and a crescent in the upper left-hand corner.

There have been some conflicting stories as to the origin of the bonnie blue flag with its one star. There is an interesting and dramatic account of what happened on January 9, 1861, at Jackson, Mississippi, when there was a debate on the matter of whether or not the other Southern states would follow South Carolina's example.

Finally in deep silence the representatives passed the Act of Secession. Then a minister made an earnest prayer. After its conclusion, an enthusiastic young Southerner entered the hall, carrying a beautiful blue silk flag with a white star in its center. This banner had just been made by his wife and was first displayed here at the convention. It is said that all the delegates arose as a salute to the flag, while the spectators gave the ensign a vigorous welcome with loud cheers. For over four months this simple blue flag was the only one around which the seceding states could rally. Some writers emphasize the fact that South Carolina had adopted such a flag and that it was her banner that had been the inspiration for "The Bonnie Blue Flag."

An actor, Harry B. Macarthy, called "the most prolific of the composers of popular patriotic melodies of the Confederacy," saw that memorable scene in Jackson. He was so impressed by the incident that he immediately left the hall and wrote "The Bonnie Blue Flag," a song that would make him famous and that won him enthusiastic acclaim in every important place in the South where he introduced it. For the melody he used a traditional old tune which his ancestors may have sung in Ireland—"The Irish Jaunting Car."

At the time he composed the song, Harry Macarthy was twenty-seven years old. He was an English singer and vaudeville star, a good vocalist and actor. Born in England in 1834, he came to the

United States in 1849. In his acting, he took the name of the "Arkansas Comedian." His connection with Arkansas is not clear, although he dedicated his greatest hit to Albert Pike, Esq., "Poet-Lawyer of Arkansas." As a stage performer Macarthy was well-known for his "traditional costume of a low-set collar, ruffled shirt and wristbands and diamonds galore."

There is some question about when and where Harry Macarthy first introduced his new song "The Bonnie Blue Flag." Most sources agree that he wrote it early in 1861, and that he introduced it and used it as the highlight of his "Personation Concerts" that same year in Jackson, Mississippi. Its success was assured when he sang it there, in the spring of 1861, to a large audience composed mostly of Southern soldiers. Because he rendered the piece "with infinite spirit and effect," Macarthy received instantaneous response; soon he was being hailed as the leading theatrical entertainer of the Confederacy.

In September of that year, Harry Macarthy was using the number at the New Orleans Academy of Music. Troops on their way to the battlefields of Virginia filled the house and greeted his singing of "The Bonnie Blue Flag" with vociferous applause.

The following year, 1862, he was performing in Mobile, Alabama. There is extant an eight-page program of his productions in that city. Next fall he played at the Broad Street Theater in Richmond, Virginia. Macarthy remained there until some time in 1863. In December he had an engagement in Wilmington, North Carolina, and then returned to Richmond in April, 1864. His wife, Lottie Estelle, accompanied him on his theatrical tours.

As Macarthy performed through the South, his "Bonnie Blue Flag" became the "Star-Spangled Banner" of the secessionists. Macarthy's success in the Southern concert halls and theaters was assured by this composition alone. Soon the number with its "catchy music and simple chorus" was being sung by countless marching Rebel troops and also by thousands of civilians.

"The Bonnie Blue Flag," which created such a sensation all through the Southern states, began with this stanza:

We are a band of brothers and native to the soil,
Fighting for our liberty, with treasure, blood and toil.
And when our rights were threatened, the cry rose near and far—
Hurrah for the Bonnie Blue Flag that bears a single star.

CHORUS
Hurrah, hurrah for Southern rights, hurrah!
Hurrah for the Bonnie Blue Flag that bears a single star!

In the other five stanzas the composer praised the eleven states
that had already seceded: South Carolina, Alabama, Mississippi,
Georgia, Florida, Texas, Louisiana, Virginia, Arkansas, North
Carolina, and Tennessee. His song ended with this soul-stirring
stanza:

Then here's to our Confederacy, strong as we are and brave,
Like patriots of old, we'll fight our heritage to save;
And rather than submit to shame, to die we would prefer;
So cheer for the Bonnie Blue Flag that bears a single star.

This song was written as "a parade of secession" and reflected
the rising tide of Southern hopes after the one star had grown to
eleven. Soon Macarthy and others were writing additional lines to
the original song, begging other Southern states to defect, notably
Missouri and Kentucky.

One stanza was a plea to Missouri to "add your bright star to
our flag of eleven." In another, the South was advised to

Make room upon the Bonnie Blue Flag—
Kentucky makes thirteen.

Numerous men from Missouri and Kentucky had left these
states and enlisted in the Confederate forces. But the states themselves remained in the Union although they were represented by
stars in the Confederate flag. Finally the seventh stanza, containing
these lines, was added to the original six:

Sing praises to the God of hosts, our cause is waxing strong,
Our flashing steel shall pay the price of ransom for the brave . . .

When the Southerners were trying to influence more states to
join their cause, some Northerners retaliated by writing lines to the

tune of "The Bonnie Blue Flag." One of the best ones was "A Reply to the Bonnie Blue Flag"; the words were written by a Mrs. Sterret and the music by H. M. Frank.

During the years between 1861 and 1864, there were six different editions of the song published by the A. E. Blackmar Firm, besides three new arrangements. The piece was also published in the North and in England.

The popularity of "The Bonnie Blue Flag" continued all through the Civil War and throughout the Southern states. When New Orleans was captured, on April 28, 1862, by the Union forces, Major General Butler was in command of the town.

The defiant citizens resented the occupation; they sang the song continually and taught their children to do so. It was heard so often, "with such perplexing enthusiasm," that General Butler became quite annoyed. Finally he issued a proclamation that any man, woman, or child who sang or whistled "The Bonnie Blue Flag" would be forced to pay a fine of $25. "In addition to this penalty, all the copies of the song that could be found were destroyed and publishers were prohibited from publishing it in any form." It is reported that Major General Butler confiscated the plates, destroyed all copies, arrested the publisher, A. E. Blackmar, and fined him $500 for continuing to print "The Bonnie Blue Flag" after it had been officially banned.

There were several pieces written in the South that were sung to the tune of "The Bonnie Blue Flag." Probably the most popular one, and the most proudly sung parody, was called "The Homespun Dress" (or "The Southern Girl"). It was the work of Carrie Bell Sinclair of Augusta, Georgia. Her work was known all over the Southern states and has become part of our American folklore.

Since the South lacked industries, the people soon felt the need of cloth for suits and dresses. Therefore old looms and spinning wheels that had not been used for many decades were brought out of attics. At once the Southern women went to work seriously. They spun the yarn, dyed it, and wove it into cloth.

One source states that the inspiration for the song "The Homespun Dress" came from the fact that at a dance given in Lexington, Kentucky, for Morgan's Cavalrymen, the ladies of the town appeared in their homespun dresses.

Miss Sinclair wrote her song in 1862 or 1863. It first appeared in a book of Southern songs as early as 1864, but it was not published as sheet music until after the war had ended. One version of the song, "The Southern Girl," sung to the air of "The Bonnie Blue Flag," told of a girl who refused to marry a Northern soldier because her brother had been killed in the conflict.

After the overwhelming success of "The Bonnie Blue Flag," Harry Macarthy tried to duplicate it, but without much success. He wrote "Missouri," or "A Voice from the South," which some one termed a Western "Maryland, My Maryland." In it the composer pleaded with the state to join the Confederacy. This piece was published by Blackmar in seven printings.

Discarding the bonnie blue flag with its single star, the Confederacy used three different banners during the Civil War. The Confederates chose the stars and bars on March 4, 1861, first unfurling it at Montgomery, Alabama. It had a red field with a white stripe in the middle third and a blue jack with a circle of seven stars.

Because of its similarity in color to the Union flag, there was conflict at the Battle of Bull Run. Then General P. G. T. Beauregard designed the second Confederate flag which had a red field with blue diagonal cross bars holding thirteen stars.

In May 1863, at Richmond, the official flag was adopted by the Confederate Congress. It was white, and twice as long as wide. The union contained the flag designed by General Beauregard. On February 4, 1865, a broad red stripe was added at the extreme right so that the banner would not be mistaken for a flag of truce.

When this flag, the stars and bars, succeeded the bonnie blue flag, the Southern song writers had a new theme. They praised "Freedom's New Banner" in various lyrics.

Harry Macarthy also wrote a song about it, called at first "Our Flag and Its Origin, Southern National Song"; later its title was "The Origin of the Stars and Bars." But it was not so popular as his "Bonnie Blue Flag." After the end of the war, Macarthy wrote a parody on his masterpiece, in which he suggested "the wisdom of reconstruction."

One source asserted that Macarthy dashed off his first and best song just because he needed an encore, thus "cashing in on the developing martial spirit of his Southern audiences." Some also remarked that the song writer's "patriotism brought him large profits."

A British citizen, Macarthy did not serve in the Southern forces. It is alleged that he left Dixie "when the Confederate armies met their final reverses." For this he lost caste and was subjected to much censure.

In the Augusta, Georgia, *Register,* in 1864 or 1865, a reporter wrote he had just heard that Harry Macarthy was in Philadelphia. This announcement was followed by a scathing poem of thirty lines supposed to have been written by Harry himself. In it he boasted of the "humbug" Southern songs he'd composed; that he had dodged the dogs of war and had come off "without a single scar." The poem also showed him as confessing that his object had been to fill his purse. But now he was in the North—

> Your glories I will sing.
> So "Hail, Columbia, Happy Land!"
> May Lincoln reign your king!

Not much is known of the details of Macarthy's later life, except through his published songs and theatrical advertisements. He performed on the stage for several more years. He also wrote some "undistinguished" pieces, but he never recaptured the sensational success of his "Bonnie Blue Flag." He did not return to the South, but died, in 1888, in Oakland, California.

During the exciting Civil War days "The Bonnie Blue Flag" played an important role in inspiring and stimulating the South by firing its imagination. But in spite of this, William A. Heaps declared "it possessed no unusual quality to insure its permanence, even had the Confederate cause been triumphant."

Today, as one writer commented, no grouping of the banners of the Southern Confederacy is complete without the bonnie blue flag which inspired Harry Macarthy's song. And this ensign remains dear to Southerners and is perhaps the best known unofficial flag.

The Bonnie Blue Flag

Harry Macarthy

Irish Tune
"The Jaunting Car"

1. We are a band of broth-ers, and na - tive to the soil, Fight - ing for our lib - er - ty With treas - ure, blood and toil; And when our rights were threat-ened, The cry rose near and far: "Hur - rah for the Bon-nie Blue Flag, That bears a sin - gle star!

2. First, gal - lant South Caro - li - na, no - bly made the stand; Then came Al - a - ba - ma, Who took her by the hand; quick - ly Mis - sis - sip - pi, Geor - gia and Flo - ri - da, All raised on high the Bon-nie Blue Flag, That bears a sin - gle star!

3. Ye men of val - or, gath - er 'round the Ban - ner of the Right, Tex - as and fair Louis - i - an - a, join us in the fight; vis, our loved Pres - i - dent, and Steph - ens, States-man rare, Now ral - ly 'round the Bon-nie Blue Flag, That bears a sin - gle star!

4. And here's to brave Vir - gin - ia! the Old Do-min - ion State With the young Con - fed - 'ra - cy at length has linked her fate; pelled by her ex - am - ple, now oth - er states pre - pare To hoist on high the Bon-nie Blue Flag, That bears a sin - gle star!

Chorus
Hur - rah! Hur - rah! for South - ern rights, hur - rah! Hur - rah! for the Bon - nie Blue Flag, That bears a sin - gle star.

9

*

"Maryland, My Maryland"

James Russell Lowell read the poem "Maryland, My Maryland" by James Ryder Randall, written during the Civil War. The noted New England writer praised it highly, saying it was the best poem created during the conflict between the states. Some critics regard this as "too high praise," but it is true that "Maryland, My Maryland" today remains one of our most popular state and patriotic songs.

James Ryder Randall, "a man of lovable characteristics and traits," whose masterpiece has immortalized his name, was born in the city of Baltimore, Maryland, on New Year's Day, 1839. He received part of his education in his native town but obtained his bachelor's degree at Georgetown University in Washington, D.C. Afterward he traveled for a few months in Central America and several South American countries.

Then he settled at Pointe Coupée Parish in Louisiana, about a hundred miles north of New Orleans. At Poydras College, a Creole school, Randall taught classes in English while he was still quite young. He was deeply interested in poetry and wrote verse, some of which was published in the New Orleans *Delta*.

On April 16, 1861, soldiers of the Sixth Massachusetts Infantry left Boston for the "beleaguered" national capital. They were marching through Baltimore on their way to the railway station on Saturday, April 19. Some Southern sympathizers, it is said, opened fire on the Northerners. The Union soldiers fired into the crowd, with the result that three soldiers and nine civilians were killed. Many others were wounded during what is alleged to have been the first bloodshed of this conflict.

The young Professor Randall down in Louisiana read an account of this tragedy in the *Delta*. He was horrified by the killings, especially as one of the first to fall was an old friend, a college classmate. This tragic happening had a strong impact on the sensitive young Marylander. Years later he told Brander Mathews, whose article was published in *Century* magazine, how he came to write the stirring poem.

That night of April 23, 1861, young Randall couldn't sleep. He kept thinking of his beloved native city of Baltimore, of his family, his friends, and of those who were "locked in the struggle of brother against brother." He tossed about in bed, reliving the terrible news he'd received that very day. At midnight the poet got out of bed, lighted a candle, and sat down to express in verse his inmost feelings about this dire castastrophe. Randall loved his native state so dearly that he wrote the words of "Maryland, My Maryland" with real patriotic fervor. Later he declared that some unknown spirit seemed to possess him as he dashed off the stanzas and brooded over "the stark horror of that senseless strife."

Little did James Randall realize he was writing words that would inspire the entire South and not just his native state—words that America has long remembered and cherished. In the stillness of that spring night, the young teacher "created a battle cry for the state he loved so dearly," containing these lines:

The despot's heel is on thy shore, Maryland, my Maryland . . .
Avenge the patriotic gore that flecked the streets of Baltimore . . .

James Ryder Randall poured out his very soul in his exhortation to his native state. He praised her former courage and begged her to take her stand with the states that had already seceded. He declared:

> Thou·wilt not cower in the dust . . .
> Thy gleaming sword shall never rust . . .
> Thou wilt not yield the Vandal toll . . .
> Thou wilt not crook to his control . . .
> For life and death, for woe or weal,
> Thy priceless chivalry reveal . . .
> And gird thy beauteous limbs with steel . . .

Then the poet urged Maryland to join the ranks of other Southern states:

> Come! to thine own heroic throng
> That stalks with liberty along,
> And ring thy dauntless slogan song,
> Maryland, my Maryland.

James Randall's original poem contained nine stanzas, but now, only three or four of them are found in our song books. The next day the young professor read his latest work to his English classes, where the students received it with much enthusiasm and begged the poet to get it into print as soon as possible.

At once Randall sent it to the New Orleans *Delta,* where it was published in full on April 26, 1861. It was widely copied in almost every newspaper in the South. It became immensely popular, and James Randall "woke up one morning and found himself famous." The poet was amazed by its immediate acceptance and "the widespread and instantaneous popularity of the lyric I had been strangely inspired to write."

(Not long before its first publication in the *Delta,* C. D. Jenkins, the editor, had sent Randall some poems by James Clarence Mangan. The metrical form of one of Mangan's poems, "Karaminian Exile" was the one used by the Maryland poet when writing "Maryland, My Maryland.")

His poem was first published in Baltimore in a pro-Confederate paper, the *South,* and was sung there to the tune, "Manormandie." Thousands of broadsides were printed with this melody and distributed throughout the city, where it was hailed as the finest battle cry of the Confederacy.

In Baltimore one of the leading pro-Confederate families was the Carys, including Hetty and Jennie. A cousin, Constance, had married Burton Harrison; the latter, a Yale man, had given Jennie his college song book.

Some Yale students had written Latin verses, including a song called "Lauriger Horatius." This was sung to the tune of the old German folk song of the Middle Ages, "O Tannenbaum, O Tannenbaum" ("O Christmas Tree, O Christmas Tree"). This old song praised the hemlock tree which many German families took into their homes at the Yuletide and then decorated and lighted with wax candles.

When the Cary sisters read Randall's poem, they were delighted with it. At once Jennie realized that the "Tannenbaum" melody was a perfect musical setting for the new song. All that was needed was an additional "Maryland, My Maryland" in the chorus.

The two Cary sisters belonged to a group called the "Monument Street Girls" who were Southern sympathizers. They had been looking for "an appropriate new patriotic song" for the Baltimore City Glee Club.

In June, 1861, the group met at the Cary home (the mecca of those who sympathized with secession) to try to devise ways and means of helping the Southern cause. Jennie Cary wanted a song that would "encourage and fire the Southern heart." Her sister Hetty stood up during the meeting and read the lines of Randall's poem, "Maryland, My Maryland" with such fervid eloquence that all were thrilled by it. The members agreed that day that the German melody was just the one for Randall's verse.

The poem was acclaimed by all present, and they made the decision to publish it. When one person, Rozier Delany, objected because of the nearness of Fort McHenry, Rebecca Nicholson said: "My father is a Union man, and if I am put in prison, he will take me out."

At once Miss Nicholson took the words and music to the Baltimore firm of Miller and Beacham, who published "Maryland, My Maryland" in their collection of pro-Southern songs. John Ryder Randall's name did not appear on the first edition. The arrangement was credited to "C. E." and some believed this was coincidental. The initials, "C. E." were those of Charles Ellerbrock, a Maryland musician. It is stated that he did arrange the piece for publication. A note said the tune was adapted from "O Tannenbaum, O Tannenbaum."

(Charles Ellerbrock was not only pro-Southern as a composer —so one source states—but he also served as a soldier in the Confederate forces.)

Thus the melody which was "in praise of friends and loyalty" became the "Marseillaise of the Confederacy," as Vice-President Alexander Stephens termed it.

There is a story extant that on July 4, 1861, Jennie and Hetty Cary with their brother and several friends "ran the blockade" from Baltimore to Orange Court House in Virginia. This visit occurred soon after the first Battle of Manassas. General Beauregard, who had been informed of the work of this group in Baltimore and of their untiring efforts on behalf of the Southern cause, invited them to his headquarters in the vicinity of Fairfax Court House and sent them passes and an escort of his soldiers.

Captain Sterrett, a Cary relative, prepared a place for the party to stay: an encampment of tents. That evening they were serenaded by the famous Washington Artillery Band of New Orleans, aided by men singers. After the musical numbers, Captain Sterrett thanked the Southern musicians and asked if they could render them any service in return. At once came the reply, "Let's hear a woman's voice!"

It was then that Jennie Cary stood at the door of a tent and "under the cover of darkness" responded by singing the new song,

"Maryland, My Maryland." The Southern troops were so pleased with her rendition that immediately the refrain "was caught up and tossed back from hundreds of Rebel throats."

As the last strains died away that night, the soldiers shouted: "We will break her chains—she shall be free. Three Cheers and a Tiger for Maryland!"

There were no dry eyes that night in camp; also no other song ever received such a dramatic beginning on the very field of battle as did James Ryder Randall's "Maryland, My Maryland," which soon became the "national war song" of the South. "Born in Louisiana and wedded to its music in Maryland," it had a very fitting introduction to Confederate troops in the state of Virginia.

James Randall enlisted in the Confederate Army but was soon discharged as he was found to be afflicted with tuberculosis. After the war was over, he became editor of the *Constitutionalist* in Augusta, Georgia, and later edited the *Chronicle* in the same place. Randall also acted as the Washington correspondent for the *Chronicle,* serving as secretary to Representative William H. Fleming and later, in the same capacity, to Senator Joseph E. Brown of Georgia.

Randall's poems were widely praised. As the author of "Maryland, My Maryland" with its continuing popularity, his fame as a poet was assured. However, it was not until some time after his death on January 15, 1908, in his adopted city of Augusta, that his poems were assembled and published in one volume.

Besides the two editions of "Maryland, My Maryland," published by Miller and Beacham at Baltimore, there were eight Confederate editions. Mathew Page Andrews once stated that the story saying that Randall received $100 for his noted song was false, and that the poet never was given any "direct" payment for his poetical works.

However another writer says this assertion seems to be contradicted by the notice that appeared in the Blackmar advertisements:

> Having disposed of the copyright to my poem "Maryland, My Maryland," to Messrs. A. E. Blackmar and Bro. I hereby certify that their edition is the only one that has my sanction and approval.
> —Jas. R. Randall

Since its writing, many critics have given much commendation to "Maryland, My Maryland." For instance, Mathew Page Andrews called the Randall composition "a work of rare patriotic fervor and completely Southern in both origin and sentiment."

It has also been said that the song was second in popularity among Southerners only to "Dixie"; that it was to the South what "John Brown's Body" was to the North. It was often heard in Maryland, which was supposed to be neutral in the great Civil War conflict. In 1899, the Savannah *Press* maintained that Randall's poem stood out as "the most beautiful war lyric of modern times."

In the Southern states during the war, not much poetry of real merit was produced. Their music in general was indicative of tastes now outmoded in the development of American culture. "But 'Maryland, My Maryland' has joined a group of soul-stirring patriotic songs."

It is true that his native state did not heed James Ryder Randall's exhortation, for Maryland remained in the Northern fold. Also the poet never again lived within the borders of the state he loved so much. Yet the song he was inspired to create is today one of the best-known ones of all those composed during the tragic conflict.

After the war was over, it was sung at Confederate reunions and is well known to succeeding generations of Southerners. And Randall had the honor of having his work adopted by the state of Maryland as her official hymn, "the only state in the Union that has such a distinctive anthem."

Maryland, My Maryland

James R. Randall

1. The des-pot's heel is on thy shore, Mar - y-land, my Mar - y-land! His
2. Hark to an ex - iled son's ap-peal, Mar - y-land, my Mar - y-land! My
3. Thou wilt not cow - er in the dust, Mar - y-land, my Mar - y-land! Thy

torch is at thy tem - ple door, Mar - y-land, my Mar - y-land! A -
Moth - er State, to thee I kneel! Mar - y-land, my Mar - y-land! For
gleam - ing sword shall nev - er rust, Mar - y-land, my Mar - y-land! Re -

venge the pa - tri - ot - ic gore That flecked the streets of Bal - ti - more, And
life and death, for woe and weal, Thy peer - less chiv - al - ry re - veal, And
mem - ber Car - roll's sa - cred trust, Re - mem - ber How - ard's war - like thrust, And

be the bat - tle - queen of yore, Mar - y-land, my Mar - y - land!
gird thy beau - teous limbs with steel, Mar - y-land, my Mar - y - land!
all thy slum-b'rers with the just, Mar - y-land, my Mar - y - land!

10

*

"Tenting on the Old Camp Ground"

Of all the songs produced during the Civil War period, perhaps the most poignant and appealing is "Tenting on the Old Camp Ground" sometimes known as "We're Tenting Tonight." Walter Kittredge wrote both the words and music. One source says that this composition more than any other has in it "the heart experience of the man who wrote it." His song truly represents "the spontaneous outgoing of a full heart."

The beloved piece begins with these words:

> We're tenting tonight on the old camp ground,
> Give us a song to cheer
> Our weary hearts, a song of home,
> And friends we hold so dear.

An unnamed writer once declared: "Walter Kittredge gave to the world this song, not of war, but of peace, not of hatred, but of love, which touches the deep places in human nature. He was not a soldier, as is generally supposed."

The composer was born in Merrimac, New Hampshire, on October 8, 1832, the tenth child in a family of eleven boys and girls. It is true that many New England farms were noted for their stony hills that were not too productive of needed crops. But it appears that in various cases during its early years the region did produce some large families.

From his childhood Walter Kittredge had a good ear for music and as a small boy showed his love for it. He picked up all his musical knowledge by himself. For he never attended a music school, had no lessons from any teacher, nor was he given any special training in the subject. Once he wrote:

> My father bought one of the first seraphines [a species of melodeon] made in Concord, New Hampshire, and well do I remember when the man came to put it up. To hear him play a simple melody was a rich treat, and this event was an important epoch in my child life.

However, by the time Kittredge was twenty years old he was giving concerts and singing ballads. Then in 1856, he began his lengthy association with the well-known Hutchinson Family Singers of Milford, New Hampshire.

In 1863, the singer received his draft notice and fully expected to go to the front at once, leaving his young wife and little daughter behind. But during his childhood Walter had been afflicted by rheumatic fever. So the draft board refused him, apparently not only because of his poor health, but as one authority asserted, because the board members felt he would be of more service to the Union cause and its fighting men as a singer with the Hutchinson group than as a soldier.

Thus, the composer of "Tenting on the Old Camp Ground," the "hauntingly plaintive" Civil War song, never served as a member of the Union Army. However, it was the receipt of his draft notice that was responsible for his creating the beloved ballad.

One source asserts the inspiration for the outstanding composition came while Kittredge was expecting to go into the service, and that it was really his farewell to civilian life.

The song was completed in one evening in 1863, when the whole nation was war-weary and longing for peace, and is really a peace song. It promptly struck a responsive chord with soldiers and public, for its plaintive melody seemed to express a sentiment that no other song had caught.

Although Kittredge was "loyal to his heart's core," the thought of leaving his home and little family saddened him. Also as he was of a poetic nature, his soul revolted against the thought of war and its horrors.

The night after he had been rejected he slept fitfully, and when he awoke in the middle of the night "the burden of dread" was still foremost in his mind. In the solemn stillness of the night, Walter thought of the battlefields and of the many young men who had already given their lives. Some had been killed in battle, while others had died of diseases in camps. The thought of countless unknown graves, of wives and children wearily waiting for the end of the struggle, and of soldiers in camps who knew that this night might be their last one on earth bore heavily on his mind.

These conflicting emotions kept the singer awake. Finally he felt compelled to get up and put his thoughts on paper. The first stanza reveals his purpose, not only to bring cheer to others, but to help comfort his own heart. A friend, Dr. J. M. French, once reported:

On the night of his rejection by the examining board at Concord, he returned to his home and sought rest, but found it not. As he lay there, sleepless, thinking over the events of the day, he saw a picture forming in the minds of the soldiers on the camp ground, of whom he himself might have been one, had he not been rejected. Little by little, the ideas and even the very words of the song began to crowd themselves into his brain.

Next the melody to accompany the words began to shape itself, and took its place along with the words. So strong was the impression made upon him that he gave up the idea of sleep, took paper and pencil and began to write both the words and the music; and in a short time, the whole song was written out, so nearly perfect that very little change was ever made in it afterwards.

In later years there was some question as to when the song actually was composed. In pursuing this query, a writer and lecturer, Colonel Nicholas Smith, wrote Kittredge. He received the following letter on May 2, 1897, from the composer at his home in Reed's Ferry, New Hampshire:

> I take this time to give you a history of "Tenting on the Old Camp Ground." I wrote the words and music at the same time, one evening, soon expecting to go down South to join the boys in blue, and I desired to have something to sing for them, as that had been my profession for a few years before the war. I think I wrote the song in tears, thinking of my wife and little daughter; but I was not accepted, when examined by the physician. He thought I could do my part better to sing for Uncle Sam, so I kept writing and singing for Liberty and the Union. The song was composed in 1863 and published by Ditson, Boston, in 1864.
>
> —Walter Kittredge

After his rejection, since he was a singer by profession, he devoted his efforts to working with the Hutchinson family as they traveled about the country, singing patriotic, religious, antislavery, and temperance songs. They had audiences both of civilians and of soldiers.

It is said that the tune of "Tenting on the Old Camp Ground" came easily to the composer. As soon as he had copied the words and music, he started out to try to sell his composition. But, like some other famous songs, it did not find immediate publication. The first Boston publisher to whom Kittredge offered it turned it down. He said he wanted something "more militant and patriotic" than this song with its theme—"Many are the hearts that are weary tonight, / Wishing for the war to cease."

Finally the singer went to Lynn, Massachusetts, to consult his good friend Asa Hutchinson. The noted singing family lived on High Rock in Bird's Nest Cottage. The two men discussed the matter of publication, and asked John Hutchinson to sing the solo. Asa took the bass part, and the children joined in the chorus. All members of the family were enthusiastic about Walter's fine composition. Then Asa Hutchinson and Walter Kittredge made a contract that the former should arrange the song properly, and when they got it published each would receive 50 per cent of the profits.

Soon the Hutchinson family put on a series of concerts on the crest of Old High Rock. Tickets of admission were only five cents! There were several ticket sellers stationed at different approaches, and they were busy supplying tickets to the great crowds of people who came from all the nearby towns.

They also concocted some homemade lighting. During the day the Hutchinsons had wound balls of old cloth and soaked them in oil. They put them in pans and placed the pans on posts arranged at intervals about the crest. The lights burned for an hour or more; then boys who were standing by replaced them.

Thousands of persons attended these Hutchinson concerts. On the opening night Walter Kittredge sang "Tenting on the Old Camp Ground," on the top of Old High Rock. This was its first public hearing.

It is reported that the success of the song was instantaneous, and that Asa Hutchinson had no trouble persuading the Oliver Ditson Company in Boston to publish it. At once the piece was so sought after that over 10,000 copies were sold during the first three months. Both civilians and soldiers responded favorably to this "sincere and spontaneous composition," for the entire country was longing for peace.

Hutchinson and Kittredge shared equally in the returns. A Hutchinson biographer later stated that Asa received more money for this piece than for any other of the numerous songs featured by the popular singing organization. During the long, bloody Civil War, hundreds of copies were sold. As casualty lists lengthened, it gained mass appeal, as the sincere and universal longing of all Americans—Northern and Southern—was for peace.

Soldiers loved the song, for it well expressed their feelings—what they thought about home, family, friends, the lost happiness of peacetime, and of comrades gone forever. In addition to its heartfelt sentiments, "Tenting on the Old Camp Ground" had a "plaintive melody." Also the "delightful harmony of the chorus" appealed strongly to them.

In order to have material to sing to the Union soldiers, Kittredge compiled a small book of his own songs, including "No Night There" and "When They Come Marching Home." But this volume was not very successful. None of his other works ever approached the success of "Tenting Tonight. . . ." His fame rests securely on this one, sincerely inspired composition.

For many years Kittredge sang with the Hutchinsons. Each summer he spent at his home, Pine Grove Cottage, near Reed's Ferry in New Hampshire, where he died on July 8, 1905.

Since the Civil War and as long as there were remaining members of the Grand Army of the Republic the song, "Tenting on the Old Camp Ground," was perhaps the most popular one when old veterans got together at their annual encampments. These aged soldiers would wipe away the tears as they sang the stanzas that recalled bygone days, brave comrades gone, and loved ones left at home.

Even today this Kittredge composition has retained as much popularity as any other Civil War song, if not more. And it is highly regarded as "a splendid peace song." Although the composer expressed the feelings of men of his time a century ago, it is just as appropriate today, for the same desires appeal to human beings now.

> Many are the hearts that are weary tonight,
> Wishing for the war to cease.
> Many are the hearts, that are looking for the right,
> To see the dawn of peace.

One Sunday evening in 1896, a Mrs. Grasheider sang "Tenting on the Old Camp Ground" at Trinity Church in Chicago. The effect on the audience was so remarkable that it inspired an article in the Chicago *Tribune* about the influence of the composition in the Civil War. It caused many to shed tears as they recalled the battle scenes of the war. "The melody is of that peculiar quality which will prevent the song from ever growing too old to reach the emotions of the human heart."

Colonel Nicholas Smith, one evening in 1894, was lecturing in Kansas City, Missouri, on the history of our patriotic songs. In the large audience were several former members of the Confederate Army. A popular singer, Captain Henry, sang in "a tone full of genuine feeling" Kittredge's noted composition and asked the audience to join in the refrain. Colonel Smith remarked later about this occasion:

> It was extremely affecting to hear the large gathering of old soldiers give expression to their sentiment by singing this song of affection with a perfect union of hearts as well as of voices. I cannot recall another instance when the chorus of "Tenting on the Old Camp Ground" was sung with more soul-feeling, with finer rhythm, or with more sensitive harmony than by that audience composed of the Blue and the Gray.
>
> "Tenting on the Old Camp Ground" is not an animating battle piece, of course, but is peculiarly touching in sentiment and plaintive in melody; and many thousands of soldiers, in the monotony of camp life and on weary marches, when thoughts of home burdened the mind, found relief in its pathetic notes and in the delightful harmony of the chorus. Such a song has a powerful hold upon human feelings. It touches the better part of our natures, and "Tenting on the Old Camp Ground," though not a song that has made exciting history, will be long and affectionately associated with the patriotic struggle for liberty and union.

We're Tenting To-Night

Walter Kittredge   Walter Kittredge

1. We're___ tent - ing to - night on the old camp ground,
2. We've been tent - ing to - night on the old camp ground,
3. We are tired___ of war on the old camp ground,
4. We've been fight - ing to night on the old camp ground,

Give us a song to cheer Our___ wear - y hearts, a
Think - ing of days gone by, Of the loved ones at home that
Man - y are dead and gone, Of the brave___ and true who've
Man - y are ly - ing near; ___ Some___ are dead and

song of___ home, And___ friends___ we love so dear.
gave us the hand, And the tears___ that said "Good - bye!"
left their___ homes, ___ Oth - ers been wound - ed long.
some are___ dying, ___ Man - y___ are in tears.

Chorus

Man - y are the hearts that are wear - y to - night, Wish - ing for the war to

cease, Man - y are the hearts that are look - ing for the right, To

see the dawn of peace. Tent - ing to - night,
(Last verse) Dy - ing to - night,

Tent - ing to - night, Tent - ing on the old camp ground.
Dy - ing to - night, Dy - ing on the old camp ground.

11

*

"Carry Me Back to Old Virginny"

Today if you should ask the average person to identify the writer of the beloved and famous song, "Carry Me Back to Old Virginny," his answer no doubt would be, "Stephen Foster."

Some years ago, when Dr. James Francis Cooke, editor of the musical magazine, *Etude,* made such a survey, 90 per cent of the persons who answered the question believed that Foster, the white Northerner who wrote such nostalgic, intriguing songs of the South, was the composer.

However, the man who really composed "Carry Me Back to Old Virginny" and other such lilting favorites as "Oh, Dem Golden Slippers" and "In the Evening by the Moonlight" was a Negro named James A. Bland.

Although he created about seven hundred songs, some of which are still sung today by millions of people everywhere, the composer died a pauper in Philadelphia in 1911. He was almost completely forgotten until recently. Although an excellent singer and banjo player, he could not get into a minstrel company at first because of his color. Therefore he turned to song writing for which he had an exceptional talent. Bland not only became popular in his own time, but today several of his compositions are considered among the finest of American folk songs.

James A. Bland will always be remembered for his "Carry Me Back to Old Virginny" which was made Virginia's state song in 1950. It is said that this work had almost been forgotten until the noted singer Alma Gluck revived it and made a recording of it. This, in addition to the fact that Negro songs, "both genuine and written in Negro style," by white musicians, have brought this ballad to permanent popularity. Today "Carry Me Back . . ." has been published in various forms for different voices and instruments: it has also become very popular as "canned" music.

Someone has said that James Bland was more fortunate than many of his race as he grew up in better circumstances than other Negroes of his time. He was born on October 22, 1854, in Flushing, Long Island, near New York City. His father, Allen M. Bland, a native of South Carolina, came from a long line of freed slaves and had attended school at Charleston and at Oberlin College. He is said to have been one of the first Negroes in the United States to graduate from college. Later Allen M. Bland was the first president of Wilberforce College at Xenia, Ohio.

James A. Bland's mother also was born of free parents in Wilmington, Delaware, but she did not have as good an education as her husband. When he got a position as engineer in the United States Patent Office in Washington, D.C., the Bland family lived near the Negro institution, Howard University. (One source states that Allen Bland was the first Negro to have a government job and that he served as a post office examiner.)

Young James Bland fell in love with music at an early age. Once when he was quite young, he saw an old Negro playing a banjo and singing to it. The boy was simply captivated by what he had heard that day; he determined that he too would have a banjo and sing to it. However it was some time before his dream came true. Finally, when he was a tall, slender boy of twelve—after the family had moved to the national capital—his parents managed to buy him an $8 banjo. This event made him very happy.

After getting the instrument, James spent so much time playing it that he sadly neglected his school studies. Mr. Bland became quite disgusted with his son's continual playing and singing. But he couldn't stop him, for the boy was a "natural" as far as music was concerned.

In the summer evenings, when the weather was favorable, James and his friends would stroll around and sing to the music of his banjo. Almost every afternoon he could be found in Lafayette Park near the White House. Because of his sweet voice and skillful playing, young Bland attracted much attention with his songs, some of which he had composed himself. The well-dressed people who passed along on their way to fashionable clubs or restaurants often tossed the youthful performer small coins. Even at an early age, James was "enough of a showman to glory in an audience."

One day a gentleman stood and watched him for some time. Then he went up to him and praised his singing and playing. He was General James Allen, and he introduced the young musician to his friend, John Chamberlin, a leading hotel proprietor. The top personalities in Washington society used to gather at his hostelry.

Bland was only fourteen when he first performed for Chamberlin. But the latter at once recognized the boy's unusual musical ability. Therefore he hired James to sing and play not only in the afternoons, but also in the evenings, for the entertainment of his distinguished guests. There was some opposition on the part of Mr. and Mrs. Bland in regard to their son's taking on this work; however they needed the extra money as there were twelve youngsters in the Bland family.

Although there were so many children to educate, Allen Bland especially wanted James to have the advantage of a college education. At sixteen, the youth entered Howard University. But he refused to apply himself to his studies, for he wanted to spend the major part of his time on music.

At Howard University James organized glee clubs and also put on musicals at different Washington churches. He was tall, good looking, and light brown in color; he had dignity and poise. As he dressed well, James soon became known among his college mates as the "Beau Brummell" of the campus; this no doubt increased his popularity with the girl students.

Often while at the college, young Bland went to various hotels with his banjo and entertained Cabinet members, United States senators, and other important personages. Even though he was not a success as a student, Bland had the satisfaction of knowing that people did enjoy his playing and singing.

Gerstenburg's Music Hall at Newspaper Row on Fourteenth Street was a rendezvous for prominent Washington residents, including the President. Sousa and his band performed here, and also young James Bland. As he wanted to learn all the current popular songs, he attended the theater as much as possible and listened carefully to the music. Much of it he didn't care for; so he decided to write his own lyrics and melodies.

Howard University was a very strict religious institution when James was a student there. The faculty disapproved of "minstrels, vaudeville, and anything to do with the theater." During Bland's second year there he wanted to put on a musical show, but the authorities would not permit him to do so.

After he had staged his production downtown for a week, he made the decision that college was not for him. He did not graduate from Howard University as his parents were eager for him to do, for he was determined to make music his life work. And above everything else, James Bland wanted to become a member of a minstrel troupe.

One day while the youth was singing and playing his banjo in Lafayette Park, Professor White, an old, white-haired Negro, who was a teacher and music composer, heard him and asked where he had gotten his songs. Then James admitted they were his own, but he didn't know how to write them down.

Professor White invited him to come to his home where he would teach him to do so. Bland went there for several months and worked hard under the older Negro's excellent direction. His teacher praised his work and told him he had a great God-given talent for creating music which he must continue to cultivate. Also, Professor White very wisely advised the young musician against worshiping success.

One source states that while Bland may have crossed over into the state of Virginia and seen part of it as a young man while living in Washington, D.C., there is no actual record of his ever making an extended tour there. Another writer has said that Virginia actually was only a symbol to him of a haven where "he could live with his people far from the bitterness of an unkind white world."

On the contrary, another authority tells of his friendship with a Negro girl, Mannie Friend, and of their visit to see her grandmother in Virginia. The two young people were very congenial. "She challenged him; she acted as a spiritual force over him . . . she became almost as important to him as his music."

Frequently they would take afternoon walks together, and in fine weather they enjoyed sitting in Lafayette Park. At first James hesitated about playing and singing his songs for Mannie, but she encouraged him in his song writing and also in his great desire to be a minstrel man.

The girl often talked to him about her old home in the Tidewater region of Virginia, where she had been born of slave parents. Mannie described to James how the slaves would gather in front of a cabin in the moonlight and sing songs together. This no doubt gave the young musician the idea for one of his most popular songs, "In the Evening by the Moonlight."

The young musician begged Mannie to take him to see her grandmother in Virginia. (After the Civil War the elderly woman had been allowed to stay on in her cabin.) Although the two friends didn't have money for the trip, Mannie succeeded in getting their transportation. John McGregor, overseer on the plantation where her grandmother lived, was loved by all the Negroes. It happened that he had just arrived in Washington with a load of tobacco; so he agreed to take James and Mannie back with him.

It was a two days' journey, with an overnight stop in the city of Richmond. All along the way the musician fairly reveled in the lovely Virginia landscape. And as they drove slowly along, he strummed his banjo and sang some of his own compositions. Bland was especially thrilled by the songs of the various birds, and those of the mockingbirds were most appealing. He also enjoyed seeing the many cotton and corn fields along the way.

At the end of the trip, Mannie had a happy reunion with her grandmother. That afternoon, the two young visitors strolled down to the James River and sat on the bank, with their backs against a tree. Bland looked around him contentedly and absorbed the pleasing details of his surroundings.

It is said that the result of this visit was the composition, "Carry Me Back to Old Virginny," perhaps his best-loved song. The story goes that later on, after the youth had returned to Washington and had just taken part in a performance, he was not able to sleep. So he got out of bed, picked up his banjo, and worked on a tune he had been thinking about all day. A few hours later he had completed the words and music of his never-to-be-forgotten song.

As mentioned before, Bland's overwhelming desire while still at Howard University was to be a black-faced end man in a minstrel show. In 1874 this type of entertainment was at its peak, and the versatile end men were the star performers. However, even though the Civil War had brought freedom to the slaves, there was still much racial discrimination. It is rather ironical that talented Negroes were not admitted as members of the black-faced minstrel troupes.

One of Bland's classmates at Howard University said later that the musician had been sheltered "from the feeling against the Negro"; that he was shocked and hurt by the insults he received during the year and a half he tried unsuccessfully to crash the white man's field.

The youth almost worshiped George Primrose, the celebrated soft-shoe dancer, star of Skiff and Gaylord's Minstrel Show. One day while in Lafayette Park, James was playing his banjo and singing a new song he had just created. A man on a nearby bench introduced himself as John Ford, owner of the noted Ford's Theater, where President Abraham Lincoln had been assassinated.

He told the young musician that he wanted him to meet George Primrose. For Ford had realized at once that Bland was "a natural-born artist"; that his songs were good, and that he should be given a chance. He soon contacted Primrose and told him of his discovery. At first the latter didn't want to bother meeting the Negro youth. However, Ford persisted and late in October, 1874, when Bland was twenty years old, Primrose gave him an interview.

Bland told the star he was doing some entertaining at local clubs and restaurants to make extra money while attending Howard University. But he emphasized the fact that what he really wanted most in life was to be a musician and minstrel man like Primrose himself.

The latter asked James to play and sing some of his own pieces. When the youth responded, the two listeners stared at each other in amazement. Now they were both thoroughly convinced that Bland really had exceptional talent. The musician then asked if he could play something he had written about the state of Virginia. When he had strummed his guitar and sung "Carry Me Back to Old Virginny," the men had tears in their eyes. One writer has reported that Ford and Primrose were astonished and "captivated by the beauty and simplicity of the new song."

Primrose told the young musician he was sorry he could not take him into his own minstrel troupe as all its members were white men. But he did introduce him to Billy West, his partner in the Haverly Minstrels. The star also told James he would use "Carry Me Back to Old Virginny" on his opening night the following week in Baltimore.

That day at the theater, the two men asked him to repeat the number. They called in the members of the company and all joined in singing the song. At first Primrose was somewhat suspicious as to the originality of the composition because it sounded so much like the music of Stephen Foster, who had died ten years before.

However, James Bland did manage to convince him that he really had written it. Both Ford and Primrose agreed that the Negro musician possessed a talent similar to Foster's.

Bland was overwhelmed by the sudden and unexpected success of his composition about Virginia. On the way home he stopped to tell his teacher, Professor White, the good news. The latter took up his violin, played the piece through, and urged the young Negro to keep on composing.

The afternoon the minstrel troupe was rehearsing his work, James sat quietly in the darkened theater; he was thrilled to realize that his dream was actually beginning to come true. Soon he called to see Mannie, who was delighted to hear of his success. Now, she told him, he was "part of the world." He called the composition "our" song, and gave Mannie credit for helping him create it. Later it was said: "Neither of them realized that the song born that day on the bank of the James River was to become Bland's greatest composition."

After this initial success, Mannie knew that she would never have him; that music would always be first in Bland's life. And it is said that from this time on the young Negro girl saw very little of him.

(One writer has given a different account of how "Carry Me Back to Old Virginny" was written: he wrote that one night the youth was walking in Philadelphia, "penniless, hungry, and heartsick." Finally he entered a saloon in the colored district, went to the back room, and sat down at an old, battered piano. According to this version he stayed there all night, and by morning he had completed his immortal song.)

"Carry Me Back to Old Virginny" was first heard in public in the city of Baltimore. The audience—so the story goes—clapped, stamped their feet, and demanded seven encores. The composition immediately became a great success, and Bland's friends were enthusiastic about it.

However, E. P. Christy and other minstrel-show owners were not pleased by its popularity. For in the heyday of minstrelsy, it was customary for the star, or the owner of the show, to claim that the songs he used were his own. For example, Christy declared he was the composer of "Old Folks at Home" (with permission of Stephen Foster).

A lawyer friend of Bland got "Carry Me Back . . . " copyrighted. But it seems that the composer sold it for a small sum; one source says he got only $250 for both lyrics and tune. (Later on when he was poverty-stricken, the song was still selling well. But the Negro writer did not receive any royalties from it.)

It has been stated that Christy had much influence with the newspapers of that era, and he persuaded the critics to "pan" the work severely. However, as has been said, "the plaintive sadness of the melody" had universal appeal. Even cowboys, driving cattle north from Texas over the famed Chisholm Trail to market used to sing "Carry Me Back to Old Virginny" to calm their restless animals.

On March 4, 1881, when James A. Garfield was inaugurated as President, a band, playing the song in march time for this occasion, swung down Pennsylvania Avenue. The composer was in the reviewing stand and happily received the plaudits of those around him.

The title of this song was not a new one, for Christy's Minstrels had a piece with the same name, but with entirely different words. It was a strange coincidence that the Negro composer happened to hit on the identical title; however, his composition far outlived the Christy one.

Victor Herbert—so it is claimed—was sure that Stephen C. Foster had written "Carry Me Back to Old Virginny," but the noted orchestra conductor, Theodore Thomas, was able to convince him that the composer was, in truth, a young Negro.

Bland finally got a chance to make his dream of becoming a minstrel man come true. A little company of Negroes was playing at Niblo's Gardens in New York to small audiences, and Bland was happy to be accepted as a member of this troupe. Gradually he learned show business; and he was also permitted to use some of his original works in the performances, including "Oh, Dem Golden Slippers" and "Carry Me Back to Old Virginny."

Billy Kersand, one of the all-time "greats," acted as end man with Bland as his assistant. This was a very successful year for the newcomer; his songs were yielding good royalties, and he declared himself "reasonably wealthy." Whenever Bland was part of a minstrel show, he appeared in black face; at other times he used no make-up.

At the close of his first season in New York, Bland went back to Washington, for he wanted to see Mannie, whom he had really missed. But after his meeting, his interest in her waned; from this time on his greatest and only love, which was show business, claimed his entire time and attention. And someone has remarked: "No woman ever won his heart because music was the one great love of his life."

In the early 1880's, Bland went to Europe with a minstrel company in which he and Billy Kersand were the end men. English patrons were different from American ones in that they seemed to prefer the all-Negro minstrel troupes to the white ones.

The British were thrilled by the productions of this company. Bland was the hit of the show, "the rage of London," and also of the music halls outside of the metropolis, in Scotland and Ireland. His "Carry Me Back to Old Virginny" thrilled his appreciative audiences. Many were already acquainted with the music of Stephen C. Foster, but it was the first time they had had the opportunity of hearing Negro minstrels sing songs of the South.

Many of the British listeners believed that the Negro's numbers were the work of Foster, as Bland's name did not appear on the sheet music. The composer naturally wanted recognition for his compositions. Therefore in London and elsewhere, when Bland performed at numerous charitable benefits, he used his own materials.

When the Prince of Wales—later on, Edward VII—heard of this unusual musician, he invited him to give a command performance at Buckingham Palace. The royal family enjoyed Bland's distinctive offerings. It is reported that the prince applauded vigorously, and from then on became one of Bland's greatest admirers and supporters.

When the minstrel troupe prepared to return to the United States after several months of very successful touring throughout the British Isles, Bland told the members of the company that he planned to remain in London and live abroad the rest of his life. He liked the city, and the people there liked him. He had made numerous friends and was highly acclaimed as the outstanding entertainer of the time.

Bland's decision to stay abroad may have been influenced by the harsh treatment he had received at home. During his stay in Europe, his salary was as much as $10,000 per year, a fabulous sum for that era. He also added much to this income by producing more songs.

It happened that there were also no race barriers in London; so the Negro composer was able to rent a flat in an expensive and exclusive residential district of the metropolis. In addition, he kept a fine carriage and some good horses. He continued to dress well; he was considered one of the best-dressed men in town and always carried a gold-headed cane. Since he was so sought after as an entertainer, his agent was able to book him at the best night clubs and restaurants in the city.

The musician also went to the Continent where he gave many performances, including several in Paris and Berlin. The Germans especially liked Bland's ballads. They were also intrigued by his banjo playing, for they had never seen such an instrument before.

James was a very restless man, always on the go. By 1890, he was known not only in the United States but in Great Britain and on the Continent. The composer lived in Europe for about twenty years, only returning occasionally for a brief visit to his native land. Until the last years of his life he managed to enjoy himself, but he was saddened by the fact that minstrel shows were on the wane, for vaudeville was taking its place.

After "Carry Me Back to Old Virginny" had become a universal favorite, Bland was in great demand in Washington, D.C., as an entertainer. He often played and sang at dinners too among his own people and was invited to perform at Negro weddings. Gradually it is said "a spirit of spirituality" crept into some of his compositions; for example, "Oh, Dem Golden Slippers."

Harvey's Restaurant, at the corner of Eleventh and Pennsylvania avenues, was the rendezvous of the celebrated Canvasback Club. Bland wrote the songs for the annual dinners of this distinctive organization. Private parties of distinguished personalities were served by the owner on the second floor. It was here that the composer played his lovely song "In the Evening by the Moonlight" for a hundred club members, including Grover Cleveland (before he became President), who was very enthusiastic about Bland's compositions. Robert E. Lee was also a member of this outstanding group.

After the great success of his "Carry Me Back. . . ," the composer was termed the "World's Greatest Minstrel," and also the "Melody Man." He dubbed himself the "Best Ethiopian Song Writer in the World." He was expert in choosing good titles for his pieces. But once he made the statement that while it was easy for him to do the words and titles, he often had difficulty writing his melodies.

Bland was continually spurred on in his composing by his overpowering love for music, and so he kept turning out countless sentimental ballads. Of these some were copyrighted; many were not. It is said that only fifty-three of his probably seven hundred works were copyrighted in Washington, D.C., along with a few in the British Museum.

As a recognized composer, Bland's songs were eagerly sought after by musical publishers for use in minstrel shows and also for barbershop quartet singers. He was "the darling of the music publishers"—not only recognized as a top musical performer but also as a versatile and prolific composer, often turning out a song a week. Between 1878 and 1881, he created "Going Home," "In the Evening by the Moonlight," and "Oh, Dem Golden Slippers." The last two, together with "In the Morning by the Bright Light," sold 100,000 copies during their first years.

Among Bland's other works were "Father's Growing Old," "The Old Homestead," "Tapioca," "The Farmer's Daughter," "Christmas Dinner," and "Way up Yonder."

Although the composer never married, he loved children. In Washington, he was often seen surrounded by a crowd of youngsters, some of them his sister's children. Bland expressed his love for boys and girls in several compositions. He often helped in charitable shows, and for several summers he staged outdoor productions with youthful performers. At times, Bland was asked to write special songs for political campaigns; one of these was "You Gotta Stop Kicking My Hound Around."

As was customary in those days, new songs were plugged by various singers, so that the public might become acquainted with them. Bland's songs were often performed by such top minstrels and good friends as Billy Emerson, George Primrose, and Billy Kersand. It is said that Bland sometimes made as much as $5,000 annually from his works.

It seems that Bland was not only "a composer, lyricist, jokester, skit writer, and banjoist"; but he was also an inventor and improved the banjo. This peculiarly American musical instrument was invented during the days when slavery was in existence in the South. The composer added a fifth string. He found this increased the richness of the tone and also made the banjo more versatile. The five-stringed instrument became known as the Bland Banjo.

Although he had poured out many of his feelings for home in his immortal ballads and had enjoyed wealth and fame in Europe for twenty years, James Bland felt a strong longing to be with his own people again.

While living in London the composer had spent money recklessly for fine clothes and elegant living. Like many other artists in show business, the musician had been more than generous in helping others less fortunate than he. And they had soon learned that James was "an easy touch."

When he decided to return to his native land in 1901, Bland gathered his meager belongings together and without telling his London friends good-by set sail for the United States. Practically all he had on leaving were the clothes on his back, and enough money for the fare.

When he arrived home he found few minstrels. The demand for minstrel songs had ceased. The day of the minstrel show was rapidly passing away. Also, his name and fame as a song writer had been forgotten, even though some of his works—his "plaintive Negro ballads"—were still being used at performances. But it seemed that no one knew or cared about their composer.

In Philadelphia, where some minstrel groups still enjoyed popularity, Bland tried to join a company but was not accepted. "Disconsolate, penniless, forlorn," he went to Washington, where the word soon got around that the formerly famous song writer was broke.

A friend of Bland's boyhood, William Silence, came to his aid. He encouraged him to go on with his song writing, and allowed him to work at a desk in his office. But apparently the old magic had disappeared and there were few people left who appreciated Bland's compositions. However, he did succeed in getting a commission to do the musical score for *The Sporting Girl,* which he managed to complete. It is said that for this work he received $250; this was probably his last musical composition. Even though his friend, William Silence, tried to help him, the composer became quite despondent. He went back to Philadelphia, and very little is known of how his last years were spent.

When the end came in 1911, at 1012 Wood Street, it is said that everything was against him. He was living in "dismal lodgings," the weather was quite unfavorable, and he had caught a bad cold.

(Some say he had tuberculosis.) In May the famous minstrel man "took his last curtain call" at the age of fifty-seven years.

The Philadelphia newspapers carried no notice of his death and no tribute was paid the composer even though some of his songs such as "Carry Me Back to Old Virginny," were still popular both with young and old. Thus the Negro writer who had followed "the song in his heart," and had delighted the people of two continents by his inimitable banjo playing and singing, passed away "unwept, unknown, and forgotten." James Bland at his death left no will, no property, no letters, nor any personal papers.

A few friends tried to raise the necessary $15 for his burial expenses, but they could collect only $5. A good-hearted undertaker offered to take care of the funeral for this small sum. So James Bland was buried in the pauper section of a small Negro cemetery at Merion (Bala-Cynwyd) just outside the city of Philadelphia. As the hearse passed along that day it attracted little attention. No one realized that a really great individual had died.

Years passed, and the small cemetery in Merion was abandoned. Weeds grew over the graves, including that of Bland, and its site was completely forgotten.

During the decades of the 1930's, Dr. James Francis Cooke of the Oliver Ditson Music Company (and editor of the musical magazine, the *Etude*), kept receiving inquiries as to who James Bland, composer of "Carry Me Back to Old Virginny," was. Often some one would ask if Bland was a pen name of Stephen C. Foster.

Dr. Cooke was eager to discover as much as possible about this comparatively unknown song writer. So he got in touch with various persons and discovered they had never heard of Bland, but had always credited Foster with certain songs. The editor spent several years trying to find out about Bland, but the *Dictionary of American Biography* and other reference books carried no material about him. Dr. Cooke interviewed elderly persons who might have had some knowledge of the song writer's life. He also contacted people at music schools and older members of music publishing firms. Some did say they had heard that the composer of "Carry Me Back . . ." had been a Negro, but they weren't sure.

It is an interesting coincidence that during the same period when Dr. Cooke was doing his investigating and trying to ferret out facts about Bland's life, the location of his grave, etc., another person, Dr. Kelly Miller, a professor of economics and mathematics at Howard University, was engaged in a similar search. Dr. Miller too believed that Stephen C. Foster had written the pieces that were really composed by Bland. Finally an old Negro, a federal employee in Washington, told Dr. Miller that James A. Bland had indeed written several familiar American songs, including "Carry Me Back to Old Virginny."

At once Dr. Miller was intrigued by the unknown composer, and was quite surprised to learn that James had been a student at Howard University—the very institution where he had been teaching for many years. The professor informed Dr. Cooke that the musician had been buried in Merion Cemetery. The latter had searched through several local graveyards in and around Philadelphia without success. When he heard the correct location, he was surprised to find that the site he was looking for was practically in his own neighborhood.

It was in June 1939, that Dr. Cooke made an exciting discovery after his search of many years. Although he had gone over Merion Cemetery, he decided to try once more. When he came across a badly neglected grave, covered with weeds, poison ivy, and an accumulation of trash, he cleared all the debris away. He was then thrilled to see on the stone the inscription he had long been looking for:

JAMES A. BLAND, 1854–1911

Thus at last he had located the grave of the famous song writer. Dr. Cooke was able to get in touch with Irene Bland Jurix, Bland's only surviving sister, and she added much to his knowledge of her brother's life.

Dr. Cooke and Dr. Miller worked for years on the same project; then they pooled their findings and told the world of the hitherto unknown life of James A. Bland. If it had not been for their untiring efforts, the grave might not have been discovered or credit given him. In addition, the finding of his burial place gave decided impetus to the belated movement to afford the Negro composer the recognition he so richly deserved.

Finally, after thirty-five years of neglect, the crumbling gravestone in the small Merion Cemetery gave way to an impressive granite memorial. On July 15, 1946, the memory of James A. Bland's long forgotten existence and accomplishments was recalled with dignified ceremonies. It was the Lions' Clubs of Virginia that raised the necessary funds for the monument. And it was through their efforts and those of Dr. Cooke and Dr. Miller that James A. Bland received this fitting tribute. Many prominent persons were present that day, including Governor Tuck and Senator Harry F. Byrd, both of Virginia. Mrs. Jurix was also at the dedication.

The district governors of the Lions' Clubs placed a wreath on the stone, which bears this inscription:

JAMES A. BLAND

Oct. 23, 1854–May 5, 1911

NEGRO COMPOSER WHO WROTE

CARRY ME BACK TO OLD VIRGINNY

and 600 other songs.

ERECTED AND DEDICATED BY

LIONS' CLUBS OF VIRGINIA

July 15, 1946

On that occasion, at least partial amends were made for the long years of neglect. In his eulogy, Governor Tuck declared:

. . . James Bland has put into ever-ringing verse and rhyme an expression of the feeling which all Virginians have for their state.

"Carry Me Back to Old Virginny" tells in an inspiring song the innate patriotism and love of native heath of all our people, white and Negro alike.

Harry F. Byrd, the noted United States senator, also praised the composer:

> It is almost inconceivable that a man who was not born and raised in Virginia could capture the nostalgic air that is evident in the lyrics and music of "Carry Me Back to Old Virginny." To have done so is a tribute to his genius just as much as it was to Foster's ability to compose "Swanee River," which many of his biographers claim he never saw.
>
> The story of James Bland is a testimonial to the greatness of America—a testimonial to the land in which an individual with ability and enterprise can make himself heard and his talents recognized.
>
> . . . may we pay tribute to a fellow American whose love of country gave us one of our best loved state songs.

And Dr. Francis Cooke asserted that day:

> When God sees fit to endow a man with greatness, He does not ask the color of his skin, nor his race. . . . And now, at last, one of America's greatest troubadours no longer lies in a forgotten and neglected grave.

The Lions' Clubs of Virginia, besides furnishing the monument, set up music scholarships for Negro students in the state that James A. Bland had made famous by his outstanding song.

Following the dedication at which the song writer was honored, some music companies published new editions of his works, and record albums were made. One source states that attempts were made to interest Henry Ford in perpetuating the life and works of the Negro composer. However, Ford, so it was stated, was not completely convinced that Bland and not Stephen C. Foster *had* written "Carry Me Back to Old Virginny."

Although Bland has never been given ample praise for his works, the millions who love and sing his music are "a testament to the fact that he is not unsung." It is true that he did not reach the fame that has been accorded Foster; yet he wrote many of the most popular songs of the 1870's and 1880's. And they were actually Negro songs composed by a Negro. Today many well-known music critics hail Bland as the second greatest writer of Southern songs. It is believed that the main reason for the never-ending appeal of his "Carry Me Back . . ." is that the state serves as a symbol for home—"no matter where one's home may be."

Carry Me Back To Old Virginny

James A. Bland

1. Car-ry me back to old Vir-gin-ny There's where the cot-ton and the
2. Car-ry me back to old Vir-gin-ny There let me live— 'till I

corn and 'ta-toes grow There's where the birds war-ble sweet in the spring time
with-er and de-cay Long by the old dis-mal swamp have I wan-der'd

There's where this old dark-ey's heart am long'd to go There's where I lab-ored so
There's where this old dark-ey's life will pass a-way Mas-sa and Mis-sus have

hard for old Mas-sa, Day af-ter day in the field of yel-low corn
long gone be-fore me, Soon we will meet on that bright and gold-en shore

No place on earth do I love more sin-cere-ly,
There we'll be hap-py and free from all sor-row,

Than old Vir-gin - ny, the state where I was born.
There's where we'll meet and we'll nev-er part no more.

12

*

"America, the Beautiful"

On the last cruise of the R.M.S. *Queen Mary* from South-ampton, England on Sunday, October 31, 1967, to her permanent home in Long Beach, California, the captain as usual read the Church of England ritual. At closing, the passengers, with the author among them, sang "God Save the Queen" and "America, the Beautiful."

It was a bit surprising that the "Star-Spangled Banner" had not been selected. Perhaps those who planned the service thought "America, the Beautiful" was more fitting.

One source states that of our three national anthems, "America, the Beautiful" is "by far, the worthiest," while another declares it reveals marked "religious and social implications"; furthermore, it is "one of the most moving and popular of American patriotic songs."

Nowadays, usually only the first stanza of "The Star-Spangled Banner" (concerned with war and bombs) is sung, while the last is unsung—the one which contains references to our religious ideals.

In comparing "America" or "My Country, 'Tis of Thee" with "America, the Beautiful," we note that the former with its "rocks and rills" is a distinctive New England product. But Katherine Lee

Bates in her "America, the Beautiful" evokes the spirit of the entire country. She spans it "from sea to shining sea." In addition, the poet refers to our history from the day of the Pilgrim Fathers to "the unlimited future." Miss Bates's distinctive poem, as one writer has well said, expresses for millions of our population ". . . their loftiest ideal of patriotism. . . . Its popularity is the most fitting of memorials for a poet whose patriotism was akin to mysticism."

In *Patriotic Songs of America,* a booklet published by the John Hancock Insurance Company, the anonymous author asserts:

> Among our American songs, none surpasses in nationalistic idealism "America, the Beautiful." In it Katherine Lee Bates has caught the beauty, majesty, and immensity of this country of ours, with its opportunity and high privilege for all; and throughout the hymn there shines a faith in human brotherhood.

This inspiring song of national scope strangely enough was created by a New England college teacher and writer, Katherine Lee Bates. She was born into a cultured family in Falmouth, Massachusetts, on August 12, 1859. (Her birthplace there is marked by a commemorative tablet.) As a child she loved the sea. And in this picturesque, old-fashioned seaport, living with her closely knit family, the young girl became deeply imbued with patriotic ideals. It is said that her love of country was intensified when she went as a freshman to Wellesley College—then just in its second year—where she found the campus "a paradise still fresh and wild."

In 1880 she completed four years' work, receiving her A.B. degree, and for a few years was a high school teacher. In 1885 she was chosen as instructor by her alma mater. And in 1891, after obtaining her master's degree, she became a professor of English literature at Wellesley. Here she taught until she retired in 1925 as professor emeritus. Her own school, as well as Middlebury and Oberlin colleges, conferred doctoral degrees on her.

In 1928 at the National Education Association convention in Chicago, a chorus of young girls—representing twenty different nationalities—sang her inspiring anthem, "America, the Beautiful," to honor the composer, who was present. This was a well-deserved tribute, not only for her beautiful song, but also for the high educational ideals she had so long fostered.

The eminent educator was very popular with her students. One of them, in the Wellesley magazine, the *Echo,* wrote a humorous biography containing these statements:

> Professor Bates was born midway between ex-President Roosevelt and William J. Bryan, at Falmouth, Massachusetts, where her cradle may be seen on exhibition in the Town Hall.
> She entered Wellesley College 100 years after the Declaration of Independence, and graduated as president of her class.
> Since then, Miss Bates has followed the profession of a teacher, whenever she couldn't help it.

This remarkable and unusual teacher rejected many of the pedagogical methods of the 1880's and 1890's, for she wanted most of all to impart to the students in her classes "the sense of great imaginative literature as something dynamic and potent."

Because of Katherine Lee Bates's "original and flexible" ways, she was influential in changing American teaching methods. She had a strong influence not only at Wellesley but also upon the new cause of higher education for women in the United States. And her students later pioneered, and in their own teaching helped spread her ideas that literature is "a vivid experience, and not material for footnotes." However, Miss Bates did arouse some opposition with her new concepts. At one time, it is said, Wellesley threatened to dismiss her from the faculty as she did not conform to their strict religious ideas.

While teaching literature at Wellesley—and also in her writing—Katherine Lee Bates aided American poetry in many ways. She was the founder of the important New England Poetry Club, which met both in Boston and on the college campus. By means of her activities in this group, and through correspondence, she guided the destinies of various poets. At Wellesley she also started a permanent series of readings and lectures by eminent American and foreign poets.

Miss Bates believed thoroughly in the enriching experiences of travel, and she inspired her pupils by accounts of these journeys. She spent several summers in Europe, one year in Spain, another in the British Isles, and a third in Syria, Egypt, and Switzerland. Her many trips were the sources of ideas for her varied writings; these included travel reminiscences and books of poems. She did some translations, too, and made adaptations for children, besides doing stories and plays for them.

Katherine Lee Bates wrote important books for and about the teaching of literature. These included the editing of many English classics which became "treasured familiars" both in high schools and colleges. For collateral reading her students enjoyed her delightful *Spanish Highways and Byways*. This outstanding educator's notes and commentaries in her text books reveal her widespread knowledge and appreciation of literature.

Among her works are *The College Beautiful and Other Poems* (1887); *Rose and Thorn* (1888); *Hermit Island* (1891); *English Religious Drama* (1893); *American Literature* (1898); *Spanish Highways and Byways* (1900); *Gretna Green to Land's End* (1907); *Story of Chaucer's Canterbury Tales Re-told for Children* (1909); *America, the Beautiful and Other Poems* (1911); *In Sunny Spain* (1913); *Fairy Gold* (for children) (1916); *Sigurd* (1919); *The Pilgrim Ship* (1926); and *America, the Dream* (1930, after her death).

Until her retirement in 1925, Miss Bates continued to write poems about her beloved country, for patriotism was one of her most distinctive characteristics. In the volume, *America, the Dream,* her opening poem is "To My Country." It begins with these lines:

> O, dear my country, beautiful and dear,
> Love does not darken sight . . .

In it she speaks of America as the "Ultimate Dream of Time," and again, as in "America, the Beautiful," she emphasizes the importance of brotherhood. This same book contains verse about the discoverers of our land, the colonial people, the Revolutionary War, the development of the young republic, and of World War I. In her poem, "Cannon Fodder" (of the last-mentioned period), Miss Bates inveighs against the sacrifice of our youth to the demands of war. She prays in "Our President"

> God help him;
> Ay, and let us help him too . . .

And the poet begs her fellow Americans to have faith in our country's

> . . . divine young vision of mankind's
> Freedom and brotherhood . . .

Another World War I poem, "Our Flag," is a tribute to the "Red, White, and Blue." She declares this ensign is "the passion of a people vowed to freedom." In "Freedom's Battle Song," she calls for loyalty to the flag while its sons are fighting and that Lincoln's words, "of the people, by the people, for the people" shall prevail over all the earth. Also in her stirring poem, "How long, O Prince of Peace, how long," she refers to the "wild war" that was then feeding "on earth's glorious youth."

In 1893, when the Columbian Exposition was held in Chicago, Katherine Lee Bates decided to visit more of the United States. Up to that year she had seen little of her native land outside of New England. After spending some time in Chicago, she journeyed to Colorado Springs where she stayed for several weeks and taught in a summer school. One day, with a party of friends, the poet climbed into the "Prairie Wagon" which made its way slowly to the top of snow-capped Pike's Peak. The group could not stay there long, for the air was too thin for some of the travelers.

Miss Bates was completely awed and inspired by the grandeur of the scene before her and the magnificence of the country. That day she experienced something she'd never known before; she did not realize that this day would prove to be one of the most important of her entire life. As she looked out for miles in every direction, she was thrilled; it seemed as if she were standing on the very roof of the world. Away to the west and north was a great expanse with mighty ridges and valleys, while vast plains stretched out toward the state of Kansas.

Miss Bates was simply enthralled by the sight. After living in New England, she began for the first time to realize the great extent of her native land. She stood there and was overwhelmed as she gazed at "purple mountain majesties"; then a rush of love for America surged up within her. The result of this unusual experience was her creation of the immortal poem, "America, the Beautiful."

That evening, back in Colorado Springs, the poet thought over her awesome experience. And then she wrote the first version of her poem while the thrilling event was fresh in her mind. However, she put her notebook away, went back to her college work in New England, and didn't get the poem out again until two years later.

"America, the Beautiful" first appeared in print on July 4, 1895, in a magazine called the *Congregationalist*. At once there were numerous requests that it be set to music. Silas G. Pratt made the first setting to the original words; later the writer revised the poem, making some important changes.

Miss Bates felt strongly that it should be sung to a familiar melody so that all could join in singing it. Although it is said that sixty original settings have been composed for "America, the Beautiful," the one chosen and most often used is "Materna," the tune of "Oh, Mother Dear Jerusalem." This was the work of Samuel A. Ward. One authority advises that the hymn be sung "with fervor and devotion" and that the refrain, "America, America," be especially stressed.

This unforgettable poem vividly reveals the poet's love for our diverse scenery; for example the "amber waves of grain," "purple mountain majesties," and "the fruited plain." The author also pays tribute to the hardy pioneers whose love for freedom was outstanding, and to the unselfish patriots who made the supreme sacrifice that others might have their equal rights and opportunities. She ends each stanza with an impassioned prayer that our country may thrive under God's guidance; that its people will cherish high ideals; and that real brotherhood will prevail "from sea to shining sea."

As we read the words, we note that Miss Bates mentions "spacious skies," new to her New England eyes. It was in the West that she got her first views of really wide-open spaces. Although she had seen small grain fields, they were nothing to compare with the miles and miles of "amber grain." Mt. Washington, in New England, was low in comparison with Pike's Peak which is over 14,000 feet in height.

When the poet realized all this abundance and vastness, she was inspired to pray that God would "shed his grace" on it [her country], and that its people would live under laws, realizing that liberty is not license. Next she refers to the great conflict—the Civil War—when men gave their lives to liberate others.

Finally, she thinks of the problems of her own time; for example, the contrast of the magnificent Court of Honor, center of the Chicago World's Fair, and the hovels in many city slums. Again she prays that true brotherhood will bring about a better future for all of America's citizens.

Katherine Lee Bates died in March, 1929, but she will long be remembered for the poem which "voices for millions their loftiest ideals of patriotism." (And many believe that "America, the Beautiful" should have been selected as our national anthem instead of "The Star-Spangled Banner.")

Covert and Lawfer in their *Handbook to the Presbyterian Hymnal* pay this tribute to "America, the Beautiful":

This is not only one of the most popular, but also one of the most beautiful of our patriotic hymns. It is patriotism at its best. . . . The last stanza gives an exalted picture of the dream of the patriots and of the nobler, freer, and more brotherly America for which every true patriot longs and prays.

It would no doubt warm the heart of Miss Bates to know that each morning, far out on the Pacific Coast, while the "Red, White and Blue" banner ascends the flag pole, the grounds of Taft Junior College echo with the sounds (played on the campus chimes) of her hymn, while these young Americans re-affirm their patriotism and their faith in this great land of ours. Surely no one has described it more beautifully than Miss Bates did in her song, "America, the Beautiful."

Helen J. Bean in an article, "America's Mountaintop Hymn," said:

> Katherine Lee Bates put into her song not only a description of what she saw, but also her dream of a great America. . . . Its words are a reminder that we have a hymn dedicated to the greatness of America and to the principles of human liberties and freedom.

America, the Beautiful

Katherine Lee Bates

Samuel A. Ward

1. O beau - ti - ful for spa - cious skies, For am - ber waves of grain, For
2. O beau - ti - ful for pil - grim feet, Whose stern, im - pas - sioned stress A -
3. O beau - ti - ful for he - roes proved In lib - er - at - ing strife, Who
4. O beau - ti - ful for pa - triot dream That sees be-yond the years Thine

pur - ple moun - tain maj - es - ties A - bove the fruit - ed plain! A -
thor - ough-fare for free - dom beat A - cross the wil - der - ness! A -
more than self their coun - try loved, And mer - cy more than life. A -
al - a - bas - ter cit - ies gleam, Un - dimmed by hu - man tears! A -

mer - i - ca! A - mer - i - ca! God shed His grace on thee, And
mer - i - ca! A - mer - i - ca! God mend thine ev - 'ry flaw, Con -
mer - i - ca! A - mer - i - ca! May God thy gold re - fine, Till
mer - i - ca! A - mer - i - ca! God shed His grace on thee, And

crown thy good with broth - er -hood, From sea to shin - ing sea!
firm thy soul in self - con-trol, Thy lib - er - ty in law!
all suc-cess be no - ble-ness, And ev - 'ry gain di - vine!
crown thy good with broth - er -hood, From sea to shin - ing sea!

13

*

"The Lord's Prayer"

Albert Hay Malotte, American organist, composer, and song writer, wrote one of our most cherished compositions when he created the distinctive musical setting for The Lord's Prayer. Once he remarked about it: "It's the most important thing in my life; I feel it is the result of a very deep inspiration. Sometimes I almost think God is back of it."

This versatile musician, Albert Hay Malotte was born in Philadelphia on May 19, 1895. He was of Huguenot ancestry; and it is said that each generation of the family had produced some musicians. The Malottes were religious; grace was said at each meal, and on Sunday attendance at church was customary.

Malotte's father was choirmaster at the Tioga Presbyterian Church. The young son began his musical career in the choir of the St. James Episcopal Church in Philadelphia as a boy soprano soloist. Its director was Dr. W. S. Stansfield, with whom young Albert studied for some time. An English organist, this outstanding teacher realized the boy's possibilities and "took him under his wing."

Malotte always gave his teacher the credit for giving him his musical start, and stated:

He was my teacher in voice, piano, pipe organ, theory, harmony —all the phases of music I could assimilate at that time. In each of our lives, someone influences and affects us in all that we do later. I was fortunate to find such a cultured, distinguished gentleman to guide me.

Malotte said that once, when on a hunting trip in Alaska, he was scouring a slough, hoping to find geese. In this marsh was an intricate maze of channels, and it took some time and hunting to discover the right one. He declared that "discovering Dr. Stansfield was like finding that main channel."

At fifteen, Malotte published his first musical composition. He had a close friendship with Victor Herbert, who cut and corrected some of the youth's early pieces. At the age of sixteen, Malotte wanted to follow a theatrical career and become an actor. However, since he had a desire to see the West, he went instead to Wyoming where he spent some time as a cowboy on a cattle ranch.

Malotte was certainly a many-sided character, for in his younger days he was a prize fighter. Later he loved to joke and brag about one encounter he had with Jack Dempsey, in Memphis, when he was an amateur light-heavyweight. He would chuckle heartily, then tell that after the brief encounter the champion threw his arms around the young fighter's shoulders, danced to his corner and swung out of the ring. Albert followed him on "rubber legs," and afterward ruefully said: "That exhibition bout almost finished me! It did finish my boxing career."

In spite of making some sidetracks, Malotte became an accomplished organist and decided to make this his life profession. Returning to the East, he played in several movie theaters. During the winter season of 1926, he was concert organist at the Plaza Theater in London. He also studied in Paris with Georges Jacob.

This young musician had a decided case of wanderlust, and by the time he was twenty, in 1915, he had played his way around the globe. He had traveled through Central and South America, visited seventeen European countries, and had seen the important places of the Orient.

For some years he made a living as an organist before beginning his composing career in earnest. He did some light operas, piano solos, and scores for various musical pieces, before going out to Hollywood. Up to this time his works included two popular songs, "For My Mother" and "The Song of the Open Road," which had soon become a favorite number with singers all over the country.

In his leisure time, Malotte wrote (while earning his living as an organist and recording artist) the original music for two ballets, unusual works for an organist. These compositions were *Carnival in Venice* and *Little Red Riding Hood*. They were staged in Hollywood Bowl in 1934 by the noted Ernest Belcher. The audiences were delighted and there were loud calls for the composer, but Malotte (who was sitting in the back row) did not respond. He didn't want to be seen as there were big holes in his shoes.

This was quite a lucky break for him, and it was because of his ballet *Little Red Riding Hood* that he attracted the attention of Walt Disney. The musician became a member of the staff at the Disney Studio, where he remained for four years. There he wrote and directed his own musical scores for about eighteen *Silly Symphonies; Ferdinand, the Bull; The Ugly Duckling;* and also for several feature productions. Thirty of his songs were published by Schirmer's.

Since Malotte had been reared in a religious family, he had long been familiar with the words of the Lord's Prayer. Someone remarked that the prayer had been solace for him "through all his ups and downs." Once, as many other boys have done, young Albert ran away from home. Finally he sent his father a message, asking for forgiveness, and also for money to pay for the return fare.

He was on a train bound for home after receiving a loving message and the necessary railway fare. One writer says that it was on this journey that young Malotte actually began to compose the musical setting for the Lord's Prayer. And it is inferred that he kept repeating the words in rhythm with the noise of the wheels; also that he compared the Heavenly Father with his earthly one who so graciously had forgiven him and urged him to return home.

During the following years the words were with him continually. He made five round trips across the Atlantic and on shipboard exulted in the strong winds and heavy seas. He would stand in the bow of the ship, with the wind and rain on his face, and repeat the words of the prayer. And it was this same repetition that helped him earn his flying license when he made his first solo flight, in 1921, in a two-seater Boeing.

After the musician had become a successful composer in Hollywood, he felt again the urge to write a musical setting for the Lord's Prayer. Years before he had worked out the chords and harmonies for it. Now the melody also began to shape itself.

One day Albert telephoned his friend, Conway Tearle, and asked him, "What would you think if I wrote music for the Lord's Prayer?" The latter seemed a bit doubtful, but the composer insisted that he really must do it. "I feel so grateful to God," he added. He did not know if it had ever been done before, but he knew he had a real compulsion to do this work. (Someone has said that Schirmer's, the great music house, had already published eighteen versions of "The Lord's Prayer," but none had been successful or popular.)

One day as Malotte was walking down a street in Hollywood, he saw an open church door. It was the most natural thing in the world for him to enter the sanctuary. There he dropped down on his knees and prayed reverently for guidance in his work. "Hallowed be Thy name; Hallowed be this music for Thee," he chanted.

Then at his parents' home in 1935, Malotte spent hours of intense work. He allowed no distractions until he had completed the setting, in which "every bar expressed the depth of his worship." Finally when he had at last completed the score, he called in his father and mother who had taught him the Lord's Prayer in his early childhood.

Malotte played the melody and sang for his parents the immortal words which Christ, centuries before, had given the world from a hilltop in Galilee. A long silence followed his presentation. Then both his father and mother threw their arms around him; they were so moved, they could not speak.

The next decision the composer had to make was who would introduce the new composition. Some months before, he had met the noted baritone and opera star John Charles Thomas. The latter had sung Malotte's "Song of the Open Road" and was delighted with it. The result was that the two had become close friends.

At once the musician mailed the manuscript to Thomas, then vacationing in Florida. The singer was enthralled by the piece, and made arrangements to sing it on the radio on a national hookup. Immediately he wired his friend Albert about his plans. So at a designated time the composer and two friends listened as Thomas, in his rich, full voice, sang to the world for the very first time the inspiring and beloved Lord's Prayer set to Malotte's music.

The baritone was so taken by its beauty that he sang it many times, endearing it to the hearts of people everywhere. "It has remained there ever since, wafting again and again the longings of a soul to the Almighty." In 1939, at Carnegie Hall, New York, Malotte accompanied Thomas in a recital of his own songs. Once when he was asked why he had set the Lord's Prayer to music, the composer replied, "You can't answer a question like that intelligently—it came from within."

One source has asserted that the Lord's Prayer can also be called the Disciples' Prayer, for Jesus gave it to his disciples as a proper and fitting sort of petition. It embodies those qualities which Christ believed a prayer should have: "It recognizes the greatness and majesty of God, and it pleads for His kingdom to come. It also asks for the forgiveness of sins and for spiritual and physical help."

That Malotte's setting is "manly" music is stressed by one writer. This explains why it is at its best when performed by a male voice. However, the composer, "a robust mystic," also finds God in ethereal things: "the fragile petal of a pale-blue flower, the gray mists overhanging the hills, the splendor of a red-gold sunset. . . ."

"The Lord's Prayer," with its outstanding setting by Malotte, has been heard in millions of homes and churches; it continues its phenomenal popularity after more than thirty years. Today it is heard more than ever at church services.

Malotte was a prolific and versatile composer, with more than eighty published compositions to his credit. They vary greatly; for example, the scores for Disney productions are quite a contrast to his religious pieces.

The latter include settings for the Twenty-third Psalm, the Beatitudes, Psalm 91, and an oratorio, *The Voice of the Prophet,* containing passages from the works of several Old Testament seers. The last-named was played by the Los Angeles Philharmonic with a full symphony orchestra and a chorus of 160 voices. Another of Malotte's works is *The Sound of the Trumpet,* based on the life and work of Jeremiah.

While "The Lord's Prayer" is no doubt this composer's best-known work, he was not primarily a composer of religious music, although it had been an important part of his life ever since his childhood days as a choir boy in Philadelphia. Among his late scores for movies were *The Big Fisherman, The Enchanted Forest,* and *The Lady and the Tramp.*

Among other compositions was the song "Brotherhood," chosen in 1951 by the National Conference of Christians and Jews to be used in connection with nationwide observance of Brotherhood Week. Another work was the music for *If Thy Light Be Darkness,* a play by Phyllis Benbow Beardsley. This was intended for performances in Protestant churches across the United States and tells the story of man's struggle to find his faith.

During the last years of his life, Malotte, who believed he did his best work when free from outside influences, was a free-lancer. He lived and worked in his home in Hollywood; forty-three steps and a winding road led up to it. Often, it is claimed, he would brood over an idea for months or even years. Then after writing fourteen or fifteen drafts, he would burn them.

Once for several months, Malotte worked on a play, *The Legend of the Mesa,* his first attempt in this medium. In it he tried to stress not merely the importance of tolerance, but of a respect for the beliefs of others. The writer did this by showing the simplicity and beauty of the faith of the Hopi Indians. It all came about because of an unfriendly glare which had been directed at Malotte and his wife while traveling in Arizona. The former related the incident:

> We were driving east, and stopped about sundown at Winslow. I parked our new convertible and noticing an Indian sitting on the corner watching us, I carefully locked the glove compartment and everything before we left the car.
>
> As we passed this man, I happened to look into his eyes. What I saw there was hatred of generations of Indians for whites. It affected me deeply and I can still clearly see his face.
>
> This play resulted. I hope and pray it will bring about a fuller, better understanding of white people for Indians, and a greater respect for their beliefs.

After this experience, he wrote a synopsis of the play and returned to Arizona. There he found both whites and Indians friendly to him personally, but the latter at first seemed indifferent to his basic idea. Malotte knew he needed to spend much more time there so that he would understand those people well enough to write about them.

Through friends at Winslow, Albert met the chief snake priest of the Hopis and other tribal leaders. Later he stated that as soon as the natives realized he was "a human being," they all got along well together. He saw their dances in ceremonial dress and became well acquainted with Hopi customs and their way of life.

Later on, the writer invited a Hopi to come to Hollywood where he had him record several important Hopi songs. And he put into his play the many things he had learned by living among the Hopis. He declared: "I hope it will be received by the Hopi people—if they ever see it—so that they are glad they offered me their friendship."

During his last years, Malotte continued to study and write various works, known for their "perfection and craftmanship." It is said that his own voice studies had given him a greater knowledge and understanding of the problems singers have to meet in their profession. His wife, Marguerite, shared in his achievements. "We are extremely happy . . . or I couldn't spend twelve to fourteen hours a day composing," he said quietly.

Even though Malotte is no longer alive (he died in 1964), the "melody lingers on" of "The Lord's Prayer," a work that has touched the hearts of countless numbers of people of varied ages and religious faiths. It has been sung in churches, synagogues, at political meetings, etc., and whistled on the street by a bootblack. And, without doubt, it will continue to live as long as men appreciate inspiring music and feel the need of spiritual communication.

14

*

"God Bless America"

The noted American song writer Irving Berlin has been producing successful compositions for more than half a century. It is claimed that he played the leading role in the evolution of the popular song from early ragtime to jazz. Many of his best-loved pieces, such as "Always" and "All Alone" are just simple melodies filled with tender sentiment. His greatest tribute to American music has been stated by one authority in this way: "He gave a new direction to the popular song—away from the set formula, and toward greater freshness and originality." And Irving Berlin's patriotic song, made popular on the radio by Kate Smith, has taken a firm hold on the hearts of countless Americans. This is his enduring and beloved "God Bless America."

Irving Berlin was born Israel Baline on May 11, 1888, in Temun in Siberian Russia. His father, Moses Baline, served as cantor at their synagogue but had a difficult time trying to support his wife and nine children—eight boys and one girl. In their district, Jews were often persecuted; Cossacks swept down on the village, bringing with them destruction and death.

Cantor Baline heard from relatives in the United States that he and his family would have a much better chance of making a living in the New World. The mother was especially eager to emigrate to America so that their children could get an education, and thus have a better life.

On an unforgetable day in the year 1892, when Irving Berlin was just a small boy four years old, a band of roving Cossacks descended on Temun. They killed or injured many Jews and ransacked their synagogue. The Baline family fled from their home and hid on the outskirts of the town, from where they saw their house burned to the ground. Following this terrible incident, Moses Baline knew he and his wife and family must leave Russia.

They were finally able to make their way to New York City, where relatives met them. Their first miserable home was a dark, crowded basement. Some time later, the Baline family was able to move to a less crowded flat in a very poor neighborhood on the Lower East Side of New York. Here over half a million persons lived in dreadful conditions.

The bewildered father was appalled by their surroundings—"the crowded slums, abject poverty, and the exploitation of labor." Often he wondered why he had left his old home in far-off Russia. In New York he found the prices of everything excessively high and living conditions unbearable. Even though he had managed to secure several jobs, such as cantor, meat inspector, and teacher of Hebrew to Jewish children, he had a difficult time providing for his large family. So Irving Berlin's early days were spent in dire poverty.

All the youngsters had to help by selling papers or working in sweat shops. Naturally their education was neglected. This caused the parents much grief for they felt that their children had little hope of a better life.

In 1896 Moses Baline died—a saddened and disillusioned man—baffled by the strange environment into which he had brought his young family. The mother did her best to hold them together. In the evening each child passed by her and threw into her lap the small coins he had earned that day at various jobs.

Irving was able to attend school only two weeks during his childhood. He helped the family by selling newspapers on the Lower East Side. But the family disliked one way he had of adding to the needed income, so he did not feel comfortable at home.

He had a sweet voice and enjoyed walking past the cafés and saloons in Chinatown. When he stopped and sang a song before one of them, customers threw pennies to him. Irving tried to explain to his mother just what he really was trying to do: to get acquainted with some one who might help him get a job singing in a theater. But she was horrified at the idea of his making money by singing "common songs" in saloons.

After thinking it over, the youth decided to leave home without telling the family, and try to become "a singing troubadour." The first night away he slept under a staircase, and next morning began his search for work.

Along the Bowery, young Irving heard that a blind singer named Sol needed a guide. For some time the boy took him into saloons, then gathered the coins after the blind man had performed. The first day Berlin earned twenty-five cents; later when he sang with the older man, he received as much as fifty cents a day. This was enough to pay for a cheap bed and some food. Afterward he had other work, and for some time managed to exist by his own efforts.

In 1906, at eighteen, he got his first real and permanent job as a singing waiter in Pelham's Café, in the heart of Chinatown. This was owned by a Russian, Mike Salter. The place, opened in 1905, had a free-lunch counter and was quite popular; even celebrities visited it at times. Young Irving's work was to clear tables, and after closing he had to sweep the sawdust floor. His salary was small but steady. Best of all, each evening the young singer had the chance to entertain the patrons with popular songs.

The pianist at Pelham's was Nick Nicholson. Once when the Prince of Battenberg came to the restaurant, the drinks were all on the house. The distinguished visitor told Irving he had enjoyed his music and offered him a $5 bill. But the youth refused it. As a consequence the incident reached the press, and for the first time in his life the young man saw his name, "Israel Baline," in print.

An important thing occurred at Pelham's that influenced him greatly. The pianist had written a melody for which Irving wrote the words. This became the song, "Marie from Sunny Italy." When the piece was published by Joseph Stern & Company, his assumed name, "Irving Berlin," made its first appearance on the cover. From it he realized exactly thirty-seven cents. But he was pleased that he had a published song even though it was not a great success.

One day when Berlin was caught sleeping at his work, he was promptly fired. Luckily he soon had another job as a singing waiter, at Jimmy Kelly's café in Union Square, not far from Tony Pastor's Music Hall. While employed at Kelly's, he kept on writing lyrics; his second song was "Queenie, My Own." The melody was written for him by a pianist who just happened into the saloon. A good-hearted owner allowed the budding musician to use an old piano in the rear of his place. There Irving would work out his compositions. He could not read music, or play except in the black keynote of F.

One day his mother surprised him while he was working there. She had been looking everywhere for him and begged him to return home. Mrs. Baline promised she would no longer interfere with his plans for a musical career; so the son went back to live with her. (In the following years as he prospered, he bought a comfortable home for his mother—with the rocking chair he had promised her in his childhood. When she died, in 1922, he chanted the Kaddish for her as he had promised years before.)

In those days before radios or television sets, songs became known and popular by being plugged at different places. Berlin was paid $5 a week by Harry Von Tilzer, a Tin Pan Alley composer and publisher. From the balcony of Tony Pastor's, he would sing the chorus of the piece just performed by a vocalist.

One day a song-and-dance man asked Berlin to write an amusing ditty in Italian dialect, for which he would pay him $10. There was an Italian marathon runner, Dorando, who had been defeated by an Indian. Irving used this incident as his theme for the piece, "Dorando." When the singer refused to take it, the young writer sold it to Ted Snyder's publishing house for $25. This song went over well, but some time passed before Berlin had enough self-confidence to write his own melodies.

His next work, "Sadie Salome, Go Home," was a real success and impressed Ted Snyder, who offered him a contract as a lyricist. He not only would receive royalties on his productions, but would have a drawing account of $25 a week. This ended his work as a singing waiter. Then at only twenty-one in 1909, Irving Berlin went confidently into Tin Pan Alley. This New York street, Twenty-eighth Street between Fifth and Sixth avenues, was where most of the leading music publishers were located. It is asserted that Ted Snyder by taking on Berlin changed the entire course of popular music in the United States.

Pure ragtime, some sources say, did not reach New York until World War I. However, almost twenty years before, in the middle of the 1890's, "coon" songs were popular in the metropolis. It is said that the first authentic published piece of ragtime was "Georgia Camp Meeting." This was the work of Kerry Mills, and was later followed by "The Maple Leaf Rag," composed by Scott Joplin.

Irving Berlin was fascinated by this kind of music; and in 1911 it led him to create the most successful song of his early career—"Alexander's Ragtime Band." This introduced and made ragtime popular all over the United States. The composer liked this piece, but felt it had no commercial value as it was in defiance of the years' old tradition of Tin Pan Alley. For up to this time the sentimental ballad was still the most popular type. In this field were four top composers: Harry Von Tilzer ("The Bird in a Gilded Cage"), Ernest R. Ball ("Love Me and the World Is Mine"), Victor Herbert ("In Old New York"), and George M. Cohan ("Give My Regards to Broadway").

However, the public did not agree with Berlin in his opinion about "Alexander's Ragtime Band." The result was that this song "infected the entire country like an epidemic." It was ample proof of the composer's real ability. "Ragtime caught the spirit of the times." Perhaps no other song has ever had so strong an impact on American life. By 1915, over 2 million copies had been sold.

Ballads gradually lost their popularity as ragtime superseded them. The latter also changed dancing customs. The steps were simpler; more people could master them; and dancing was indulged in not only in the evening, but also by day.

"Alexander's Ragtime Band" came about in the following way. Berlin, in 1911, was asked to join the Friars' Club and to make a personal appearance. Some time before, he had created a piece, "Alexander and His Clarinet." He got it out of his files, made a few changes, and renamed it, "Alexander's Ragtime Band." Although it was well received when first sung, it wasn't until a singer named Emma Carus introduced it in Chicago that it really became an outstanding success. Within a year she "had the entire city throbbing to the rhythms of 'Alexander.'" In less than a year, it was "the most widely sung, played, and danced-to song of the period." Also its success brought a flood of ragtime pieces to Tin Pan Alley.

(On February 12, 1924, when Paul Whiteman gave his long-remembered jazz concert in New York, George Gershwin's *Rhapsody in Blue* was heard for the first time and "Alexander's Ragtime Band" was on the same program. And twenty-seven years after it had been written, it gave its name to a moving picture featuring a cavalcade of Berlin songs.)

After this first important success, Berlin produced one song after another. Almost any incident could give him an idea for a lyric. The chance remark of a friend, "My wife's gone to the country," resulted in that long-time favorite of the same name which sold over 300,000 copies. In 1914, the composer went into a new field of activity by writing the complete score for the Broadway musical *Watch Your Step,* starring the popular dancing pair Irene and Vernon Castle.

When World War I threatened and political tensions increased,

Berlin used his compositions to spur patriotism in his fellow Americans and to aid in selling war bonds. On April 2, 1917, President Wilson urged a declaration of war on Germany. The composer's doctor had told him that his chronic nervous indigestion would keep him from Army service. However, the musician was surprised when he was accepted and sent to Camp Upton. There life was quite different from what he had been enjoying.

One day, General J. Franklin Bell called him in to his office and told Berlin he needed about $35,000 for a service center for his men. He asked Irving if he could write and stage an Army show to raise the necessary funds. At once, the composer went to work on the requested production, writing the entire score himself from his own personal experiences in the Army. *Yip Yip Yaphank* opened on July 26, 1918, in New York, at the Century Theater.

He appeared in the performance, sitting before a pail of potatoes, singing "Poor Little Me, I'm a K.P." He was also dragged from his cot and out of the tent by the morning bugle call. So the song, "Oh, How I Hate to Get up in the Morning," became the hit of the entire production. One reporter commented on this successful production: "Thus a little sergeant, drawing $40.00 a month as producer, author, actor, and composer, delivered to General Bell a check, not for $35,000, but for $80,000."

After the First World War was over, Irving Berlin left Ted Snyder, in 1919, to open his own publishing house, which soon was a thriving business. He also drew a salary of $2,000 a week for making personal appearances at vaudeville theaters. One of his loveliest songs, "A Pretty Girl Is Like a Melody," was introduced in the *Ziegfeld Follies*.

With a partner, Sam Harris, Irving Berlin built the Music Box Theater where outstanding *Music Box Revues* were produced; in one of them was his popular piece, "Say It with Music." Productions at this theater attracted great crowds, houses were sellouts, and four productions grossed over $2 million. It was at the Music Box that Grace Moore got her start as an opera singer.

When the stock market crashed in 1929, Berlin's fortune was swept away. At first he became panicky, for he realized now he would have to depend on composition for a living, and he wasn't sure he had enough creative ability left. But fortunately "his fertility was as rich as ever," and in the next decade he wrote *Face the Music, As Thousands Cheer,* and *Louisiana Purchase.*

Irving Berlin had the distinction of not only producing a hit show for World War I, but twenty-four years later he was asked to write another show after we entered the Second World War in December, 1941. At that time he was fifty-three years old, wealthy, and a world-famous composer.

Again he went to Camp Upton, where he spent much time observing life in the second great war. He had an outstanding assistant, Ezra Stone, known to millions as "Henry Aldrich" on the popular radio program. By hard work, they got the production, *This Is the Army,* completed, and on Independence Day, 1942, the first performance was given in New York. Philip Dunning, drama critic for the New York *World-Telegram,* wrote: "There will never be a service show to beat it, and it is doubtful if there will be a Broadway musical presented during the duration that will halfway approach it for sheer entertainment and wallop."

This show had everything: "love, sentiment, broad burlesque, dynamic production features, and nostalgia." In one scene they went back to World War I. Again Irving Berlin was dragged from his bed to sing, "Oh, How I Hate to Get up in the Morning!" Also the number, "This is the Army, Mr. Jones," was a great hit.

The company toured the entire United States with the production as a stage play, and in Hollywood it was made into a movie. Then the troupe went to England, Ireland, and Scotland. Berlin wrote a special number for this trip—"My British Buddy." The tour cleared $350,000 for British charities.

It was the intention to disband the company in London, but the composer begged General Eisenhower to let him take it to the fighting men on the European continent. General Marshall gave the order which permitted the show to move on to Europe. As they went into combat areas, the cast did their best to cheer the men in spite of the grave personal danger.

After going halfway round the world the production visited the Pacific area and Australia. The final performance—after three years and three months—was given on October 22, 1945, in Honolulu. The company had entertained 22 million GI's, and *This Is the Army* contributed over $10 million to Army and Navy welfare funds.

Following the Second World War, Berlin was soon back at work, composing and producing such memorable shows and films as *Top Hat; Annie, Get Your Gun; Call Me Madam; Miss Liberty; Holiday Inn;* and others. It is said he has produced songs and scores for twenty Broadway productions. Some of his most popular pieces include "Remember," "Blue Skies," and the show-stopper, "There's No Business Like Show Business," which has virtually become "the battle hymn of the theater."

Irving Berlin has been called "one of the most original and graceful lyric writers in the song industry." His works have had a continuous and enduring popularity. It is said that he usually writes his lyrics first and then fashions melodies best suited to the words.

Of all the hundreds—some say, a thousand—of songs he has written, the following eight are said to be his own special favorites: "Alexander's Ragtime Band," "I Love a Piano," "Always," "Say It with Music," "A Pretty Girl Is Like a Melody," "Easter Parade," "White Christmas," and "God Bless America."

Berlin, in strong contrast to some of our other composers, has always been well paid financially for his work. His weekly royalty from *Annie, Get Your Gun* was $2,500, while the film, *Easter Parade* netted him $600,000. In his field, he has topped all others in financial returns.

"GOD BLESS AMERICA"

During the 1930's, threats of war were troubling European countries. As a result, more Americans became conscious of their blessings in living in a free nation like the United States.

When Irving Berlin reached New York again in 1938 after a stay in Europe, Kate Smith, the popular radio singer, asked him to write a new patriotic song for her to sing on her Armistice Day program that year. She wanted lyrics that would express the increasing awareness many Americans were feeling about "the glory and grandeur" of their native land.

Berlin, who had been observing at first hand reactions in wartorn Europe, had always strongly expressed his feelings of gratitude toward his adopted country and his pride in her. Therefore he was glad to try to grant Kate Smith's request. For Irving's parents had brought him from a terrible life in Russia to this great country. No one had asked him about his ancestry, but had taken him, Irving Berlin, at his own worth.

At once the composer set to work to create a song that in part, at least, would repay the great debt he felt he owed to the United States. But for some unexplained reason, he could not compose a melody that he thought was suited to his new lyric.

One day, while struggling over the matter, he had a sudden idea. During World War I, he had written a number, "God Bless America," for his show, *Yip Yip Yaphank,* which he had finally decided not to use in the production. He believed then that the song did not suit that occasion; also he thought it would be "gilding the lily" to represent Americans as going off to war singing "God Bless America."

So Berlin had just put the song away in his files, and had forgotten about it until Kate Smith contacted him for a piece suitable for her Armistice Day broadcast. Then he got out "the yellow and frayed manuscript," made a few changes, and handed it over to Miss Smith. He assured her he didn't think it was much, and that maybe it wasn't what she wanted. However, if she could use it, she was welcome to do so. It didn't take her long to read it. She was more than delighted with it and declared that Berlin had written a second "Star-Spangled Banner." When she introduced the new song on the radio, it was an immediate hit. And it is still one of our best-loved patriotic songs, especially popular on our national holidays.

As the Second World War erupted soon afterward, Berlin's song helped to boost patriotic feelings among many citizens. By means of recordings, "God Bless America" was heard in motion picture houses, at various public meetings, and at numerous sports events. It was featured at both presidential nominating conventions in 1939. The following year, 1940, the National Committee of Music Appreciation chose it as the best work of the year. For this fine, rousing song expressed what many Americans were feeling about their native country. When Kate Smith popularized it, it became "something of a national anthem."

In Great Britain, "God Bless America" was sung in preference to "The Star-Spangled Banner" as our true national hymn. (The latter had a third stanza—not usually printed today—in regard to our British foes during the War of 1812. Also there were references in that song to "bombs bursting in air" during time of war.)

Although it is reported that "God Bless America" netted Berlin more than $250,000 in royalties, he refused to capitalize on patriotism; he turned the entire amount over to the Boy Scouts, Girl Scouts, and the Campfire Girls for their character-building projects. The composer is to be honored for thus proving his gratitude to the United States by his generosity, and for giving all of us his most inspiring, patriotic song—"God Bless America."

Berlin has been paid several well-deserved honors. In 1943, for example, the National Association for American Composers and Conductors gave him a citation, declaring he was "the outstanding composer of popular music."

The productions of this master song-maker did not go unnoticed by the government to which he was so devoted. In 1945, for "his unstinted and untiring" devotion to the war effort during World War II, General George Marshall decorated Irving Berlin with the Medal of Merit at the express direction of President Harry S. Truman.

Five years later, on his sixtieth birthday (in 1948), Berlin was honored when a scholarship in his name was set up at the Juilliard School of Music in New York. And in 1954, President Dwight D.

Eisenhower signed a bill authorizing a gold medal for the song writer "in recognition of his services in composing many popular songs, including 'God Bless America.' "

The secret of Irving Berlin's enduring popularity is his priceless gift for creating fresh, simple melodies with appealing lyrics. And "his inexhaustible melodic inventiveness has produced successful songs for over half a century."

He was a close friend of George Gershwin and encouraged the latter in his musical composition. Gershwin once remarked of Berlin: "His songs are exquisite cameos of perfection. Each one is as beautiful as its neighbors. Irving Berlin is America's Franz Schubert."

When the eightieth birthday of Irving Berlin came around on May 5, 1968, he was given a superb salute on the Ed Sullivan television show. As reported by the columnist Earl Wilson, the affair opened with a filmed greeting from President Lyndon B. Johnson. During the show there were tears in the eyes of the noted song writers who had gathered to pay homage to Irving Berlin. Sammy Cahn, the writer of many noted hits, remarked afterward, "Know why we were crying? Because we didn't write those songs!"

And the climax of this tribute to one of America's greatest and most beloved song writers came when Irving Berlin went on stage and sang his incomparable "God Bless America."

15

*

"Ballad of the Green Berets" and Others

From earliest times, music has played a major role during wars. Out of each conflict in which we Americans have engaged, songs have originated which in several cases became immensely popular, and are still sung today. In World War I, it is said that no song achieved greater popularity than the inspiring "Over There."

George M. Cohan, the well-known singer and actor, became quite unhappy soon after the beginning of World War I because he was too old "to join up." However, he at once decided he *could* do something to aid the war effort. He had written a new marching song; so he asked permission to put on a show and sing it for the GI's of Fort Myer near Washington, D.C.

Cohan's request was granted. He walked briskly up on the stage of the recreation room where the soldiers had gathered. Then he asked the men if they'd like to hear a new song never before heard in public. There was not much response, but in spite of this George M. Cohan sang his latest number with all his heart and soul. At its conclusion, the soldiers gave little applause. The result was that the composer thought it was just a "dud" and told his audience: "I guess you're right. That song is just a bugle call. So long now, and God bless you!"

That night, as he went back to his home in New York, Cohan was discouraged. He believed his piece was an absolute failure. Little did the composer know that within a few weeks this same song would be sweeping through the entire United States. And it wasn't until several months later that he learned the reason for the lack of enthusiasm at Fort Myer. The night he had sung there, the soldiers were dead-tired as they had been out all day on a strenuous march. They were so exhausted they could hardly keep their eyes open to say nothing of getting enthusiastic over a mere song.

The composition that had received such a chilly reception at Fort Myer was George M. Cohan's great hit—that stirring number, "Over There," for which he later received a Congressional medal.

Authorities say more songs came out of World War II than from any other conflict in which we have engaged. Every branch of our armed forces had its own individual song. Some used their traditional numbers, while others had new songs composed by noted musicians.

Arthur Loesser's well-known "Ballad of Rodger Young"—so one source states—sets forth our American ideals in war. It tells of the heroic part the average GI played in it. This song praises "a little man" of the infantry, who on an island in the Solomons, gave his life that his company might live on to fight the enemy. Therefore, this is

. . . a paean of praise, not to any one man, but to all the little men in the war—the little men who in Europe and in the Pacific plowed their way through mud, pain and death to give our country the victory.

"Praise the Lord and Pass the Ammunition" originated with Rev. William Maguire. As bombs were falling on Pearl Harbor, the priest looked up and shouted the never-to-be-forgotten words to the GI's. This stirring order inspired the song, and in the early days of World War II it was set to music. This unusual composition "gave hope and courage when hope and courage were needed the most."

In May, 1954, Governor Goodwin Knight of California met at Anaheim, California, with military heroes, many Navy chaplains (come to honor their former comrade), and about 25,000 citizens. The occasion was a memorial service for Father William Maguire. Among the notables present from Hollywood were Maureen O'Hara, Tyrone Power, Janet Leigh, Leo Carrillo, and Loretta Young. For some time before his death, the gallant priest had served as chaplain at St. Catherine's Military School in Anaheim. During the memorial service, a squadron of Navy planes flew overhead, two hundred cadets from the school marched with their band, and Governor Knight paid a fine tribute to the beloved chaplain. The event also was a fund-raising affair to provide a suitable memorial for Father Maguire.

After 1908 "The Caissons Go Rolling Along" was the official Army song for many years. It had been written by Brigadier-General E. L. Gruber. As the Army wanted a newer and more suitable song, they initiated several contests. For over twenty years they tried to find a suitable replacement but without success. Finally the field commanders were asked which one they preferred, and "Caissons" was the winner.

Word was sent out asking for new lyrics to the old tune. One hundred and forty sets came in. "The Army Goes Rolling Along" was chosen, and it became official on November 11, 1956.

The song "Marching Along Together" attained great popularity during the Second World War. It was written by Franz Steiniger, a native of Vienna, Austria, and a godson of the noted Franz Lehar. The composer now lives in Hollywood, California. He is a conductor and has created pieces for motion pictures.

His march is still popular around the world after more than thirty years. Steiniger wrote the music, but the lyrics were the work of a Britisher named Eddie Pola. The song was introduced here by

Kate Smith. It received much acclaim and was recorded by many orchestras, including that of Paul Whiteman. "Marching Along Together" is said to have been President Franklin D. Roosevelt's favorite march. It became the theme song of the Women's Army Corps (WAC's); and it was featured on many stage and radio shows.

Tedd Thomey, a *Press-Telegram* reporter, said that one day when Franz Steiniger was playing in a Long Beach café, listeners asked him to play his "Marching Along Together." At the conclusion of the number, a stranger asked him if he *really* had written the march.

When Steiniger said it was his own composition, the man shook his hand and told the composer the story of how his work actually had saved his life and those of several comrades. They were on Leyte in the Philippines during World War II. He and a dozen other Americans had been cut off behind the enemy lines. They had floundered through the jungle for several days. Some of their number had been killed; others, wounded. The soldiers were so exhausted that they were ready to give up the difficult struggle.

Suddenly one GI began to sing "Marching Along Together," and at once the others joined in. Then they started to move more rapidly through the jungle. The ex-soldier told Steiniger: "It was a miracle. Your song saved all our lives. It lifted our morale so high that we broke back through the lines and rejoined our regiment. . . ."

Strange to say, no songs came out of the Korean conflict. And though there have been numerous compositions protesting our involvement in Vietnam, no songs in praise of our men fighting there were written until recently. Then Staff Sergeant Barry Sadler of the United States Special Forces produced his inspiring "Ballad of the Green Berets." One writer, Linda Mathews, said that few war songs have gained recognition in recent years: "But S/Sgt. Barry Sadler, who could not even read music, has gotten the most mileage out of the Vietnam War."

This song writer was born in Carlsbad, New Mexico, on November 1, 1940. After his father's death, Barry and his brother wandered through several western states with their mother. Once the sergeant stated he had lived in perhaps twenty-five different towns. One year he attended seven or eight schools, but he dropped out of school at fifteen when he was in the tenth grade.

At seventeen, the young boy decided to enlist in the Air Force and his mother had to give her consent. He was accepted at Denver, Colorado, in June, 1958. He was sent to Lackland Air Base near San Antonio, Texas, and there received training in radar. Sadler spent his eighteenth birthday in Tokyo after he was shipped to Japan. He became expert in karate and earned the black belt in judo.

From his childhood on he had enjoyed listening to music, and in his traveling around the Southwest he had had ample opportunity to hear western and Mexican songs. In the Air Force he learned to play the guitar, and after his enlistment was over, he and a drummer buddy formed a combo with a Negro piano player. They tried to make a living playing anywhere they could. But this didn't prove successful financially, so Barry Sadler decided to re-enlist— this time in the Army.

In his leisure time in the Army, he enjoyed strumming his guitar and making up words to go with tunes he improvised as he went along. Often he would finish a song in ten or fifteen minutes, and later he would try to polish it up a bit. Barry would say to a buddy, "Just give me a subject." At once he'd start to play and sing, and in no time at all he had concocted another number.

He himself describes his pieces as "kind of intermediate between ballad and country-western, with maybe a little calypso." The sergeant said he began to write his own songs because he had a hard time trying to play other people's music. His first audiences were his fellow GI's in the barracks. They liked his songs and encouraged him in his efforts.

Back in the service Sgt. Sadler volunteered for the Airborne Unit as a paratrooper, and began work just after New Year's Day,

1963. From this he went into the United States Special Forces—
"The Army's elite Green Berets." He had his training at Fort
Bragg, North Carolina, at the John Fitzgerald Kennedy Special
Warfare Center. President Kennedy visited Fort Bragg to inspect
the training of the Green Berets, and was more than pleased with
what he saw there. He gave this outstanding group a big boost and
told the men to wear their green berets proudly as "a mark of
distinction and badge of courage."

After eleven months of diverse and strenuous training, Sadler
passed all the tests and won the right to wear the coveted green
beret. As a combat medic he received special training at Brooke
Army Hospital and the Medical Center at Fort Sam Houston.

The highly trained Green Berets specialize "in guerilla fighting
and they proudly wear their hard-won insignia, the green beret." In
1962 these men were the first Americans to be in combat in
Vietnam. They go out on missions of counter-insurgency and work
directly with the South Vietnamese soldiers. Besides doing guerilla
warfare, they also start "civic-action programs to help improve their
[the Vietnamese] standards of living."

The Green Berets also set up camps along infiltration routes and
train the Vietnamese to watch for enemy activity. Sometimes they
attack small enemy groups that manage to enter the country. The
Special Forces carry on military activities behind enemy lines, such
as demolition and fighting in the jungles and mountains.

A book reviewer, Bill Slocum, in speaking of Robin Moore's
The Green Berets said: "The Special Forces Fellows are the finest
fighting men—and men—that we have anywhere. Robin Moore,
who fought with them, gives a wonderful picture of their terrifying
work." Robin Moore trained with the group at Fort Bragg and also
engaged with them in hand-to-hand fighting in Vietnam. On the
jacket of his book is the unidentified photograph in color of Barry
Sadler. In *Green Berets* the men are praised as "fantastic fighters"
who . . . tangle with women spies, traitors, torturers, bandits
and tribesmen. . . ."

Another writer, Peter Derrig, in his book, *The Pride of the Green Berets,* tells of the experiences of a Captain Cunningham and his Special Forces team as they hunt the Viet Cong in the jungles. The jacket carries this paragraph:

> The Green Berets are America's greatest fighting guerillas, especially trained for all-out war, dedicated to total victory. And they hunger to win that victory—despite the cruel cunning of the Viet Cong, restraints imposed by the Pentagon, and the undependable fighting spirit of their Vietnamese allies.

Although the exploits of these superb fighting men have been highly appreciated and praised by most Americans, a few have criticized the establishment of what they call "an elite corps of American fighting men." Some have even compared them to Adolph Hitler's S.S. troops. A newspaper publisher, Walter Ridder, reported of one such dissenting group:

> As a necessary adjunct of suppressing the American counter-insurgency units, whose trade mark is a green beret, the deluded students and teachers want the "Ballad of the Green Berets" tossed off the air.

Ridder declared that to try to link the United States Special Forces with Hitler's men is ". . . a deliberate distortion and a purposeful twisting of facts, both military and historical." He maintained, too, that the authors of such letters ". . . are engaged in a transparent effort to besmirch the United States effort in Vietnam and to throw the slimiest kind of mud at our fighting men."

This newspaperman also asserted that society has always had "an elite section of men" who do things better than others. As examples he cited the famous Cold Stream Guards in the British Army and the United States Marines. The latter have always regarded themselves as "the elite of the American military services," and no one has ever likened these groups to Hitler's men. Mr. Ridder concluded: "The men with the green berets are performing their difficult and distasteful job with honor. To compare them to the hoodlums of Hitler's S.S. is arrant stuff and nonsense."

After Americans became acquainted with the outstanding work of the Green Berets in Vietnam, it was not surprising that a motion picture was made in their honor, and filmed at Fort Benning, Georgia. This movie, *The Green Berets,* honors the United States Special Forces. An advertisement for it contained these words: "They had to be the toughest fighting force on earth . . . and the men who led them had to be just a little bit tougher."

On July 4, 1968, John Wayne and David Janssen, the stars of the movie, were honorary marshals of the annual Fourth of July "Salute to America" Parade in Atlanta, Georgia. While the two actors received loud cheers from the spectators, "the loudest outbursts from an estimated 250,000 was for the stern-faced soldiers in combat garb."

There were some attempts to block this procession by "about twenty hippie-type demonstrators," but they had to give up the attempt when "several huge Army earth-moving machines lumbered their way." However, two antiwar pickets did manage to get into the line. They were carrying a sign reading WAR AT ANY PRICE.

At the premiere of the *Green Berets,* John Wayne was greeted by a large crowd. In his speech he declared: "We hear there are a lot of things wrong with America. Critics seem to forget there are a million things right about America." The actor also designated the Fourth of July ". . . as a day to stop crying about what's wrong and to start thinking about what's right."

While the performance was going on, anti-war adherents paraded up and down outside the theater in Atlanta. In some other places there were also objections to the picture. *The Green Berets* received varied criticisms from reviewers. An article in *Time* contained this statement:

> In his own blunderbuss way, John Wayne has tried to make the war comprehensible. But except for the technical excellence of a few

gory, glory-hallelujah battle scenes, *Green Berets* is strictly for the hawks.

An interesting report came from Japan, where John Wayne's movies have long been popular. *Green Berets* drew great numbers in Tokyo; many in the audience were young people of the age that protests the war in Vietnam. In a Japanese magazine, *Shukah Ashahi,* the reviewer, Jun Izawa, declared that while the movie was in bad taste, the theaters never had had it so good. "And this in the midst of anti-Vietnam War campaigns by students and unionists." (However, his article also stated that the Japanese go in large numbers to view propaganda films from North Vietnam, and also eagerly attend performances of the Red Chinese "cultural troupes" that visit Japan.)

When *The Green Berets* was first shown in Atlanta, John Wayne presented the commander of the Special Forces with a seven-foot memorial weighing two and a half tons. It was sculptured by the Jones Brothers of Barre, Vermont.

This depicts an engraving of the famous beret worn by the Special Forces; below it is the United States emblem and the Green Beret crest and at the bottom is the Special Forces shoulder patch. The inscription reads:

> IN TRIBUTE TO THE MEN OF THE
> GREEN BERET, UNITED STATES
> ARMY SPECIAL FORCES, WHOSE
> VALIANT EXPLOITS WILL EVER
> INSPIRE MANKIND.

While training as a combat medic at Brooke Army Hospital and Medical Center at Fort Sam Houston, Barry Sadler met his future wife, Lavona Edelman, of Lehighton, Pennsylvania. As a WAC, she was training for operating room nurse. Following a five weeks' courtship they were married on July 18, 1963. Their son was born on December 3, 1964, just before the sergeant had to leave for Vietnam.

While serving his own comrades in Vietnam, Sadler also helped sick natives. In his own words, he did "anything from treating insect bites to delivering babies for villagers." One day, while leading a patrol of native tribesmen, Montagnards (mountaineers), from a camp southeast of Pleiku, in the Central Highlands of Vietnam, the sergeant stepped on a razor-sharp bamboo stick, or punji pole, left in a pit by the Viet Cong. He tried to clean the wound; then went on to finish his patrol duties.

Back in the camp, the wound developed a massive infection, and also his left leg was partially numb. He soon discovered that his Green Beret days were over. He was sent to Clark Field Hospital in Manila for treatment. One day an officer visited him and gave him this piece of news: "Sergeant Sadler, you're going home; you're a lucky man!"

After reaching the United States, he was given a desk job (still wearing his green beret) at Fort Bragg, North Carolina, where he had received his intensive training. There he finished his period of enlistment, which ended in the spring of 1967.

Of course he could no longer do parachute jumping; however, after his leg was better he taught some hand-to-hand fighting. He was also kept busy with recruiting, speaking, and singing at patriotic meetings all over the United States and in the Canal Zone. He has shared the platform with Vice-President Humphrey and many other civic and military V.I.P.'s. But after his nine years in the Air Force and the Special Forces, Barry Sadler hated to leave the service where he had had so many unusual experiences.

In 1967, the Macmillan Company published Barry Sadler's autobiography as told to Tom Mahoney. It is entitled *I'm a Lucky One* and is "a uniquely American story" of "an uncommon young man" in his twenties who managed to pack "a heap of living" into a short period of time.

The book gives a fascinating picture of the training and combat experiences in the United States Special Forces—the "Green Beret way of fighting in Vietnam." Sadler says that he wrote many of his songs for the buddies who did not return and at the end of the book he lists their names. On the jacket of *I'm a Lucky One* are these words: "The soldier who wrote 'The Ballad of the Green Beret' tells what it's like to train in today's Armed Forces, to fight as a Green Beret and to strike it rich as a balladeer."

As mentioned earlier, Sadler delighted in playing his guitar and improvising songs. One day, so the story goes, a soldier who had fought in Korea asked the sergeant why he didn't write a song about his buddies. Barry set to work at once, and in just a few minutes he came up with the first version of his greatest hit—"The Ballad of the Green Berets."

As time passed more stanzas were added, one by Robin Moore. In this song Sadler pays tribute to the unique achievements of "the fearless men" who wear "silver wings upon their chests." The final stanza of the recorded version is of a young wife whose Green Beret will not return to her. But his final message to her was to put silver wings on their son's chest—"Make him one of America's best."

In 1963 Sergeant Sadler mailed $3 to Washington and got his ballad copyrighted. He kept on writing other pieces about his buddies, and made some tape recordings which he sent to New York, but without success. The next year a Lieutenant Gittell tried to interest music publishers in Barry's works.

In 1965, in Saigon, the sergeant was asked to make a tape of "The Ballad of the Green Berets," and also to write a song about General Delk, known as the "Flying General."

When the song writer was back in the United States after his stay at the hospital in the Philippines, he continued to try to arouse interest in getting his compositions published.

Finally his long-continued efforts were rewarded. In 1965 the R.C.A. Victor Company asked him to make a record of "The Ballad of the Green Berets," and also to record an album with twelve tunes. One source stated that the sergeant records his songs in "a lack-luster tenor . . . with a backing of R.C.A. trumpets or fiddle and humming voices," singing such pieces as "Here's the Mail That Came Today" or other songs connected with ordinary incidents in the life of a Green Beret soldier.

The recording came out on January 1, 1966, and was an immediate success as was the album that followed. At once Barry Sadler was in great demand for personal appearances to feature his compositions on top television shows. It is stated that within three months "The Ballad . . ." had sold over 2 million copies, and that Sadler had received two gold records on one show. Innumerable copies of the sheet music, piano rolls, and tapes have also been purchased.

Many other singers besides the composer have recorded "The Ballad . . ." and other of Sadler's pieces, and they have been played by leading orchestras. The noted conductor Arthur Fiedler opened his first 1966 program of the celebrated Boston Pops Orchestra by playing "The Ballad of the Green Berets." For this special occasion, the affable conductor wore a green beret.

Sergeant Sadler and his wife are now "fixed for life." They paid off their mortgage and bought a color television set. It is admirable the way the young soldier has taken his stupendous success; for he is extremely modest about his unusual achievements. He stated that he could buy a three-story house if he wanted to, but said this may be "a flash thing" and people may forget him after a couple of years. He added: "I hope I have enough character not to let this thing blow my head out of proportion."

Perhaps the most noteworthy thing the young song writer has done is to set aside a percentage of his income to establish the Barry Sadler Fund to provide full college scholarships for children of deceased or disabled veterans. At the close of his book, *I'm a Lucky One,* he expresses the hope that others will join him in aiding this worthy project.

The veteran of the Special Forces also has the hope for his ballads that ". . . many years from now these songs . . . will be recalled as a true expression of the Vietnam combat soldier's feelings during the time of that fierce encounter."

Henry Belk, editor of the Goldsboro, North Carolina, *News-Argus,* predicted in 1967 a long life for "The Ballad of the Green Berets" and pays the song this tribute:

> Sadler's ballad is the one song which has come out of the war in Vietnam which will live. . . .
>
> World War I had a flowering of popular songs which still thrill the gray-haired men of that period, and indeed touch a spot in the hearts and minds of men of later generations.
>
> Sadler's "Ballad of the Green Berets" sprang full-blown from a lonely heart far from home. It came naturally from the heart of Sergeant Sadler and instantly was a national success. . . . Patriotism, be it said, has no greater stirring of emotion than from the Sadler "Beret" unless it is the National Anthem, or "The Battle Hymn of the Republic." . . .
>
> The Vietnam War has produced a song which will live long. It will live as long as "The Long, Long Trail," "White Christmas" or any other song you can name. . . . Already it has captured the heart of the nation, and is deepening the patriotic feelings of millions. . . . "Ballad of the Green Berets" causes chills to run up and down your spine. It has a mournful note that makes you see and feel war in all its strangeness.

16

*

Some American
Christmas Songs

Comes the merry month of December and "all through the house" we hear from radio, television, or record player the carols that have become more familiar with the passing years. And along our streets, from stores and cafés, our ears are continually assailed by sounds of holiday melodies. Some are new compositions being tried out in the perennial effort to find another lasting best-seller like "Rudolph, the Red-Nosed Reindeer."

Even though we tire of this constant dinning, we love to hear, or join in singing, our beloved favorites—the "glorious carols that have lived on, with increasing favor during the years." For as one writer has said: "The warmth and joy that is Christmas is always greatly magnified by the everlasting beauty and charm of music."

While many of our favorite carols are of foreign extraction, several popular ones did originate in the United States. These include "It Came Upon a Midnight Clear," by Dr. Edmund H. Sears (1810–1876); "We Three Kings of Orient Are," by Rev. John H. Hopkins, Jr. (1820–1891); "I Heard the Bells on Christmas Day," by Henry Wadsworth Longfellow (1807–1882); "There's a Song in the Air," by Josiah G. Holland (1819–1881); "O Little Town of Bethlehem," by Bishop Phillips Brooks (1835–1893); and the popular Negro spiritual, "Go Tell It on the Mountain."

"JINGLE BELLS"

Of the origin of one of our favorite holiday carols, "Jingle Bells," there has long been some doubt. Strange to say, in many song collections it is marked anonymous, or no notation as to the composer is made. However, in the Salem, Massachusetts, *Evening News* of December 24, 1964, there was an article about the origin and composer of this song.

It stated that James Pierpont wrote both the words and the lyrics. He was also the author of other musical pieces, but none ever became so popular as "Jingle Bells." The composer was the son of Rev. John Pierpont, who in 1859 was pastor of the Medford, Massachusetts, Unitarian Church.

Now for many years this "gay and lively tune has been as much a part of the Yule season as the sacred carols known and loved by young and old."

The story goes that during the 1850's young Pierpont called Mrs. Otis Waterman's attention to his song. She was an amateur singer and had a piano in her home—something that was not too usual in those days.

One evening, Pierpont sat down at her instrument, and told Mrs. Waterman he wanted her opinion of a little piece that had been running through his head. After he had played and sung it for her, Mrs. Waterman was delighted with the composition. She called it "a merry little jingle," thus helping the song get its title.

Now more than a century has gone by, and "Jingle Bells" has attained more popularity than its composer ever dreamed. It is a favorite that we love to sing at the holidays, and in some parts of our country, merry sleigh bells still ring out through the crisp air during this happy season.

One writer has said that James Pierpont "was an obscure, otherwise unsuccessful man, whose contribution added much to the festive spirit of Christmas."

Jingle Bells

J.S. Pierpont

1. Dash - ing through the snow in a one - horse o - pen sleigh
2. Day or two a - go I thought I'd take a ride, And
3. Now the ground is white, Go it while you're young;

O'er the fields we go, Laugh - ing all the way,
soon Miss Fan - ny Bright was seat - ed by my side; The
Take the girls to - night, And sing this sleigh - ing song; Just

Bells on bob - tail ring, Mak - ing spir - its bright, What
horse was lean and lank, Mis - for - tune seem'd his lot, He
get a bob - tailed nag, Two - for - ty for his speed, Then

fun it is to ride and sing a sleigh - ing song to night!
got in to a drift - ed bank, and we, we got up - set.
hitch him to an o - pen sleigh, and crack! you'll take the lead.

Chorus

Jin - gle Bells! Jin - gle Bells! Jin - gle all the way! Oh, what fun it is to ride in a

one horse o - pen sleigh! Jin - gle Bells! Jin - gle Bells! Jin - gle all the way!

Oh, what fun it is to ride in a one - horse o - pen sleigh!

"WHITE CHRISTMAS"

When Bing Crosby was asked by a company to make a record of "Adeste Fideles," he thought that since he was only a crooner, it wasn't fitting for him to do so. But he was finally persuaded to make it, and millions have enjoyed his rendition of this Yuletide hymn.

Also, when urged to record "Silent Night," again Crosby was hesitant, believing it didn't really belong in the carol category. However, his chief reason was that he felt it was not right for him to take money for making such a record; he declared it was like "cashing in on the Church or Bible."

Finally, his brother, Larry, suggested a solution; he could set up a fund for children in China who were being cared for at American missions. So for several years the royalties from "Silent Night" were used for this purpose. In addition, during World War II, Larry Crosby used some of the proceeds to finance an entertainment unit that performed for our soldiers at various camps.

But of course the song which to millions really means Christmas is "White Christmas," by Irving Berlin, "which has become a modern Christmas carol by popular acclaim."

Berlin is indeed a versatile lyricist and composer. He wrote not only (in the opinion of many) our best war song, "This Is the Army, Mr. Jones," and its finest patriotic one, "God Bless America," but he also created the most touching sentimental song of the war years—"White Christmas."

According to one source, there was a real revolution in Christmas music, when in 1942 for the first time Bing Crosby sang this composition.

That year Metro-Goldwyn-Mayer bought the song from Berlin; at first he had intended to use it in a Broadway musical show. Instead it was put into the screen play *Holiday Inn,* in which

Crosby and Fred Astaire had the leads. It is said that Berlin had written "White Christmas" while sitting near his swimming pool.

The plot of *Holiday Inn* included a song for each important American holiday, including "Let's Start the New Year Right"; "Abraham" for Lincoln's birthday; the "Easter Parade," from *As Thousands Cheer;* "Song of Freedom" for July 4; "Plenty to Be Thankful For" for Thanksgiving; and "White Christmas."

And of these varied numbers, the last-named was the most popular and an immediate hit. On the first edition of the sheet music scenes from *Holiday Inn* were shown. Now, many years afterward, most Americans would consider our annual Christmas celebration a total loss if they didn't hear or sing this popular holiday classic.

Crosby once commented that he had had something to do with the third Christmas song, "White Christmas," which during the holidays "booms out of department stores over the heads of shoppers and corner Santa Clauses." He likes it because it is truly "a great song with a simple melody." As this Berlin composition was the biggest hit of *Holiday Inn,* it has almost replaced his records of "Adeste Fideles" and "Silent Night." Here is the way Crosby told of the beginning of "White Christmas":

> . . . against a backdrop of artificial snow, I stood beside a comely young lady, named Marjorie Reynolds, and raised my sleepy baritone—unknowingly beginning what has become a kind of Yuletide tradition, along with "Silent Night." The artificial snow blanketed the set for a movie, called *Holiday Inn,* and the song, if you'll remember, was "White Christmas."

Then the famous crooner did a bit of philosophizing about a truly "white" Christmas, and spoke of sharing as revealing the true spirit of the Yule season; and he concluded with these words: "I'd like to see some of this snow of mutual sharing last through the spring, summer, and autumn, too."

When "White Christmas" was released in 1942, most Americans were feeling quite sentimental, for our young men were going off to fight in World War II, in various parts of the world. So the circumstances under which this song was introduced were conducive to its winning immediate and lasting popularity.

During the lengthy conflict, American soldiers in different theaters of war sang this song, some as they fought their way through the jungles on Pacific islands; David Ewen declares that these homesick men ". . . sang 'White Christmas' as they sang no other song, because in singing it, they felt themselves, momentarily, brought a little nearer home."

During this world conflict, Bing Crosby made a tour of several weeks in Europe. Often his troupe gave three shows a day for the soldiers; they visited various hospitals, and helped cheer the wounded. Later the singer declared: "The look on the faces of the men we entertained was better than money from Paramount. . . . My big song was 'White Christmas.' . . . It was a tough song to sing, but it was asked for, wherever I went."

This touching, distinctive ballad sold more than 2 million copies in its first year. It is one of Irving Berlin's most well-loved and successful songs. During this period the same number of records was purchased; by the end of its fifth year, three times as many were bought.

Even though "White Christmas" was composed over twenty-six years ago, it is said that today it is still the favorite Yule composition. In 1963, *Variety* stated: " 'White Christmas' is probably the most popular of any song copyright in the entire world."

One source reports that Irving Berlin once said he would not take "seven figures" for the copyright. Since it came out in 1942, it has averaged between 115,000 and 125,000 sales of copies of the sheet music annually and has been translated into nine other languages. Including instrumentals, about 6 million copies have been bought. A few years ago it was said that more than 21 million recordings had been purchased. In 1968 it was reported that Bing Crosby holds the record for the biggest sale of a single record—16 million copies of Irving Berlin's "White Christmas."

Even though some may look upon "White Christmas" with a bit

of disdain and term it a tear-jerker, it is said to cause even the most hardened traveling salesman (away from his home and family at the holidays) to have a case of the sniffles. The ballad retains its immense popularity, and is heard in lands around the globe. And to the countless people who sing the familiar words, "I'm dreaming of a white Christmas," many cherished memories of past holidays become vivid again.

"RUDOLPH, THE RED-NOSED REINDEER"

Then, in 1949, like a bolt from a clear sky, came that irresistible ditty, "Rudolph, the Red-Nosed Reindeer," written and composed by Johnny Marks. This composition set Tin Pan Alley to work during the following years, trying to produce a rival, or as one writer put it: "All Tin Pan Alley took off on a wild goose chase after Rudolph down the Christmas Sky, trying to find a similar smash."

So, each year, there's a new rash of holiday songs. Here are a few of the many titles: "Santa Claus Is Coming to Town," "Frosty, the Snowman," "How'd You Like to Spend Christmas on Christmas Island?" "All I Want for Christmas Is My Two Front Teeth," "Christmas in Killarney," "I Saw Mommy Kissing Santa Claus," "Silver Bells," "You're All I Want for Christmas," "Winter Wonderland," and "Santa Claus Is Riding Through the Sky."

There have been numerous other American Christmas songs, of varied types; some are serious, many otherwise; in his best Mr. Magoo voice, Jim Backus relates the fervent wish of one husband—at least—that his wife spend the holidays with *her* family so *he* can have a Happy New Year.

Each year thousands of lyrics for holiday songs are sent to the music publishers; but "few are chosen." One authority in this line asserts that it is "the toughest business in the world."

An executive at Capitol Records reported that when the song, "Hang Your Wishes on a Tree" (by Marian Boyle and Eddie Gales) was published, it was the only one of its type selected; it had been chosen from between five hundred and six hundred sent in that season. He said, too, that every publisher is looking for a *big* Christmas song. If a person is lucky enough to write such a composition, "It's just like having an annuity policy."

It is uncertain business backing a new song, and it may take years to get it well established in public favor. It is said that novelties sell better than ballads. This accounts for the long-continued success of such numbers as "All I Want for Christmas . . ." and "Rudolph. . . ."

Therefore it's no wonder that times along Tin Pan Alley are feverish. Song writers are wracking their brains for new ideas, and music publishers and recording firms are hoping one of their writers will come up with a piece that will be a hit at record counters and in juke boxes.

Some years ago Hugh Mulligan wrote: "The tinsel-taunted tunesmiths . . . tantalized by the lingering success of 'Rudolph, the Red-Nosed Reindeer,' as they say in the song, just go nuts at Christmas."

He said they really let their imaginations run wild and turn out impossible creations; they use every possible animal in that kingdom, place them in various climates and impossible situations, in the vain hope that such nonsense ditties will get their efforts "a place in the sun," and like "Rudolph . . ." be heard round the world.

However, despite all these attempts, "Rudolph . . ." each year outsells all others. And no matter where you happen to be on December 25—in Turkey, Tokyo, or Timbuktu—you're sure to hear this ditty.

Perhaps you wish that Santa Claus had bought a space ship, instead of using that timeworn sleigh, drawn by the "eight tiny reindeer" and personally conducted through the fog by a small red-nosed animal. It is stated with authority that some kiddies have actually played this record for fourteen hours straight. The result, in one case at least, was that the distracted father smashed the record with all "the vigor of a Carrie Nation."

The story and song have been translated into many languages; it is known by such names as these: in Madrid, "Rudolfo, el Reno de Nariz Roja"; in Paris, "La Petit Renne su Nez Rouge"; and in Norway, as "Rudolfe, Er Rod Om Malem."

Here's the way the story of Rudolph—and later the song—came about. The book was written by Robert L. May, a graduate of Dartmouth College and a member of Phi Beta Kappa (also the father of six children). He was working in Chicago in the advertising department of Montgomery Ward, and he did this piece for a holiday giveaway.

The whole thing began when, in 1938, May wrote some parodies for an office party given by his firm. Some weeks later his boss called him in; he told him the verses weren't too bad; then he asked him to do a Christmas story to give to their customers when the holiday season came around. This executive made two stipulations to May: At that time the story *Ferdinand, the Bull* was at the height of its popularity; he suggested that May write about an animal; second, that he put it in verse.

At once May set to work; first he read many children's books and thought about them. He decided that a happy ending would be most pleasing to youngsters as would a tale on the order of *The Ugly Duckling* or *Cinderella*.

He admits that the story didn't come to him "in a blinding flash." He finally selected a reindeer as "a natural" for the season; then came the problem of how a small reindeer could become a hero on Christmas Eve. When May suggested that St. Nicholas wasn't powerful enough to get his famous sleigh safely along the airways on Christmas Eve, he was being somewhat daring.

Also when he gave Rudolph his red nose, the boss objected. However, an artist friend went with May to a zoo, where he sketched a picture of a reindeer that actually *did* have such a nose. Therefore, the boss agreed to let the matter stay as the author had planned. When May read the completed poem to the staff, some suggestions for changes were made, but a senior member stood up and "roared approval."

In 1939—and again in 1946—Montgomery Ward gave away a total of 6 million copies of the illustrated booklet about a small animal with a beet-red nose and an inferiority complex.

When May received his copyright on the story, he began to look for a commercial publisher. He contacted Harry Elbaum, who published children's books. This man admitted that all his life he had been teased about his "big, peculiar-looking nose."

Elbaum published May's story, "Rudolph, the Red-Nosed Reindeer," and it sold a million copies during its first year. This number did not include countless coloring and comic books on the same subject.

This was the first money May had ever made outside of his advertising work. The book was, and still is, a best-seller. The writer has been astonished by the way his story "went down in history." For he felt its origin was as casual as that of two other popular Yule songs, "A Visit from St. Nicholas" and "Silent Night."

Then, for the next seven years, May gave all his time to taking care of Rudolph. (Later he returned to Montgomery Ward as editorial director of their catalogue.) A quiet, slender man, with graying hair, he is very grateful to Rudolph, for the little reindeer enabled May to get out of his crowded city apartment. Also he had no financial worries about college educations for his children.

For several years he was kept busy with varied business items in connection with Rudolph. In 1949 there were fifty products involving this reindeer on the market, including radios, flashlights, savings banks, etc. There was a technicolor Rudolph in the movies, a game based on him, and in the Gene Autry program a papier-mâché reindeer with an electrically lighted nose.

One reporter stated that during the period of increasing popularity of the noted animal, May would arrive at home eager to tell of the latest developments in the reindeer business. Finally his children got a bit fed up hearing about such products; for they wanted to tell him about *their* experiences at school and in sports.

Of course, in spite of all this, the May youngsters were happy to move from the old apartment to "the house that Rudolph built." The story goes that when May was overseeing the unloading of the furniture vans at their new home, a small boy came up and called out, "We all know you work for Rudolph," and May had to admit that he really did.

So, it is not surprising that each holiday season, on the lawn of the May home, north of Chicago, there is a flood-lit replica of Rudolph; of course he has a blinking red light for a nose.

When the reindeer was twenty years old, his creator answered a query by saying that Rudolph would never grow up; that he would always stay young, like Peter Pan; for youngsters would much prefer him that way.

In a 1964 interview May declared that while the song had made much money for Gene Autry and Johnny Marks, he himself hadn't fared so well. It was true that he had done nicely the first two years, but taxes took much of his returns.

In the May home are two hand-blown replicas of Rudolph; these are above the mantel in the living room, while in their recreation room are portraits of the animal and reindeer lamps and ash trays. These also picture the noted character that on one foggy night guided Santa's sleigh on a journey into everlasting fame. And May happily declares, "All I know is that he's always been the all-time favorite in our home."

Salvation Army band leaders say that playing "Rudolph, the Red-Nosed Reindeer" "warms up a sidewalk concert" even when "the weather is cold enough to freeze the tambourines." Also, "the loose-limbed set" like the new version, "Rudolph, the Red-Nosed Reindeer Cha Cha."

The famous little animal has been seen in the store windows of many large department stores, and has ridden in parades all over the world. He has also brought much joy to sick children in hospitals at Christmas time.

For example, at a holiday party for the youngsters at the Orthopedic Hospital in Los Angeles (an event sponsored by the Juniors of the League for Crippled Children) Santa Claus brought Rudolph with him, and this visit "put a bright glow on the children's faces."

For in a cage, mounted on a small wagon, was a real deer, just nine weeks old. Of course Santa had a big bag of gifts for the boys and girls; and the cheering presence of Rudolph made this a most successful party.

The man who wrote the popular song is Johnny Marks. He was then a struggling song writer who had composed about 750 songs; however, only a few of them had been published.

One day at a corner newsstand, he ran across a copy of *Rudolph, the Red-Nosed Reindeer*. Mr. Marks declares he was struck at once by the unusual title. Soon he had jotted it down in a small notebook, where he had about three hundred titles which he thought might possibly become songs some day. However, it was several years before he got around to trying to write "Rudolph." Finally, in 1949, after he'd worked a month on it, he completed the job, although he once said he had really spent twenty years preparing to do it.

Marks was so sure this would go over that he borrowed $25,000 and started his own publishing house, which he named "St. Nicholas Music, Inc." An unknown singer, Guy Mitchell, made a demonstration record for him. Then a friend of Marks at Warner Brothers declared it was just the song for Gene Autry.

After the latter had been contacted by Marks, he played the record, was much impressed, but still felt it wasn't for him. But his wife, luckily, helped him change his mind, for she said, "I love that song; you should take a chance on it." Johnny Marks had to wait two months for Gene Autry to decide to make the record, which is still an all-time best-seller among Columbia labels.

The first year—1949—his record of "Rudolph" sold 17 million copies, and 15 million the next. After 1949 there were seventeen other versions made, but in spite of them, the Autry record still sells no less than 150,000 each year.

Whenever a major artist records this song, at least 100,000 copies are purchased annually. By 1959 more than 29 million records of "Rudolph" had been sold and it was really big business. According to one source, it is the biggest holiday hit in the history of song business. It has been recorded by 120 different singers and translated into many other languages, including Russian.

Johnny Marks has written other popular hits, including "When Santa Gets Your Letters," "Rocking Round the Christmas Tree," "The Night Before Christmas Song," and "Everyone's a Child at Christmas." However, he admits that even though he has a Phi Beta Kappa key, it didn't open the door of success until he wrote the song "Rudolph." And he also makes this admission: "I have a constant ringing in my ears—sounds like jingle bells."

In 1959, while sitting in his office high above Broadway at the St. Nicholas Music Company, Marks spoke of the fact that "Rudolph" had passed the sales mark of "White Christmas" and reputedly declared: "I do know that 'Rudolph' flabbergasted me. Thirty-nine new recordings of it this year, over the ten years a total of two hundred."

Now this song, "Rudolph, the Red-Nosed Reindeer," is well established as a worldwide classic. During the first three years of its existence, more than two hundred pieces were written in imitation of it, but not one was a success.

Some time ago Marks decided he would never write another Christmas song. But one day, while reading some of Henry Wadsworth Longfellow's poems, he came across "I Heard the Bells on Christmas Day."

He was much impressed by its semireligious theme and the victory of hope over despair. It haunted him, for he is a person who broods over the way things are going in the world. So Marks set the words of this poem to music; then Bing Crosby made a successful record of "I Heard the Bells on Christmas Day." (A member of a music union, so the story goes, seemed puzzled by the name Longfellow, and called Marks. He said, "We don't find this guy Longfellow in our files.")

While making this recording, Crosby dryly remarked to Johnny Marks: "You had a pretty fair lyric writer on this one." After completing it, the song writer declared: "This is it. I'll never write another Christmas song." But the devotees of Tin Pan Alley remarked: "Christmas is no longer just a holiday for Rudolph's father. It's a life sentence."

One of the chief and most lasting things about "Rudolph" is that, in addition to its clever words and catchy tune, it teaches a subtle lesson. One source has asserted: "Rudolph, the young reindeer, with the bright red nose, which made him an object of ridicule, has become the favorite of young Americans." Because of his unusual nose, poor Rudolph had been shunned and mistreated by the other reindeer. But at last on that foggy Christmas Eve, Santa Claus trusted him, and showed his faith in the small animal's ability. Therefore, he had a chance to prove his talent, and to shed his inferiority complex. One sociologist has said that this song has been "the only major addition to Christmas in this country."

One of the finest things yet written about this noted song is, I believe, the editorial that appeared in *Life* magazine, in January, 1950 (also in *Time*). This really should be broadcast each year, especially in these trying times of racial tension.

RUDOLPH AND THE STINKERS*

Some two million recordings of the song, "Rudolph, the Red-Nosed Reindeer," were sold over the Christmas holidays, and we hope that the little boys and girls who played the record and heard it over and over again on the radio will stop to reflect. The reindeer around Rudolph, so the kids should note, were all too human in their behavior. They discriminated against Rudolph for not being just like every other reindeer in the herd. They called him the reindeer equivalent of wop; they drew the color line against his nose.

Came Santa Claus, a nice old fellow, who had the sense to see that Rudolph had a special gift, his luminous snoot. Santa put the gift to work, guiding his sleigh through the foggy night. In a twinkling, Rudolph became fashionable. Reindeer bigwigs delighted in showing him off at the reindeer equivalent of the Stork Club. The

* Used by permission of *Life* Magazine.

run-of-the-sled reindeer began shouting his praises, not because they really loved Rudolph, but because Rudolph was suddenly a Big Shot.

Ponder the lesson, children, that is here. Kick other people around, just because they're different in some way, and like the mean reindeer, you'll be shown up as a bunch of stinkers. Get that into your noggins and the world will be a better place when you grow up.

Rudolph the Red-Nosed Reindeer

Lyric and Music by
Johnny Marks

Ru-dolph, the red - nosed rein - deer had a ver - y shin - y nose

And if you ev - er saw it, you would ev - en say it glows.

Copyright 1949 by Saint Nicholas Music, Inc.

Bibliography

BOOKS

Bates, Katherine Lee. *America, the Beautiful and Other Poems.* New York: Thomas Y. Crowell Company, 1911.

———. *America, the Dream.* New York: Thomas Y. Crowell Company, 1930.

Bernard, Kenneth A. *Lincoln and the Music of the Civil War.* Caldwell, Idaho: Caxton Printers, 1966.

Boni, Margaret B. *Fireside Book of Favorite Songs.* New York: Simon & Schuster, 1952.

———. *Fireside Book of Folk Songs.* New York: Simon & Schuster, 1947.

Brown, C. A. *Story of Our National Ballads.* New York: Thomas Y. Crowell Company, 1931.

Burgess, Dorothy. *Dream and Deed.* Norman, Okla.: University of Oklahoma Press, 1952.

Crosby, Bing (as told to Pete Martin). *Call Me Lucky.* New York: Simon & Schuster, 1953.

Daly, John D. *A Song in His Heart.* Philadelphia: The John C. Winston Company, 1951.

Derrig, Peter. *The Pride of the Green Berets.* New York: Paperback Library, Inc., 1966.

Elson, Louis C. *National Music of America.* Boston: L. C. Page Company, 1899.

Emurian, Ernest K. *Dramatic Stories of Hymns and Hymn Writers.* Boston: W. A. Wilde Company, 1941.

———. *Living Stories of Favorite Songs.* Boston : W. A. Wilde Company, 1958.

————. *Stories of Civil War Songs.* Natick, Mass.: W. A. Wilde Company, 1960.

————. *Stories of Our National Songs.* Boston: W. A. Wilde Company, 1957.

Ewen, David. *Life and Death of Tin Pan Alley.* New York: Funk & Wagnalls, 1964.

————. *Men of Popular Music.* New York: Prentice-Hall, Inc., 1949.

————. *Songs of America.* Chicago: Ziff Davis Publishing Company, 1947.

————. *Story of Irving Berlin.* New York: Henry Holt & Company, 1950.

Farwell, Arthur, and W. D. Darby. *Music in America,* Vol. 4. New York: National Society of Music, 1915.

Fitz-Gerald, S. J. Adair. *Stories of Favorite Songs.* Philadelphia and London: J. B. Lippincott Company, 1901.

Gibbons, Crowell. *Republic U.S.A.* New Haven, Conn.: Country Press, 1961.

Hart, W. J. *Stories of Our National Songs.* Boston: W. A. Wilde Company, 1942.

Harwell, Richard B. *Confederate Music.* Chapel Hill, N.C.: University of North Carolina Press, 1950.

————. *Songs of the Confederacy.* Cincinnati, Ohio: Willis Music Company, 1951.

Heal, Edith. *The First Book of America.* New York: Franklin Watts, Inc., 1952.

Heaps, W. A., and Heaps, P. W. *The Singing Sixties.* Norman, Okla.: The University of Oklahoma Press, 1960.

Humphreys, Henry S. *Songs of the Confederacy.* Cincinnati, Ohio: Willis Music Company, 1961.

International Library of Music. New York: University Society, Inc., 1948.

Johnson, Helen K. *Our Favorite Songs and Those Who Wrote Them.* New York: Henry Holt & Company, 1909.

Luther, Frank. *Americans and Their Songs.* New York and London: Harper & Row, 1942.

Malone, Dumas. *Dictionary of American Biography.* New York: Charles Scribner's Sons, 1934.

Moore, Robin. *The Green Berets.* New York: Avon Books, 1965.

Ninde, E. S. *Story of the American Hymn.* New York: Abingdon Press, 1921.

Piggott, H. E. *Songs That Made History*. London: J. M. Dent & Sons, 1937.

Rodriguez, José (ed.). *Music and Drama in California*. Hollywood, Cal.: Bureau of Musical Research, 1940.

Sadler, Barry (with Tom Mahoney). *I'm a Lucky One*. New York: Macmillan Company, 1967.

Silber, Irwin. *Songs of the Civil War*. New York: Columbia University Press, 1960.

Slonimsky, Nicholas. *Baker's Biographical Dictionary of Musicians*. New York: G. Schirmer, 1965.

Songs and Choruses for Community Singing. Boston: C. C. Birchard & Company, 1917.

Sooneck, O. G. T. *Report on "The Star-Spangled Banner," "America" and "Yankee Doodle."* Washington, D.C.: Government Printing Office, 1909.

Smith, Nicholas. *Stories of National Songs*. Milwaukee, Wis., 1899.

Sutherland, Allan. *Famous Hymns of the World*. New York: F. A. Stokes, 1906.

Ulanov, Barry. *The Incredible Crosby*. New York: McGraw-Hill Publishing Company, 1948.

Vernon, Grenville (compiler). *Yankee Doodle Doo, A Collection of Songs of Early American Stage*. New York: J. J. Little, Ives and Company, 1927.

Wells, Amos. *A Treasury of Hymns*. Boston: United Society of Christian Endeavor, 1914.

World of Music. New York: Abradale Press, 1963.

MAGAZINE AND NEWSPAPER ARTICLES

Antrim, Doron K. "The Song that Swept the World," *Lifetime Living*, March, 1954.

"Arthur Fiedler and His Green Beret," Long Beach *Press-Telegram*, April 30, 1966.

Bailey, Albert E. "Great Hymn Writers," *Classmate*, July 10, 1949.

Bates, Joy. "Meditation," *Methodist Woman*, March, 1968.

Bean, Helen J. "America's Mountain-Top Hymn" *National Retired Teacher's Association Journal*, July–August, 1968.

Belk, Henry. "Editorial," Goldsboro, N.C., *News–Argus*, February 15, 1967.

Bengston, Bennie. "Home, Sweet Home," *Classmate*, April 29, 1951.

"Bing Crosby's Record Sales at 200 Millions," Long Beach *Press-Telegram,* October 16, 1968.

Boyle, Hal. "Yule Songs, Writers Can't Stop 'em," Long Beach *Press-Telegram,* December 15, 1956.

Bundschu, Barbara. "Rudolph's Bright Nose Changes Santa's Legend," Los Angeles *Times,* December 23, 1956.

Burkholder, Edwin V. "America's Forgotten Minstrel," *Coronet,* December, 1960.

Cerf, Bennett. "The Millionaire Reindeer," *This Week,* December 12, 1959.

Clark, William F. "Great Tribute to Eccentric Writer of Songs: Pittsburgh Joins South in Honoring Anniversary of Stephen Foster," Long Beach *Press-Telegram,* January 13, 1932.

"Composer of Prayer Dies at 69," Long Beach *Press-Telegram,* November 17, 1964.

Crosby, Bing. "A White Christmas for One and All," *Reader's Digest,* December, 1960.

"Far from Vietnam and the Green Berets." *Time,* June 21, 1968.

"Forty-nine Star-Spangled Banner Raised over National Anthem Birthplace," Long Beach *Press-Telegram,* July 4, 1959.

French, J. M. "Tenting Tonight on the Old Camp Ground," *Granite State Monthly,* 1929.

Gilmore, Eddy. "Anthem is an Old British Booze Song," Long Beach *Press-Telegram,* February 22, 1967.

Haskin, Dorothy. "He Set the Prayer to Music," *Christian Herald,* April, 1952.

"He's Twenty Years Old, but Rudolph Will Never Grow Up," San Francisco *Chronicle,* December 27, 1959.

"Injunction Issued: Try to Close Bar. Bartender Arrested for Refusal to Serve Negro Green Beret," Long Beach *Press-Telegram,* August 19, 1966.

"Jingle Bells," Salem, Mass., *Evening News,* December 24, 1964.

King, Dr. Martin Luther, Jr. "I have a dream," *New York Times,* August 29, 1963.

Kirkpatrick, James. "Is the National Anthem Too Unsingable, Warlike?" Long Beach *Press-Telegram,* August 11, 1966.

Krythe, Maymie R. "America, the Beautiful," *High School Pupil,* October, 1951.

———. "A Minstrel Walkaround," *Tradition,* June, 1962.

———. "My Country, 'Tis of Thee," *War Cry,* December, 1955.

Mason, George R. "Where the Old South Lives on," *Highway Traveler,* Winter, 1952–53.

Mathews, Linda. "The Vietnam War—a De-musicalized Zone," Los Angeles Times Sunday Magazine, *Calendar,* December 10, 1967.

"May Cut Green Beret Force in Vietnam," Long Beach *Press-Telegram,* July 3, 1968.

McCall, Denis "Taft College Students Show Their Patriotism," Long Beach *Press-Telegram,* March 24, 1968.

McCleary, Anna L. "My Old Kentucky Home," *Etude,* May, 1939.

"Monument to Honor Green Berets," Long Beach *Press-Telegram,* June 23, 1968.

Mulligan, Hugh. "Rudolph, Far in Front of Holiday Hot Songs," Los Angeles *Times,* December 7, 1958.

"My Country, 'Tis of Thee," *Together,* July, 1959.

"New Old Song," Long Beach *Press-Telegram,* April 22, 1968.

"No Time for Sergeanting," *Time,* April, 1966.

"Official Version Sought," Long Beach *Press-Telegram,* May 22, 1968.

Oursler, Fulton. "The Song You Can't Forget," *This Week,* December 27, 1953.

Phifer, Lyndon B. "Way Down upon the Swanee River," *Classmate,* April 27, 1858.

Poole, Gray Johnson. "What So Proudly We Hailed," *Trailways Magazine,* Winter, 1949.

Poos, Bob. "Wayne's Green Berets Packs in Anti-War Japanese Youths," Long Beach *Press-Telegram,* August 9, 1968.

"Proof Through the Night," Long Beach *Press-Telegram,* June 12, 1968.

Ronnie, Art. "A New War Song Is Here," Los Angeles *Examiner,* February 6, 1966.

"Rudolph and the Stinkers," *Life,* January 9, 1950.

"Rudolph Really Big Business," Long Beach *Press-Telegram,* December 22, 1959.

"Rudolph, the Reindeer Gets Due Credit," Los Angeles *Times,* December 9, 1964.

Shafer, Ovella Satre. "Patriotic Music Memos," *Conquest,* July, 1957.

Shaw, G. Russell. "A Yankee Who Sang of the South," *Southland,* November 6, 1960.

Slonimsky, Nicholas. "Stephen Foster, Minstrel," *Christian Science Monitor,* January 16, 1963.

Smith, Kate. "Only a Bugle Call," *Coronet,* March, 1954.

"Stephen Foster Didn't Write Those Songs," Magazine *Digest.*

Sutton, Carol. "Niece Wants Foster's Songs Sung As They Were Written," Louisville, Ky., *Courier-Journal,* July 4, 1958.

Swanson, Neil. "The Story Behind the Star-Spangled Banner," *Coronet,* June, 1948.

Taylor, Genevieve D. "The House That Grandfather Built," *Southland,* November 16, 1958.

Thomas, Bob. "All Song Publishers Seek Another White Christmas," Long Beach *Press-Telegram,* December 9, 1952.

Thomey, Tedd. "Pianist Told How His March Saved Soldiers," Long Beach *Press-Telegram,* November 3, 1966.

Thrapp, Dan L. "Composer Tells of Guidance Prayer," Los Angeles *Times,* March 22, 1952.

"Vet Reaps Royalties from Ballad of War," Long Beach *Press-Telegram,* February 14, 1966.

"White Christmas Still a Goldmine for Berlin," Long Beach *Press-Telegram,* December 21, 1963.

Wilson, Earl. "An Old Song for Young GI's," Long Beach *Press-Telegram,* January 16, 1968.

———. "Sammy Cahn Tells Why Writers Wept," *ibid.,* September 5, 1968.

ENCYCLOPEDIAS

American People's Encyclopedia. New York: Grolier, Inc., 1966.

Collier's Encyclopedia. New York and Toronto: Crowell, Collier and Macmillan, Inc., 1967.

Compton's Pictured Encyclopedia. Chicago: F. E. Compton Company, 1966.

Encyclopedia Americana. New York: American Corporation, 1967.

Encyclopaedia Britannica. Chicago and London: William Benton, Publisher, 1967.

Grolier Universal Encyclopedia. New York: Encyclopaedia Britannica, Inc., 1966.

New International Encyclopedia. New York: Dodd Mead & Company, 1916.

World Book Encyclopedia. Chicago and London: Field Enterprises Corporation, 1964.

BROCHURE

Patriotic Songs of America. Boston: John Hancock Insurance Company, 1928.

Index

69 70 71 72 73 8 7 6 5 4 3 2 1